I0816669

GOD'S HOMECOMING

HarperOne Titles by N. T. Wright

The Day the Revolution Began
Simply Good News
Surprised by Scripture
The Case for the Psalms
How God Became King
Simply Jesus
Scripture and the Authority of God
The New Testament for Everyone
After You Believe
Surprised by Hope
Simply Christian
The Meaning of Jesus (with Marcus Borg)
Broken Signposts
On Earth as in Heaven

GOD'S HOMECOMING

The Forgotten Promise of Future Renewal

N. T. WRIGHT

HarperCollins books may be purchased for educational, business, or sales promotional use. For information, please email the Special Markets Department at SPsales@harpercollins.com.

harpercollins.com

FIRST EDITION

Designed by Michele Cameron

Library of Congress Cataloging-in-Publication Data has been applied for.

ISBN 978-0-06-256417-7

Printed in the United States of America

26 27 28 29 30 LBC 6 5 4 3 2

*This book is dedicated with respect,
gratitude, and occasional disagreement,
to the memory of Jürgen Moltmann
(1926–2024)*

CONTENTS

Preface xi

Introduction: The Forgotten Story

Chapter 1: The Story of Scripture 3
Getting the Story the Right Way Up
Misunderstanding Heaven and the Soul
The Central Story

Section I: Starting Points and Groundwork: The Biblical Promises

Chapter 2: Filling the Earth with Glory 27
Introduction: Glory Already Present
Glory Still to Come
The Temple and God's People

Chapter 3: Creation and Temple: The Glory Comes to Dwell 49
From Genesis to David
David and the Temple

Chapter 4: The Departing and Returning Glory 72
The Glory Departs—But Will Return
Hope and Hermeneutics

Chapter 5: The Human Face of the God Who Comes 92
Introduction
Mark
Matthew
Luke
John
The Fourfold Gospel

Chapter 6: The Apparent Exceptions 114
Today in Paradise
Room in My Father's House
At Home with the Lord
Depart and Be with the Messiah
Citizens of Heaven
Eternal Life
Treasure in Heaven
In Abraham's Bosom
Till We Cast Our Crowns Before Thee

Chapter 7: The Homecoming of God: Filled with the Spirit 129
The Promise of the Spirit
God's Homecoming in the Spirit: Paul
God's Homecoming in the Spirit: Acts
The Work of the Spirit in John

Interlude: How Did We Miss the Point?

Chapter 8: Switching the Script? The Bible and the Christian Tradition 149
Changing the Story
Re-Reading the Texts
Considering the Options

Chapter 9: God's Arrival on Earth or the Soul's Arrival in Heaven? 172
The Bible and the Church
Stages of Development

Chapter 10: The Imagined Goal and the Unnecessary Journey 190
The Vision of God
So What About Purgatory?
How Can the Bible Be Authoritative?
God's Homecoming and the Human Vocation

Section II: So What? Living Within the Real Biblical Story

Chapter 11: Worship, Evangelism, and Prayer 219
Celebrating God's Homecoming: Worship
Announcing God's Homecoming: Evangelism
Exploring God's Homecoming: Prayer

Chapter 12: The Sacraments 234
God's Homecoming in the Sacramental Universe
God's Homecoming in Water: Baptism
God's Homecoming in Bread and Wine

Chapter 13: The Polychrome Church as the Sign to the Powers 256
The Problem of Divided Churches
Paul's Vision of the Church: Ephesians 2–3
Unity as the Sign of Hope: Romans 15
What the Monochrome Church Misses

Chapter 14: Life Beyond Death and the Calling of the Church 278
What Are We Waiting For?
The Double "Coming"
Between Death and Resurrection
Comfort, Comfort My People

Notes 307

Index 325

Index of Biblical Passages 341

PREFACE

As I write this it is Advent Sunday. Churches such as mine, which follow the Christian calendar, celebrate this day as the beginning of the new year. Advent looks ahead, of course, to Christmas, but it also looks way beyond that, to the promised "second coming" of Jesus. Sometimes the two get muddled up, with hymns and readings referring now to one of these and now to the other. This doesn't matter that much, because in fact the two "comings" of Jesus, Christmas and the second coming, are more closely related than you might think. The Christian calendar is not twelve but actually thirteen months long, starting with the preparation for the first coming at Christmas and ending with the preparation for the second coming. Both have to do with a theme that is larger even than either of them, but one that is often neglected or ignored: God's homecoming.

There are two mistakes people regularly make when thinking about the second coming of Jesus. The first is to imagine that Jesus will come back to our world *in order to take people away to a different place*, namely, "heaven." His second coming would then not be a "homecoming" at all, but a rescue operation, a raid on enemy territory, heading back quickly to his real and very different home. No: his final coming will coincide with the glorious renewal of all creation, so that he will come home to the heaven-and-earth world that God the father always intended.

The second mistake is to imagine that Jesus will only really become Lord of the world when he finally returns. From this point of view, the great gospel events of Jesus's birth, life, death, resurrection and ascension, and the sending of the spirit, are all designed to get people ready for his final return. Until then, he hasn't really become king, hasn't really taken his throne as Lord of the world. He hasn't really come home.

My earlier book, *Surprised by Hope*, addressed the first of these mistakes.[1] The present book is a kind of sequel, and addresses the second one.

In *Surprised by Hope* I explained how the early Christians drew on their scriptures to speak of their ultimate future hope, not in terms of "heaven and hell" but of new creation: a new heaven and a new earth, joined together into one. Within that new creation, God's people are to be bodily raised from the dead to share in the freshly rejuvenated world. Many people have found this perspective revolutionary and liberating, as I know from letters, emails, phone calls, and even conversations in the street with strangers. But during the last decade or so I have become increasingly aware that even those who have grasped the principle of new creation still tend to think within the standard western categories of people "going up to be with God." The whole Bible, however, thinks in terms of God coming to be with us. Coming to be at home.

This is, if anything, even more revolutionary, and, I believe, even more liberating. It also offers fresh ways of addressing some long-standing theological and practical questions. Having explored these themes in many guest lectures and discussions over recent years, I decided it was time to pull it all together, and the present book is the result. I regret that it is a few years later in coming than I had hoped. As with many other things just now, I blame the pandemic.

In bringing this project to fruition, I have been conscious that I am walking on a similar pathway to some other recent writers, though I have not tried to show in any detail where I simply agree with them and where I am doing something different or additional. I think particularly of the remarkable study (now in a fifteenth anniversary edition) of Steve Bouma-Prediger and Brian Walsh, *Beyond Homelessness: Christian Faith in a Culture of Displacement*, which traces a major current social problem back to the very idea of home, and with it to the idea of God's being at home.[2] I am grateful to Brian in particular for his comments on early drafts of some of this book, and I regret that I haven't been able to do more to explore the further implications, in areas such as ecology and political life, toward which he was nudging me. More recently, Miroslav Volf and Ryan McAnnaly-Linz have written *The Home of God: A Brief Story of Everything*, which draws heavily on various biblical passages in a way complementary to my work.[3] And I think particularly of J. Richard Middleton, *New Heavens and New Earth*.[4] I am grateful to Brian, Miroslav, and Richard for their help and advice with my own work. These all look back, at least by implication, to Jürgen Moltmann's celebrated treatment, *The Coming of God: Christian Eschatology*.[5] My sense, though, is that Moltmann never dived as deeply as he might have done into the relevant scriptural material, no doubt because the German biblical studies of his day did not give him as much help as perhaps they should. And Moltmann was, inevitably, still wrestling with some of the demons from an earlier period of German philosophy and theology, going back at least to Hegel, in a way that seems unnecessary or even positively unhelpful today.

I am especially grateful to those, including my son Oliver and Dr. Zack Kahler, who have read parts of the present book and given me wise and sometimes critical advice. They are not, of course, responsible for the eventual result. My editor at SPCK, Philip Law, has been reading my work for over thirty years and as always has given wise advice and help. I have been fortunate in that my new editor at HarperOne, Stephanie Duncan Smith, has provided fresh insight into how I might best present my argument. My warm thanks to both, and to the colleagues in both houses with whom they work.

In an attempt to keep the book reasonably short, I have not for the most part debated here with other scholars. Those who know the relevant fields will be able to see where I am in implicit engagement with significant alternative positions: this is particularly so, for instance, in chapter 10, where I have argued against the traditional highlighting of the "Beatific Vision," with purgatory as (often) a necessary staging-post on the way to that end. That debate, however, highlights a theme that resonates throughout the book, and to which I devote an interlude at the midpoint. Western theology as a whole, since at least the third century, has found it difficult to work with biblical categories, tending instead to find its frameworks within the philosophies of Plato and/or Aristotle and reaching for the Bible simply as a random source of illustration or proof texts. Sometimes, indeed, theologians express surprise that there should even *be* such a thing as a biblical metaphysic or worldview. This is a major problem for the wider discipline, as the gap between historical biblical studies and systematic or philosophical theology seems to grow wider all the time. I hope that setting things out as sharply as I can in this book will at least alert my many friends and colleagues in other branches of our overall discipline to the necessity of doing business with scripture itself, not simply with what much later writers have done with it, and to the possibility that fresh theological proposals, not simply more recondite footnotes, may emerge from such study.

As I have done for some years now, I refer to the holy spirit without capitalization. The word "spirit," *pneuma*, was in widespread and varied first-century use in philosophy and theology, and the meanings that Jesus and his first followers intended when they used the word had to make their own way in the marketplace of beliefs and ideas, without the benefit of, as it were, being identified by a kind of linguistic halo. Another linguistic point: like some other recent historians, when speaking of the ethnic people from which Jesus came, I have referred to them as "Judaeans" rather than "Jews."[6] People from Athens were Athenians; from Rome, Romans. As the gospel went out into the world, Jesus and his earliest followers were thought of as being from Judaea. Our modern word "Jew" has many connotations, some of them unhelpful to historical study.

Translations of the Old Testament and Apocrypha are taken from the NRSV, except that I have used the name YHWH rather than "the LORD." Translations from the New Testament are from my *The New Testament for Everyone*, 3rd edition (2023).

It seems only appropriate that I should dedicate this book, with gratitude, to the memory of Jürgen Moltmann. I was privileged to know him briefly toward the end of his long life. Even when we would disagree, his faith and hope, and tireless work, remain an example to us all.

N. T. Wright
Wycliffe Hall, Oxford
Advent Sunday, December 1, 2024

Introduction

THE FORGOTTEN STORY

1

THE STORY OF SCRIPTURE

Getting the Story the Right Way Up

Most people today imagine that the point of Christianity is "to go to heaven when you die." That's what most believers believe. It's what most unbelievers unbelieve. It's certainly what journalists, broadcasters, and popular commentators think Christianity is supposed to be all about.

They are all wrong. The point of Christianity is not that we should go to heaven. The point of Christianity is that heaven should come to us. "To earth," in Jesus's words. The story the early Christians told was not about how humans (or their souls) could, as it were, go upstairs into the presence of God. It was about how God had come downstairs to live with them—and would one day complete that operation, eventually suffusing all creation with his glorious presence. Thus, though people sometimes speak of those who have died as having "gone home" to be with God, from the early Christian point of view that is the wrong way around. The great hope is God's own homecoming. That project, long promised in Israel's scriptures, was launched with Jesus and with the holy spirit. Grasping this enables us to glimpse the true Christian hope and allow it to shape our mission and life. In much contemporary Christianity, this story has been all but forgotten. It is time to refresh our memories.

What the early Christians said about Jesus and the spirit—two of the most important topics, obviously, in the early church—meant what it meant within this story. When they spoke of salvation, they were not talking about people being saved *from* the present world. They were talking about the creator God's plan of salvation *for* the present world—with themselves, as rescued and repurposed human beings, playing an important role in that project.

This, by the way, underlines the importance of seeing the story of scripture as being basically about *things that happened in the real world*. Some have objected to the use of "story" as a basic category, fearful that it may indicate a fantasy, a mere imagined world.[1] There is of course a place for such nonhistorical stories. Jesus's parables mean what they mean without any need for us to ascertain which farm the Prodigal Son had come from, or which Galilean fields had been sown with a mixture of wheat and tares. But it is vital for the overall biblical world, Judaean and Christian alike, that the story that scripture tells, and the smaller narratives of which that larger story is made up, mean what they mean within the framework of what can be called "creational monotheism": the belief that this world of space, time, and matter is God's world, and that God is reaffirming, reclaiming, and renewing it, not abandoning it.

This is all the more important because this simple yet profound truth about God's sovereign, saving rule becoming a reality "on earth as in heaven"—the very thing for which Jesus taught his followers to pray—has been largely ignored, particularly in the Western churches (Roman Catholicism and the many varieties of Protestantism). The Eastern Orthodox churches, as often, have a different approach. Some of what I want to say in this book may ring bells in those traditions, even if my approach may seem unfamiliar.[2]

Part of the problem here, which we shall meet frequently in what follows, has been a basically platonic interpretation of the Christian gospel. This has continued to exercise a tight grip on popular imagination, but it is not what Jesus and his first followers taught.[3] Just to be clear from the start, however, we had better give a very brief summary of the key issues.

Plato lived (mostly in Athens) from around 428 to 347 BC. He remains the best known of ancient philosophers, surpassing even his pupil and critic, Aristotle. He was a disciple of the great Socrates, and his works comprise the "dialogues" between Socrates and his many interlocutors, plus a record of Socrates's trial. His many followers in subsequent centuries are normally categorized into groups, of which for our purposes the "Middle Platonism" of the first and second century AD and the "Neoplatonism" of the third and subsequent centuries are the most important. Examples of middle Platonists include the Judaean philosopher Philo of Alexander (c. 20 BC to AD 50) and the biographer and thinker Plutarch (c. AD 45–125), who was a priest of the shrine at Delphi. The best known of the Neoplatonists is Plotinus (AD 204–70), whose thought influenced several of the leading theologians of the next few hundred years, including Augustine. Plato has continued to be a significant influence ever since, not least in the Renaissance period and in the philosophies of Kant and Hegel.

There are whole libraries devoted to the many twists and turns of platonic thought from its origins to the present day. A brief summary is bound to give hostages to fortune. But the main characteristic of Platonism all through, and particularly in its influence on developing Christian thought from the third century onward, is a dualism in which the world of space, time, and matter is seen as essentially secondary to the world of the unseen and atemporal realities. The former, the world of space, time, and matter, has to do only with "appearances," which may be deceptive. The latter, the world of the unseen and atemporal realities, concerns ultimate reality, the object of real knowledge. Classic Platonism does not see the world of appearances as evil. That was an extreme view developed by, for instance, the second- and third-century Gnostics. Classic Platonism contends that the world we see and know in the present can be powerful and beautiful, but it is not the real thing, only secondary and transient. For a near-contemporary of St. Paul such as Plutarch, the whole point was that we humans have "souls" that belong in "heaven" and that are looking forward to leaving behind the present world of appearances and returning to their true home.[4]

That going-to-heaven story is, of course, what many, perhaps most, modern western Christians understand to be the Christian position. At a popular level—but it is at the popular level where most people will meet it—this view is well expressed by the poet John Betjeman:

Jesus is God and came to show
The world we live in here below
Is just an ante-chamber where
We for His Father's house prepare.[5]

This present book is my best shot at undermining this assumption.

Misunderstanding Heaven and the Soul

We could sharpen up my argument by focusing on two words that play a large role in popular Christianity but that the early Christians used quite differently: heaven and soul.

I have a personal backstory for these words. In 2003, the year I became Bishop of Durham, I published a short book called *For All the Saints*, in which I expounded briefly what the Bible says about Christians who have died. I pointed out that, contrary to popular imagination, scripture speaks robustly about resurrection to new bodily life *in the end*, and of a time in between bodily death and bodily resurrection, a time of being "with the Messiah," which we are told is "far better."[6] The *Times* of London, much to the delight of the publisher, treated my little book as a news item. The Religion reporter, Ruth Gledhill, wrote a fair and clear summary of what I had said, including the point that the Bible does not, to the surprise of most people, describe the ultimate future in terms of the soul going to heaven. But the headline writers, knowing a good "another-crazy-liberal-bishop" story when they saw one, gave the short article the strapline: NEW BISHOP ABOLISHES HEAVEN AND THE SOUL. That, of course, made it sound as though I was some kind of secularist, denying any spiritual dimension to human life, or to the future world.

Well, there have been such secularists from time to time. But nobody who reads that book, or anything else I've written, could suppose I was in that camp. Come to think of it, there are today some anxious theologians who, seeking to ward off the ravages of secularism, have made similar charges against me, and also against others who have expounded the biblical view of God's world-affirming good news. To those who have reacted in that knee-jerk fashion, I would say: please read on.

That brings us to a further necessary definition. The word *shamayim*, the Hebrew word normally translated as "heaven" (strictly, "heavens," because the word is plural), was used as loosely in the Old Testament as "heaven" or "the heavens" are used in contemporary English. Sometimes it simply means "the sky," or "what we see in the sky," especially the sky at night with its glorious display of stars and planets. Sometimes, however, it means "God's domain" or "God's sphere." This does not suggest that God lives a long way up in the sky. Some may well have imagined that, but the meaning is far more interesting. From Genesis to Revelation, the biblical view of the world is bipartite: "heaven and earth."

This phrase does not suggest that both spheres are part of the same space-time continuum, with "heaven" being simply a long way up in the sky. It assumes, on the contrary, that the two spheres were made to overlap and interlock. Rather, as we speak of a view being suddenly enhanced when the sun comes out from behind a cloud and all the shapes and colors come alive in a new way, so the space-time-matter world comes alive in a new way when we sense the presence of the Creator.

Human rebellion has darkened this perception. But the Bible as a whole envisages the Creator planning to bring the two spheres together completely at last, so that, as in the Psalms and the writings of the biblical prophets, the earth will be filled with the knowledge or glory of YHWH as the waters cover the sea, or so that, in the words of Paul, God will at last be "all in all."[7] In the present time there are moments when the heavenly dimension suddenly becomes visible to the earthly creatures. We might think of Elisha's servant suddenly seeing horses and chariots of fire around the prophet, or John the Seer looking through an open door into the heavenly throne room, not (as it were) miles up in the sky but right before his eyes.[8] What's more, the ancient Israelites understood the wilderness tabernacle and then the Jerusalem temple as specific points where heaven and earth came together. Though God might be encountered in all sorts of places—as in Jacob's ladder, for instance, or Moses's burning bush—the shrine provided a location for regular assignment. God and humans could meet one another there, with all the promise and danger that implied. Tabernacle and temple are to be seen, in the larger sweep of biblical story, as places where the final uniting of heaven and earth, the original intention of the first creation, could be anticipated in advance. In the present time, heaven was the storehouse where the Creator's plans for the future were already laid out and kept ready. They were kept in heaven against the day when they would become a reality in the new heavens and new earth.

Thus heaven is already a way of gesturing toward the belief that the Creator dwells in a complex relationship with earth and its inhabitants. Sometimes the word "heaven" then becomes a reverent way of speaking of heaven's principal inhabitant, the one creator God. Saying that "heaven rules over earth" is a way of speaking of God's sovereignty. At other times God is envisaged as being surrounded with "heavenly" courtiers, perhaps angels, dwelling like God in the nonearthly realm (though not themselves being divine as such) and ready to put his purposes into practice. But the main point of "heaven" is that it is God's sphere, intersecting with ours without either sphere being reduced to terms of the other.

The two basic meanings—the sky, and the divine sphere—should not, then, be confused. We could say that the sky functions as a *metaphor* for the divine sphere, noting (for instance) the various places where rain or snow, coming from the sky, make the earth fruitful, thus establishing a positive relationship between the two rather than a great disjunction.[9] But the wider use of the word makes it repeatedly clear that those who spoke in this way did not characteristically understand God's domain to be as far away, or as unreachable, as the stars and planets. The fact that God dwelt in a different sphere from humans did not make him distant. In fact, it allowed him to be disturbingly present and unexpectedly active.

The point I am making throughout this book can therefore be stated more crisply. Many Christian traditions have seen the ultimate goal of life as being for us humans, somehow, to go and be with God, in heaven. But the great story the Bible tells, from Genesis to Revelation, is about God's purpose and promise to come and live with us. To make his home with us, as Jesus said on the night he was betrayed.[10] In Revelation's "new Jerusalem," the redeemed will see the face of God (22:4), not because *they* have gone to dwell with *God* but because *he* has come to make his home with *them* (21:3). God's intention, from start to finish, is to bring the life of heaven, indeed the *sovereign rule* of heaven, to birth as a new reality on earth. As Paul says at one point about knowledge: the real point is not *your* knowledge of *God* but God's knowledge of you.[11] So for the early Christians as a whole the point was not whether you could find your way up to be with God. The point was God's homecoming: his coming to be with his people and his world in the person of Jesus, and his coming to live *within* his people and his world in the power of the holy spirit.

In fact—this point brings gasps of astonishment when I say

it in lectures—the New Testament *never uses the word "heaven" to talk about the destination of God's people after their death*. This can be illustrated sharply by thinking for a moment of Paul's letter to the Romans.

That great letter—arguably one of the most extraordinary letters ever written by anyone—has often been expounded in terms of a Romans Road, along which sinners may travel to be forgiven and then to go to heaven at last. But Romans only mentions the word "heaven" twice, and in neither passage is it speaking of the place, or the state of being, where God's saved people will finally end up.[12]

Paul's understanding of being saved—both the ultimate end in view and the means of getting there—is quite different from what most Christians have imagined. Yes, "salvation" is the main theme of the letter, not least its climax in Romans chapter 8, where Paul celebrates the salvation through which God's people will obtain their inheritance. But this inheritance is not heaven. It is the whole redeemed creation—a fact with considerable importance for several other key topics.[13] When people ignore this, as many have done over the years, the vital passage about the rescue and renewal of creation (8:18–30) becomes obscure and puzzling. But if we take seriously Paul's notion of creation reborn it all makes excellent sense. And the glorification of which Paul speaks in that chapter—meaning that humans will share the glory of God, as in Romans 5:2—is not a lavish description of heaven. It has to do with the saturation of human life with the presence and power of God, enabling humans to play their proper glorious role of wise stewardship within God's created order.[14] We see exactly the same sequence of thought, and the same result, in the dramatic song of praise in Revelation 5:9–10.

Thus the popular view, that the letter to the Romans displays the going-to-heaven story, is not in the text. It has to be read *into* the text from a quite different worldview. Ironically, this has often happened when the book is being expounded by people who claim to believe in "the authority of the Bible." But if we really mean what we say about biblical authority it is incumbent on us, both with Romans and with the whole Bible, to ponder the stark mismatch between our easygoing (and probably platonic) assumptions and the text itself. In one sense, the present book is simply an appeal to let the Bible be the Bible.

Take another obvious starting point. The fact that many people still understand the phrase "kingdom of heaven" to mean "God's place, which is heaven," doesn't make it correct. That phrase, which we find almost exclusively in Matthew's gospel, was always a reverent way of talking about "God's sovereign, saving rule."[15] Jesus wasn't talking about God taking people away from the present world to a kingdom somewhere else. He was talking about God's sovereign, saving rule breaking into *this* world. He was teaching his followers to pray that this would become a reality. That is because this world, God's good heaven-and-earth creation, is where God has long desired to make his home. However, the misunderstanding of the phrase "kingdom of heaven" as though it referred to a place, *other than this earth*, where God reigns, and to which he will take his people in the end, is unfortunately inscribed into church liturgies as well as hymns. Other passages and themes in the Bible have regularly been misunderstood in the same way. We will deal with them as they come up.[16]

The second misunderstood word is "soul." Again, many are shocked to hear that the New Testament *never uses the word "soul" to talk about either the real inner human identity, or the final postmortem state, of God's people.* That, however, is of course how most Christians normally think and speak. A hymn often sung in churches I have known ends with the lines:

> *O spread thy covering wings around, till all our strivings cease;*
> *And, at our Father's loved abode, our souls arrive in peace.*[17]

This way of thinking is taken for granted in some of the popular classics of modern Christian writing. C. S. Lewis's well-known book *The Screwtape Letters* assumes throughout that what matters is the "soul" of the "patient" (the human who is being tempted). That, indeed, is what we might expect from Lewis, steeped as he was in Plato. After all, as we saw earlier, it was the first-century Platonist Plutarch who described carefully how humans have souls that are currently in exile from their true home in heaven but looking forward to returning there at the appropriate time.[18] That is not what Jesus taught, or what his first followers preached.

The word "soul" appears, to be sure, in various contexts in modern translations of the Bible, usually translating the Greek *psychē* or the Hebrew *nephesh*. Twice, both in Revelation, it is used to refer to humans in an intermediate state between bodily death and bodily resurrection.[19] In Jesus's parable of the Rich Fool (Luke 12:13–21) the Authorized (King James) version has God saying, in verse 20, "Thou fool, this night thy soul shall be required of thee." But the word *psychē*, there and elsewhere, regularly refers, not to the disembodied "soul" of standard platonic imagination, but to what we would call the whole *person*.

It denotes the entire life, not some internal, invisible supposed reality that constituted a real self that could be set over against what we might call the material human being and bodily life. The same verse in the NRSV has "This very night your *life* is being demanded of you." The preceding verse, indeed, has the man patting himself on the back for accumulating so much wealth and saying to his "soul" that it should take it easy, relax, eat, drink, and have a good time. That sounds much more like the whole bodily life, rather than some inner self, settling down to enjoy a life of luxury.

In another text, Jesus warns against the danger of winning the whole world but forfeiting one's . . . well, what? Traditional translations have said "soul"; this, too, has naturally been interpreted in terms of the immortal "soul" of popular platonic imagination. But again the Greek word *psychē* is standing for the Hebrew word *nephesh*, or its Aramaic equivalent, which mean "life." It isn't hinting that Jesus was after all a Platonist. It is referring to the whole life of the person, both in the present and in the ultimate future.[20]

The Bible does, of course, often refer to what we might call the interiority of human life. Paul, in a telling passage, uses the language of spirit at this point, speaking of God's spirit bearing witness with our spirit.[21] The Psalms describe an interior dialogue between a more depressed and downcast self and another voice, another self as it were, that is offering a prophetic word of encouragement:

Why are you cast down, O my soul, and why are you disquieted within me?
Hope in God; for I shall again praise him, my help and my God.[22]

Here again the phrase "O my soul," and the Septuagint translation *psychē*, is easily read in terms of the platonic "soul." No doubt that was how many in the early church understood it. But, once more, the Greek word *psychē* is in fact regularly used where the Hebrew or Aramaic speaker would use some form of the noun *nephesh*. And *nephesh* is quite different from soul in platonic thought, and for that matter in popular speaking today. When Old Testament writers depict dead humans inhabiting the world of "Sheol," they do not refer to them—to what remains of them, that is, after the death and decay of the physical body—in terms of *nephesh* or, in Greek, *psychē*.[23]

Indeed, there are key places where we might have expected to find *psychē* in reference to the disembodied state, but do not. When Paul teases the Sanhedrin about the resurrection (Acts 23:8–9), the Pharisees assume he hasn't actually seen a risen body. They speculate that he has perhaps encountered someone in the intermediate state between bodily death and bodily resurrection, so they suggest that perhaps Paul had seen, not a "soul," but an "angel" or a "spirit." This is more striking in view of Wisdom 3:1, which does indeed speak of the *psychai dikaiōn*, the "souls of the righteous," in the intermediate state prior to the resurrection (which will be described in 3:7–9).[24] In other words, the word *psychē* was indeed available in Judaean thought to denote the state of someone supposed to be poised between death and resurrection, but the New Testament, and it seems perhaps the Pharisees as well, never used it that way. The Song of the Three hedges its bets on this one, speaking of the *pneumata kai psychai dikaiōn*, the "spirits and souls of the righteous."[25] Perhaps, like Thomas Cranmer, that great poem is here using two words to gesture toward a further reality for which precise terminology was lacking.

The exception is Revelation. When the fifth seal is opened (6:9–11), John sees "the souls under the altar"—the martyrs, crying to God for vengeance against their murderers. They are told to rest a little longer. Whatever this strange passage actually means, it contrasts with the views of Tertullian and Cyprian, for whom the martyrs had gone straight into a place of bliss—some sort of heaven indeed, though they do not call it that, nor is it yet the full new creation and resurrection. Then, in Revelation 20:4, the souls of the martyrs who had been beheaded come to life in the "first resurrection" and reign as royal priests with the Messiah for a thousand years. These are the only places in the New Testament where *psychai* is used to denote the continued existence of previously embodied humans as they await their new resurrection bodies. These puzzling references offer no support to a platonic view of an automatically immortal soul. The beings in question are not, it seems, being punished or purified, nor are we told that they are on their way to see God. They are simply required to wait patiently for God's justice to take effect on earth as in heaven.

As we'll see in the concluding chapter, it appears that the early Christians were not particularly concerned with "going to be with God" as a new reality after their death. They were much more interested in the fact that, in Jesus, and in the spirit, the God of creation and covenant had already come to make his home with them—and, through them, within his world; and that in his own resurrection Jesus had led the way into God's long-promised new creation. They believed that Jesus would return to complete the work he had so dramatically and effectively begun. That is of course one particular sharply focused point of the whole theme of this book: the incarnate Lord will come at last to complete his work of bringing all things into subjection under him.[26] In particular, the early Christians believed that God's holy spirit, having already dwelt within them in the present life, would sustain them in the closer presence of Jesus and then, in the end, raise them to new bodily life.[27]

Speaking of God making his home with his people brings us back to where we began. My argument in this book is not simply (as in *Surprised by Hope*) that popular beliefs about the soul going to heaven are unbiblical and ought to be replaced with a more robust view of creation and new creation, with humans being bodily raised to share in the new creation. The point of this present book is to suggest that, in addition, the whole idea of an immortal human soul making its way up to God is a radical distortion of biblical teaching. *The Bible speaks with one voice of God coming to live with humans.* Of God coming to *be at home* with us humans.

This story has largely been forgotten. But until we get our minds around it, and bring our teaching, preaching, sacramental and liturgical life, pastoral practice, and, not least, our personal prayer into line with this remarkable narrative and promise, we will not only be distorting the Bible's message. We will be robbing ourselves of the central reality that Jesus and his first followers were celebrating.

At its best, of course, the platonic tradition within Christianity is, from one point of view, aiming at the right end result, namely, the intimate union of human beings with the God in whose image they were made, and their invitation to live at the glorious but demanding intersection of heaven and earth. My criticism of the tradition is that, by adopting the platonic framework of heaven and the soul, it imports into the biblical narrative several themes that undermine and distort the main message of scripture, including the Christian gospel. But to make this clear we must lay out that biblical story more fully.

The Central Story

Genesis begins with the creator God making a world—a heaven-plus-earth reality—which is to be his own home.[28] To speak thus of "heaven-plus-earth," as we saw, does not mean "sky and ground." It means "God's sphere and our sphere," with the implication (already in Genesis 2 where God is walking in the garden looking for Adam and Eve) that the two were meant to overlap. Heaven is not, so to speak, "the place miles up there where God lives." God desires to live in the heaven-and-earth combined reality. That is to be his home. When the text speaks of the Creator "resting" on the seventh day, this doesn't mean simply that he stopped working, or took time off. It means that he came to "be at home" in this bipartite world he had made.

What's more, as the same passage indicates, God's desire, and his initial practice, was to be at home *with his human creatures*. God made humans in his own image, in other words, so that they could reflect his wise stewardship into the world, and join in articulating the praises of creation back to him. The idea of humans being made "in God's image" has generated enormous amounts of speculation, but at its heart it is simple. Creation—heaven-plus-earth—is designed as a *temple*, the home for the Creator. At the heart of the temple, as you'd expect in widespread ancient culture, we find the "image" that reflects the presence and power of the Creator into the world around and transmits the worship and praise of the world around back to the Creator. Anyone familiar with ancient near eastern temples would see the point at once.[29]

Putting Genesis 1 and 2 together, we find that God gives to the image-bearing creatures his own breath, his *ruach* (Hebrew) or *pnoē* (Greek). The result is that humans—like the other animals—become *nephesh chayyah*, or in Greek *psychē zōsa*, "living being."[30] This life remains the gift of God, to be returned at death, rather than a body-independent and immortal soul, existing before all time.

Genesis 1 and 2 thus describe the start of an intended ongoing project. There is no suggestion in the text, as there often has been in western Christianity, that the point of it all was to set humans a moral examination to see whether they, or their souls, might be fit to go and make their home with God, presumably in heaven—or, if not, whether he would have to send them to somewhere less attractive instead. The point was that they would live in such a way that it would make sense for *God* to come and make *his* permanent home with *them*. When the humans fail in this vocation, the Creator's plan is not to abandon the project, or to suggest that a way might be found to switch direction and have some humans leaving earth and going to heaven. The Creator inaugurates a plan whereby a people will be called into existence in whose midst God will come to live.

Thus the call of Abraham and God's covenant with him (Genesis 12–22) indicate that God will continue to work, as his original project suggested, *through* human beings, even though they are now routinely muddled and disobedient.[31] As the story unfolds, the human beings through whom God now intends to take forward his purposes—Abraham's family—are rescued from slavery in order to become the people in whose midst God does indeed come to live. The creation of the tabernacle at the end of the book of Exodus, and the glorious divine presence coming to dwell within it, offers a kind of sigh of relief, rounding off, at least for the moment, the narrative arc from Genesis 1. God made his heaven-and-earth world as a temple where he would come to dwell in person. The tabernacle is a small working model of that continuing purpose. God has come to dwell with his people, as he always intended. The ongoing story of Israel shows well enough that this is only a beginning. There is a long way to go and much work to do. But the original project is back on track.

If we take a flying leap from the beginning of the Bible to the end, we discover that the subject has not changed. There is much in Revelation 21 and 22 that we could ponder, but my point here is simple. The strapline to sum up the whole narrative is not "the dwelling of humans is with God," but *God has come to dwell with humans* (21:3). That was the point from the start. It is the point at the end. It is so important that the "loud voice from the throne," heard by John the Seer, repeats it twice more:

> *Look! God has come to dwell with humans! He will dwell with them, and they will be his people, and God himself will be with them and will be their God.*

In John's vision, God declares that he is "making all things new" (21:5). But the "new thing" in question is what creation was made for in the first place. It is what emerges once God has dealt with, and abolished, death, mourning, weeping and pain. Once God is "all in all," as in 1 Corinthians 15:20–28, his homecoming will be complete. The purpose of the original creation will have been fulfilled—including the plan that humans should be image-bearers, reflecting God into the world and the world back to God (the royal priesthood, in other words).[32] Unless we see that this has been the goal of the entire biblical story, we will never understand either that story as a whole or the key elements that make it up. And unless we think of Christian faith, and everything to do with it, as being held, poised, between the original good creation and the final renewal and restoration of that creation, we will distort and misunderstand everything in our path.

It is true, of course, that Revelation, like some other key texts, speaks of the *new* creation as somehow taking the place of the *old* one that has been abolished. But on closer examination this means that what has been done away with is the decay and corruption of the old, allowing the true nature of God's good creation to shine out as never before.[33]

This vision of renewed creation is further confirmed through the story of Jesus of Nazareth, as told by the four canonical gospels.[34] Many devout readers have been lured (perhaps by the fact that Matthew comes first in the New Testament) into the classic misunderstanding of supposing that Jesus was teaching people "how to go to heaven." This problem is not confined to one strand within western Christianity. It is common to Catholic and Protestant alike, to liberal and charismatic alike. It seems clear enough: people have long assumed that Jesus came to teach us how to go to heaven; here he is talking about "inheriting the kingdom of heaven"; well, that's what we expected. That, people think, was what we came looking for when we opened the Bible. That is what, they assume, they have found. This is where the historian is obliged to play the spoilsport, or even the killjoy. As C. S. Lewis put it, when we read a book in our own language but from an earlier century, if we find a word we don't understand, we look it up in the dictionary. But when we find a word we ourselves regularly use we don't look it up, because we assume we know what it means. We take for granted that the writer is using the word to say what we want to say when we use that same word.[35] Lewis was brilliant at teasing out unexpected meanings from early English texts and exposing the problems we run into if we don't do that linguistic homework. Ironically, he never applied the same methodological insight to his reading of the New Testament. He assumed the souls-going-to-heaven narrative. He thereby produced a somewhat uneasy clash between that sense of destination, as in *The Screwtape Letters*, and the much more robust picture of a whole new *physical* creation, as for instance in *The Great Divorce*. (The same tension is visible in Lewis's Narnia stories, where the rich theology of creation and new creation in *The Magician's Nephew* clashes noticeably with the platonic vision—which Lewis names as such!—at the end of *The Last Battle*.)

The problem is that most Christian readers, and most non-Christian readers for that matter, have had the "getting-to-heaven" narrative firmly fixed in their minds before they begin and so have read the stories that way. To say it yet again: the overarching story assumed in the New Testament is not about humans going to be with God, but about God coming to be with humans.

The conventional going-to-heaven narrative generates other problems down the line. In the New Testament, Jesus's "second coming" refers to his return to consolidate his rule over the whole created order—the rule that has already begun in his resurrection and ascension. This is clear enough in well-known passages like Philippians 3:20–21, where Jesus will come back to complete the task of making all things subject to himself, including transforming the physical bodies of those of his followers who are still alive at the time.[36] But in much of western Christianity, insofar as people reflect at all on the promised second coming of Jesus, they tend to reduce it to a brief visit for the purpose of scooping up the faithful and taking them back to heaven. The point once again, in the popular imagination, is for God's people to escape the present world, not for God to rescue and redeem it and come to make his home there with us—the vision we find in such decisive passages as Romans 8 or, again, Revelation 21 and 22.[37]

The theory of a "rapture" (Jesus coming back briefly to snatch people away with him to "heaven") has then been amplified, through a whole swathe of fundamentalist or dispensationalist Christianity, into various bizarre, cartoon-strip theories, sometimes supporting various political agendas. The Bible, I should stress, says nothing of the kind. What it does say makes views like these not only ridiculous but unnecessary.[38] The early Christians had a robust view of Jesus's ultimate return, and it was all about him coming at last to be at home as the true Lord of earth and heaven together. It is ironic that the wrong view here is often taught zealously by people who claim to take the Bible very seriously, even treating it as authoritative. But these claims are meaningless if the Bible becomes obscured or even obliterated by later traditions.

Even this very brief preliminary sketch—which we shall amplify considerably as we go on—poses a major set of questions that can be put like this. For many western Christians, including myself as I was growing up, the Bible as a whole appeared to pose a puzzle. The Old Testament seemed to be looking in one direction, focused relentlessly on what we might see as "this-worldly" issues, holding on to the promise of a "this-worldly salvation." The New Testament, however, seemed—according to preachers and teachers at least—to be looking in the opposite direction, holding out the hope of heaven, of life after death for our souls, enabling them to escape the world of space, time, and matter and enter something called "eternity." What were we supposed to say about this apparent discrepancy? I will discuss this question more fully in chapter 8, but raising it here will also serve as the bridge into our first main concern, which is to reread and reexamine what the whole text is actually saying.

Section I

STARTING POINTS AND GROUNDWORK: THE BIBLICAL PROMISES

2

FILLING THE EARTH WITH GLORY

Introduction: Glory Already Present

Christian readers of Israel's scriptures have long been puzzled that the Old Testament says so little about God's people "going to heaven when they die." One may, of course, highlight certain exceptional moments, such as Moses going up the mountain to speak with God, or Elijah being "taken up to heaven in a whirlwind" (2 Kings 2:11). One might mention the soft hint in Psalm 73 that speaks of God guiding the poet with his counsel and "afterwards" receiving him "with glory" (Revised English Bible).[1] But there isn't much more. This biblical near silence about people dying and going to heaven then gives way to the sudden promise, in what are assumed to be later strands of thought, of a very different future, namely, bodily resurrection.[2] But resurrection was never a fancy way of referring to the going-to-heaven story. It was about a new bodily life in a world at least somewhat like the present one—albeit now shot through in a new way with the presence and power of God.

So the question needs to be pressed: If we consider the scriptures to be authoritative, what should we make of the fact that the Old Testament shows little interest in people going to heaven when they die? It's time to reassess our assumptions.

Fortunately, reassessing our reading of Israel's scriptures is not difficult. From Genesis to the Psalms, from Sinai to Jerusalem, from life in the promised land to suffering in exile, our attention is drawn again and again to the mysterious assurances about the heavenly reality or dimension *already present* in this world. The earth is already the place where the Creator reveals his glory and love:

> *Holy, holy, holy is YHWH of hosts; the whole earth is full of his glory.* (Isaiah 6:3)
>
> *The earth is full of the steadfast love (*chesed*) of YHWH.* (Psalm 33:5)
>
> *The earth, O YHWH, is full of your steadfast love (*chesed*).* (Psalm 119:64)
>
> *The earth is YHWH's, and all that is in it; the world, and those who live in it.* (Psalm 24:1)[3]
>
> *O YHWH, how manifold are your works! In wisdom you have made them all; the earth is full of your creatures . . . May the glory of YHWH endure forever; may YHWH rejoice in his works.* (Psalm 104:24, 31)

This already indicates that the biblical language about "heaven" is more complex and interesting than we have often imagined. The Hebrew word normally translated as "heaven," as we saw, is plural: *shamayim*, "heavens." This already offers a hint that the biblical writers are aware, in speaking of "the heavens," that they are gesturing toward the multilayered reality that on the one hand is emphatically the domain of the creator God and on the other hand is designed to exist in mutual relationship with "earth," the abode of humans. Part of the complexity has to do with the fact that *shamayim* sometimes simply means "the skies." And part of the difficulty modern Western thinkers have with understanding the multilayered meanings of the text comes from the assumption of some kind of Epicureanism, endemic in modern Western culture, in which if there is or are a god, or gods, they are by definition a long way away, not just spatially up in the sky but in a totally other dimension from ourselves, with no real possibility of interaction. Nothing could be further from the meaning of "heaven" in the Bible. God's space and human space are indeed radically different, but they exist in a close relationship, being designed to overlap and interlock.

This emerges clearly in a passage like Isaiah 55:8–11:

> *For my thoughts are not your thoughts, nor are your ways my ways, says YHWH. For as the heavens are higher than the earth, so are my ways higher than your ways and my thoughts than your thoughts. For as the rain and the snow come down from heaven, and do not return there until they have watered the earth, making it bring forth and sprout, giving seed to the sower and bread to the earth, so shall my word be that goes out from my mouth; it shall not return to me empty, but it shall accomplish that which I purpose, and succeed in the thing for which I sent it.*

Here we see the fluidity between "heaven" as the sky from which rain and snow descend, and "heaven" as the dwelling place of YHWH—but not as a detached, unreachable space, but as the dimension from which his powerful word goes out into the "earth," the world of humans, and accomplishes his purpose of new creation. All this reinforces the appeal in the previous verses (55:6–7) to "Seek YHWH while he may be found, call upon him while he is near . . . return to YHWH, that he may have mercy." God's domain and the human domain, then, are meant to come together in fruitful symbiosis, as humans enter into relationship with the Creator and the powerful word of new creation accomplishes God's will in the world of space and time. All this stands behind Jesus's vision of God's kingdom coming "on earth as in heaven."

The texts are not blind to the problem with the idea of heaven and earth intersecting. Psalm 104 is clear, as they all are, that the earth is still dangerously infected with wickedness and corruption of various kinds. The song of the seraphim in Isaiah 6 is immediately followed by the prophet's recognition of sin in himself and the people. All this has to be rooted out if YHWH's purpose is to be completed. The Psalmists stand in the middle, on the one hand celebrating the glory of the present creation and on the other hand praying for God's world to be released from the corrosive, decaying power of evil.

That release will be brought about by the coming judgment in which YHWH, the Creator, will finally put everything right. This future event is celebrated exuberantly in various Psalms, including 96:

> *Say among the nations, "YHWH is king!*
> *The world is firmly established; it shall never be moved. He*
> *will judge the peoples with equity."*

Let the heavens be glad, and let the earth rejoice; let the sea roar and all that fills it; Let the field exult, and everything in it.
Then shall all the trees of the forest sing for joy before YHWH;
for he is coming, for he is coming to judge the earth.
He will judge the world with righteousness, and the peoples with his truth.[4]

Sometimes the two themes are joined together, as when Jeremiah warns that God's present "filling" of heaven and earth means that evildoers have nowhere to escape to:

Am I a God nearby, says YHWH, and not a God far off? Who can hide in secret places so that I cannot see them? says YHWH. Do I not fill heaven and earth? says YHWH.[5]

This tradition was retrieved in the Wisdom of Solomon, roughly contemporary with Jesus. There we find the affirmation that God's spirit fills the whole world—and that the spirit therefore knows precisely who has spoken or acted unrighteously.[6] "Wisdom is a kindly spirit," says the writer,

But will not free blasphemers from the guilt of their words . . . Because the spirit of the Lord has filled the world, and that which holds all things together knows what is said, therefore those who utter unrighteous things will not escape notice; and justice, when it punishes, will not pass them by.[7]

In these passages we observe not only the promise that everything will at the last be put right, because all that corrupts and defaces God's good creation will be dealt with. We see, in addition, that Israel's God YHWH is enthroned in heaven. This does *not* mean, despite regular modern misunderstandings, that he is detached from the present world. It means, rather, that he is ruling the earth *from* his throne in heaven—God's unseen dimension—while his breath or spirit goes out into the whole creation.

God the Creator, then, will come to "judge" the earth. That is, he will deliver earth from its corruption and wickedness and make it the place that, deep down, earth knows itself to be. That is why the trees, the field, the sea, the hills, and the animals will all be singing for joy at the thought of it. The coming judgment will not destroy the world, the good creation. It will rescue it precisely from those dark forces that are threatening to destroy it. This biblical vision comes forward into the New Testament in Romans 8:18–30, one of the major climaxes in Paul's writings, to which we shall return in due course.

The severe warning in Jeremiah 23 makes it clear that, though YHWH's basic domain is in "heaven," he is not absent from "earth." If the "fillings" of earth we saw in the Psalms are assurances of God's "loving kindness," Jeremiah's repetition of that theme provides the assurance that God knows exactly what wickedness is going on, not least among those who are supposed to be his special people.

When the Psalms speak in this way of YHWH coming to judge the earth, we would be right to see, opening up before us, the basic picture of all reality, which the Hebrew scriptures affirm in a variety of ways. YHWH, the Creator, is set over heaven and earth, with heaven being his particular domain and earth being the location, the realm perhaps, that falls under the rule of heaven and is responsible to it. Earth is in fact where God's wise, healing judgments, announced in God's own domain of heaven, are to be put into practice. Thus:

YHWH is God in heaven above and on the earth beneath.[8]
YHWH is king; let the peoples tremble! He sits enthroned upon the cherubim; let the earth quake![9]
YHWH is in his holy temple; YHWH's throne is in heaven. His eyes behold, his gaze examines humankind.[10]
YHWH has established his throne in the heavens, and his kingdom rules over all.[11]
Heaven is my throne, and earth is my footstool.[12]
The heavens are YHWH's heavens, but the earth he has given to human beings.[13]
Look down from your holy habitation, from heaven, and bless your people Israel and the ground that you have given us . . .[14]

Sometimes this, too, can turn into a warning:

God is in heaven, and you upon earth; therefore let your words be few.[15]

And sometimes it is the framework for a strong statement of Israel's call to be God's special people for the sake of the world:

Although heaven and the heaven of heavens belong to YHWH your God, [and also] the earth with all that is in it, yet YHWH set his heart in love on your ancestors alone and chose you . . .[16]

Or, again, stressing the summons to repentance and humility:

> *Thus says the high and lofty one, who inhabits eternity, whose name is Holy: I dwell in the high and holy place, and also with those who are contrite and humble in spirit . . .*[17]

The picture that emerges from all this is of a biblically rooted heaven-and-earth metaphysic. As we saw in the introductory chapter, this offers a nuanced and supple vision of a two-dimensional world. "Heaven" and "earth" are the twin halves of God's good creation, with the former hinting at further dimensions within it, as in "the heaven of heavens." In this world, the Creator dwells in "heaven," and rules from there. The "earth," which is *already* "full of his glory," though still in need of "putting right," that is, "judgment," is then the location of human beings in general and Israel in particular.

The movement between heaven and earth—one can hardly stress this enough—is almost always one-directional, from heaven to earth rather than vice versa. The one who dwells in heaven *possesses* earth, *rules over* earth, *sees* earth and all that happens on it, *knows exactly* what is happening there, *fills* earth with his steadfast love and glory, *rejoices over* all his works on earth, *promises to put right* all that is wrong on earth, and *summons earth's inhabitants* to humility, penitence, gratitude, and hope—not so that they can then leave earth and go to heaven but so that earth, filled with wise humans, will flourish as the Creator intends.

At no point—not even when Moses goes up the mountain or Elijah is taken up into heaven—is there any suggestion that the aim of the story is for human beings eventually to follow them, to graduate from their earthly existence and go to heaven to be with the Creator there, away from earth. Moses goes up in order to return and construct the Tabernacle in which God will dwell on earth. Elijah, having gone up, will (according to the prophet Malachi, endorsed by Jesus himself) return one day to bring the final warning of God's own coming. The aim of it all, then, is for the Creator to complete the work begun in creation, the work that has been continued in the twists and turns of the world's story in general and Israel's story in particular.

All this is framed, within the larger Hebrew canon, by the opening statement of Genesis, where the creator God made the heavens and the earth.[18] But it comes into particular dramatic expression when Solomon builds the Temple in Jerusalem. His prayer of dedication provides a striking statement of the mainstream scriptural metaphysic:

> *When the priests came out of the holy place, a cloud filled the house of YHWH, so that the priests could not stand to minister because of the cloud, for the glory of YHWH filled the house of YHWH.*
>
> *Then Solomon said, "YHWH has said that he would dwell in thick darkness. I have built you an exalted house, a place for you to dwell in forever." . . .*
>
> *"But will God indeed dwell on the earth? Even heaven and the highest heaven cannot contain you, much less this house that I have built! Have regard to your servant's prayer and his plea, O YHWH my God, heeding the cry and the prayer that your servant prays to you today; that your eyes may be open night and day towards this house, the place of which you said, 'My name shall be*

there,' that you may heed the prayer that your servant prays towards this place. Hear the plea of your servant and of your people Israel when they pray toward this place; O hear in heaven your dwelling-place; heed and forgive."[19]

The prayer continues, thinking ahead into the many situations that God's people may face, praying that whatever need they may have can be brought to the Temple—even from far away in exile!—and that YHWH will then hear, forgive, restore, and supply their needs.[20] This then issues in Solomon's great blessing of the people, producing general celebration.[21] Once again, there is no sense that the Temple is built, or the prayer offered, in order that the people may somehow ascend from earth to heaven. The Temple is there to be the focal point of YHWH's promise *to put his name*, his personal presence, character, and identity, in the midst of his people.[22] To know the name of God, and where this name is to be found in particular, means that Israel can call on him. The ark of the covenant, located in the Holy of Holies at the very heart of the Temple, becomes the spot at which YHWH promises to be with Israel, as he had been in the wilderness Tabernacle.[23] Will God indeed dwell on the earth? asks Solomon. His own answer seems initially to be "No, of course not," but as the prayer develops this seems to change into "Yes, in the sense that he is putting his name in this house." The New Testament, asking the same question, as for instance in the Prologue to John's gospel, gives an even more emphatic "Yes."

Once Israel's God has put his name in the Temple, then of

course priests and people can gather to be with him "to behold the beauty of YHWH and to inquire in his temple."[24] This movement (toward the temple and then into its innermost shrine) thus mirrors Moses's ascent up the mountain, not that this point is often made in the scriptures. But, the primary movement is for God to come and dwell with his people. Once he is there, pilgrimage is invited. The point of it all is not to provide a quasi-heavenly space to which humans can retreat from earth, but to celebrate God's presence with his people here on earth, and to be thereby equipped to be his agents in bringing his purposes to fruition.

The temple thus encapsulates the central metaphysical belief of ancient Israel. What later philosophically minded thinkers have referred to as "transcendence" and "immanence"—with God being (a) vastly greater than, and indeed totally other than, the created world, and simultaneously (b) richly and vibrantly present within the created world—is here seen in the familiar biblical language of "heaven" and "earth." Even heaven is not enough to express God's ultimate reality (as though one might envisage a metaphysical structure and think of God as safely contained within one bit of it). Nevertheless—as an act of grace, of covenant mercy, of the taking forward of his purposes for Israel and the world—he condescends to become present and active, attentive to Israel's prayers, in the temple. The temple becomes, as indeed ancient temples were regularly supposed to be, the place where the divine realm and the earthly realm meet. The temple is the heaven-and-earth place, the small working model of creation. As we shall see, the architecture and decoration of both tabernacle and temple bear striking witness to this.

Glory Still to Come

The filling of the Temple with the glorious divine presence was itself, in the larger context of Israel's scriptures, a pointer to the extraordinary promise that returns our gaze to the wider horizon of creation. The earth, which is in one sense already "full of YHWH's glory" (though paradoxically at the same time full of wickedness and corruption), is to be filled in a new way with the divine presence, knowledge, and glory.

Perhaps the best known of these passages, one to which Paul alludes in his letter to the Romans, is in Isaiah 11. That chapter sets out the vision of the messianic kingdom in which, under the wise and beneficent rule of the coming Davidic king, a new day of justice and peace will dawn to replace the present age of violence and wickedness. But to understand Isaiah 11 best we need to see it in the context of the earlier promises in the book. It picks up strands from 2:2–4, with its near parallel in Micah 4:1–3:

In days to come the mountain of YHWH's house shall be established as the highest of the mountains, and shall be raised above the hills;
all the nations shall stream to it.
Many peoples shall come and say,
"Come, let us go up to the mountain of YHWH, to the house of the God of Jacob;
that he may teach us his ways and that we may walk in his paths."
For out of Zion shall go forth instruction, and the word of YHWH from Jerusalem.

He shall judge between the nations, and shall arbitrate for
many peoples;
they shall beat their swords into plowshares, and their
spreads into pruning-hooks;
nation shall not lift up sword against nation, neither shall
they learn war any more.[25]

Micah adds:

But they shall all sit under their own vines and under their
own fig trees,
and no one shall make them afraid;
for the mouth of YHWH of hosts has spoken.
For all the peoples walk, each in the name of its god,
but we will walk in the name of YHWH our God forever
and ever.[26]

Though the king is not mentioned as such, the work of YHWH in Isaiah 2:4 and Micah 4:3 ("he shall judge . . .") is clearly the same as the work of the king in various prophecies, particularly Isaiah 11, Psalm 72, and so on.

This emerges clearly in the oracle in Isaiah 9. After promising that there will come a new time, free from oppression, war, and violence, the prophet declares:

For a child has been born for us, a son given to us;
Authority rests upon his shoulders;
And he is named Wonderful Counsellor, Mighty God,
Everlasting Father, Prince of Peace.
His authority shall grow continually, and there shall be
endless peace

for the throne of David and his kingdom.
He will establish and uphold it with justice and with righteousness
from this time onwards and for evermore.
The zeal of YHWH of hosts will do this.[27]

The prophecies of Isaiah 2 and Isaiah 9, taken together, point us toward Isaiah 11. There, the coming king is equipped with God's own spirit of wisdom, in order to perform the true judgment through which God will bring his intended peace to his world, freeing all creatures from oppression. The coming king will delight in the fear of YHWH, and have the wisdom to "decide with equity for the meek of the earth." In this new Eden, the wolf shall live with the lamb; the leopard shall lie down with the kid:

> *They will not hurt or destroy on all my holy mountain; for the earth will be full of the knowledge of YHWH as the waters cover the sea.*[28]

This *knowing* of YHWH, in context, sums up the passage. The whole creation will understand, at a deep, powerful level, who its Creator really is, namely, the God of peaceful, healing justice. And this knowledge will enable that whole creation to live in accordance with God's character.[29]

This vision in Isaiah 11 is repeated, with variations, in chapter 65, as part of the promise of "new heavens and a new earth" (65:17). This time, however, it is focused, not on the filling of the whole earth (and the animal kingdom) with divine knowledge, but more specifically on the renewal of Jerusalem and the delightful, peaceable lives of its inhabitants.

The promise for the whole creation is repeated in Habakkuk, in the teeth of the world's wickedness:

> *Alas for you who build a town by bloodshed, and found a city on iniquity! Is it not from YHWH of hosts that peoples labor only to feed the flames, and nations weary themselves for nothing? But the earth will be filled with the knowledge of the glory of YHWH as the waters cover the sea.*[30]

It is almost as though the prophet is borrowing this promise from happier visions elsewhere, clinging to the hope that the creator God will eventually sort out the terrible mess, confronting the chaos and horror of the world with the promise of renewal. And this time the filling of the earth will be with "the knowledge *of the glory* of YHWH." The divine glory that came to live in the tabernacle in the wilderness, and then in the temple in Jerusalem, will one day fill the whole earth, and all creatures will know it and live accordingly.

Once more this is likened to the waters "covering the sea," inviting the comment: How do the waters "cover the sea"? The waters *are* the sea. The image indicates a rich, complete "filling," where the divine glory floods into the whole creation, resulting in a knowledge in which creation in all its parts resonates with, responds to, and rejoices in the Creator's ultimate will and intention.

A similar moment, when the promise of divine glory filling the whole earth bursts in suddenly on a scene that otherwise appears full of rebellion and punishment, comes in Numbers 14. The Israelites are in the wilderness, approaching the Promised Land from the south, after two years or thereabouts of journeying away from Egypt.[31] Moses has sent twelve spies, one from each tribe, to explore the land and report back. Ten of the spies, however, offer a dismal picture: there are fortified cities, there are giants in the land, and the whole situation is hopeless. Some of the Israelites, hearing this, want to choose a new leader and go back to Egypt. Only two of the spies, Caleb and Joshua, take a positive line, insisting that conquest is well within their grasp, granted YHWH's presence and protection.[32]

YHWH's reaction to all this is anger. His glory appears, visible to all, not now in blessing but in warning.[33] Once more, as in Exodus 32, Moses has to intercede to prevent the whole people from being wiped out. God's reputation, he insists, is at stake: the Egyptians and the Canaanites already know that

> *. . . you, O YHWH, are in the midst of this people; for you, O YHWH, are seen face to face, and your cloud stands over them and you go in front of them, in a pillar of cloud by day and in a pillar of fire by night.*[34]

Moses therefore prays, not only for divine wrath to be averted, but for God's glorious power to be displayed:

> *Now, therefore, let the power of YHWH be great in the way that you promised when you spoke, saying, "YHWH is slow to anger, and abounding in steadfast love, forgiving iniquity and transgression, but by no means clearing the guilty, visiting the iniquity of the parents upon the children to the third and the fourth generation."*[35]

The answer to Moses's prayer picks up this theme of God's power and glory being displayed in all the world. The point is *not* that therefore the people's rebellion does not matter. The point is to make it plain, as with Habakkuk, that rebellion and wickedness will not thwart the larger divine purpose:

> *Then YHWH said, "I do forgive, just as you have asked; nevertheless—as I live, and as all the earth shall be filled with the glory of YHWH—none of the people that have seen my glory and the signs that I did in Egypt and in the wilderness, and yet have tested me these ten times and have not obeyed my voice, shall see the land that I swore to give to their ancestors" . . .*[36]

The message is clear. The divine glory, now residing in the tabernacle and sometimes dangerously visible there, will fill not only the holy tent (as in Exodus 40:34–35) but actually the whole earth. The people's anxiety about entering the land is therefore a trivial concern. YHWH has the power, and the settled intention, to saturate the whole world with that same glorious presence. Enabling the people to go in and possess the land, taking with them the tabernacle where the divine glory is presently residing, is simply one small step toward that larger purpose.

The final passage that showcases the same basic promise is Psalm 72. This Psalm completes the second book of the Psalter, bringing to an end "the prayers of David son of Jesse."[37] The Psalm consists of a long celebration of the wise and just rule of the coming Davidic king, and a prayer that through him the divine justice and mercy will take effect in the world.

"Give the king your justice, O God, and your righteousness to a king's son" (72:1). The Psalm shares its vision with Isaiah 11, not with the imagery of wild animals living at peace, but more specifically with justice at last being done for the weak and oppressed:

> *May the mountains yield prosperity for the people, and the hills, in righteousness. May he defend the cause of the poor of the people, give deliverance to the needy, and crush the oppressor.*[38]

This future ideal king will rule the whole world, with all other rulers coming to do him homage,[39] not because of military conquest or oppressive rule, but rather because he delivers those who have suffered under exactly that kind of treatment:

> *For he delivers the needy when they call, the poor and those who have no helper.*
> *He has pity on the weak and the needy, and saves the lives of the needy.*
> *From oppression and violence he redeems their life; and precious is their blood in his sight.*[40]

This, then, is how the promise of Isaiah 11, Habakkuk 2, and Numbers 14 is to be fulfilled:

> *Blessed be YHWH, the God of Israel, who alone does wonderous things. Blessed be his glorious name forever;* may his glory fill the whole earth. *Amen and Amen.*[41]

The image of the coming king, wise and just, bringing about the Creator's purpose, resonates at several points with the stories of, and traditions about, Solomon, who is often seen as the archetypal "son of David" as well as the model and source of "wisdom." Indeed, Psalm 72 in the Hebrew bears the heading *liShelomoh* ("to Solomon" or "of Solomon"). The various traditions converge. In 1 Kings, Solomon builds the temple so that the divine glory may come and dwell there, filling the house. In the Psalm, the future king, ruling the whole world, will do justice and mercy for the weak, rescuing the oppressed and delivering the poor, *so that the divine glory may fill the whole earth*. The parallel indicates, what we shall see again and again, that the temple is to be seen as a small working model of the whole of creation. What Israel's God does in the temple is the pointer to what he intends to do in and for the whole creation.

All this becomes suddenly far more complex when the temple is destroyed. The glory disappears; God leaves home.[42] Jerusalem is left lamenting that her God has abandoned her. What will then happen to the divine promises to Israel, never mind the whole of creation? But the tragedy of Israel's exile, including the apparent thwarting of the repeated promise about the divine glory coming to dwell amid the people, becomes the occasion for a whole new set of promises. And—just in case anyone should imagine that all this is an ancient Hebrew vision that was quite different from the beliefs of the early church—it was precisely and particularly those promises that the early Jesus-followers believed had been fulfilled in Jesus, and were being fulfilled through the spirit of Jesus at work in and through them.

The Temple and God's People

Before we get there, however, we should emphasize again the key features of the emerging picture.

First, the divine promise in all of this is not that humans will leave earth and go to heaven to join God there. It is that God will come to fill all creation, revealing his glory and enabling creatures of every sort to know him (whatever that really means for particular entities, whether rocks or rabbits, spruce trees or stars) and thereby to fulfill his purposes for them. The Psalmist speaks of all creatures already looking to God for their food; we may take this as a pointer to the ultimate knowing of which Isaiah speaks.[43] And this is then the ultimate biblical hope. Paul, quoting Isaiah 11, refers to God as "the God of hope."[44] Many in our own day find this hope—the coming of God to us, to fill all creation, rather than our leaving earth and coming to him in heaven—a surprise, to say the least. Like Abraham and Sarah being startled at the promise of a child in their old age, most people cannot imagine God doing such a striking thing. Anyone preaching on this theme is likely to find congregations saying that they've never heard such a thing before.

Second, the promises assume and reinforce the belief that the world of creation—of space, time, and matter—is in principle good, and that whatever YHWH does in the future will liberate that creation from all that has corrupted it, all that has threatened to destroy it. "New creation" will be patterned on the resurrection of Jesus, whose body was raised from the tomb never to die again. The "old," which is done away with in the "new," is the decay and mortality which, though built in to the way creation currently works, will ultimately give way to God's larger intention. This theme of new creation, modeled on Jesus's resurrection, becomes a major theme, indeed a climactic theme, in Paul's letter to the Romans.

Third, the promises are, we might say, *temple-shaped*. The Jerusalem temple, looking back to the wilderness tabernacle, functions within the larger story of the Bible as a pointer to the eventual rescue and transformation of the whole of creation. It is no accident that Jesus made the Jerusalem temple a major focus of his final days, speaking and acting out the message of judgment for Jerusalem's failure to recognize the time of divine visitation.[45] Nor is it accidental that John's gospel signals from the start that the tabernacle and the temple provide the clues to Jesus's identity and vocation. The word became flesh and *tabernacled* in our midst; Jesus spoke of the *temple* of his body.[46]

Fourth, whether in Genesis or in First Kings or elsewhere, the divine purposes for creation and for the temple (which points to creation) are put into operation *through the central human figure*. The first humans, male and female, are God's image-bearers in the cosmic temple of Genesis 1. Aaron the priest ministers at the heart of the tabernacle in Exodus 40, and then in Leviticus. Solomon leads the prayer and worship at the dedication of the temple. The promises about justice and mercy for the poor and oppressed, resulting in the earth being filled with the knowledge of God (Isaiah 11) and the glory of God (Psalm 72) are to be fulfilled through the work of the coming king.

All this leads to an initial conclusion that will be surprising to most modern Western readers. It is commonly taught and thought that, while the Old Testament speaks about God coming to earth, the New Testament reverses this and speaks of how human beings might go to heaven. But this is quite wrong. *The New Testament claims that the Old Testament's promises have been, are being, and will be fulfilled in and through Jesus and the spirit.* The hope held out in Israel's scriptures appears in retrospect like an unfinished tune, moving forward toward an as-yet-unheard resolution.

3

CREATION AND TEMPLE: THE GLORY COMES TO DWELL

From Genesis to David

The vast overall promise of the creator God filling all creation, saturating it with his splendid presence, is one of the great biblical themes. In parallel with it, Israel's scriptures articulate the second promise: that YHWH, having abandoned the Jerusalem temple, would one day come back in glory. But to understand this we have to start a long way back, with the much earlier story as told in scripture.

I assume that the biblical books where this narrative is displayed, from Genesis through to 2 Kings, were brought together, edited, and arranged, in some cases from much older material, during the time of the Babylonian exile. Fortunately for our present purposes we do not need to know in any detail when the different traditions arose, what editorial processes they underwent, or how, when, and by whom they were brought together into their final form. From a Christian point of view, what matters is that by the time of Jesus they constituted the narratival core of Israel's scriptures. They are the books that, along with the Psalms and the Prophets, shaped Jesus's sense of vocation and mission, and then his followers' sense of what his kingdom-bringing work ("on earth as in heaven") was really all about.

The case I am making in the present book, then, does not need a long display of the early history of Israel. What we need is to note briefly the ways in which the biblical promise, of God's dwelling with his people (rather than people going to live with God), emerges at key points that are then picked up (not denied, undermined, or "translated" into something else) in the later Christian writings.

We have already indicated that Genesis 1, the first creation story, is told in such a way as to indicate that creation, the heaven-plus-earth reality, is like a temple. This is where humans would meet with the divine presence.[1] In particular, temples in the ancient world routinely focused on a central, special, and often secret place where the image of the divinity was kept. The image would be the focal point of worship. People would offer sacrifices and prayers before it. In that sense, the people of the town, village, country, or wherever the temple was located would look forward to their regular pilgrimages to the shrine, the times when they could bring their homage and their hopes into the divine presence. To that extent, they would want to "go to be with the god"—as the Psalmist is longing to do in poignant poems such as Psalms 42 and 43:

> *Send out your light and your truth; let them lead me;*
> *let them bring me to your holy hill and to your dwelling.*
> *Then I will go to the altar of God, to God my exceeding joy;*
> *And I will praise you with the harp, O God, my God.*
> (Psalm 43:3–4)

But the reason they would hold on to this hope was because, in the image at the heart of an ordinary (non-Israelite) temple, *the divine presence had already come to dwell in their midst.* The image made the divinity present to the people, inviting their response of worship, loyalty, and obedience. That is why, in many ancient cultures, the idea of the image would spill out into the social and cultural life of the society, with the king being seen as the image of the divinity. Traces of this notion are still found, through to the modern period, in the idea of the "divine right of kings."

But Genesis 1 has a different story to tell. Genesis 1 sketches a metaphysic—a heaven-and-earth description of the whole cosmos—in which human beings are the image at the heart of the temple-creation. *All* human beings, we note, not just "special" ones. Female as well as male; all their descendants, not just one particular one at a time. You can read it both ways: as a democratization of a royal prerogative, or an ennobling of all humans.

Anyway, the point of creating this heaven-and-earth world, like the point of building a temple, is so that *the Creator can come and dwell there*, taking his rest, not in the sense of having nothing more to do after a busy week, but in the sense of *coming to be at home.*[2] Humans are designed to stand, like the image in a shrine, at the threshold between heaven and earth, creatures of earth and yet called to reflect heaven to earth as well as earth to heaven. "Called" here is important: this is about the human *vocation*, a much richer and more biblical category than the frequent picture of Genesis 1–3 being simply about sin. Indeed one could helpfully reframe moral discourse as a whole in terms of the human, image-bearing vocation.

This primary vocational purpose, I have argued elsewhere, is expressed at key points in terms of the royal priesthood.[3] The "royal" bit is the human vocation to look after creation, bringing it into the wise order intended by its Creator. The "priestly" bit is the summing up of creation's worship. All temples were intended to be mysterious, with the divine presence hidden behind the "image" and yet revealed through it; now, in the creation-temple, it seems that humans are designed to be the Creator's means of veiled self-disclosure. They are to be God-revealers, with God being mysteriously present with them, "behind" them, "through" them. If heaven and the highest heaven cannot contain the Creator, how much less can these humans, frail and vulnerable, be the perfect expression of his power and glory. And yet, as with Solomon's temple, the writer of Genesis is telling us that, in the human vocation to be image-bearers, God will be present and active, at work in his creation.

The point of all this ought to be clear—even though it flies in the face of most modern Christian assumptions. Genesis 1 and 2 are not describing earth as a "training ground for heaven," still less as a moral *testing* ground to see if the humans are fit to go to heaven and be at home there with God. For humans, creation is their home. It is where they belong. And *it is where God wants to be at home with them*, to give them the dignity of responsible agency within the world over which he delights. They are to know him, and to be agents of his glorious purposes for his creation.

The book of Genesis shows how this works in practice. The story eventually focuses on Joseph, to whom the book devotes roughly the same space as had been accorded to Abraham. The story of Joseph completes a kind of circle with Genesis 1:

Joseph is portrayed as the archetypal wise human, the image-bearer whose skill and intervention bring rescue, reconciliation, and hope after three generations of sibling rivalry, violence, and famine. We should not miss the narrative shock of Jacob's family finding forgiveness and new harmony after the duplicitous and near-murderous behavior of Isaac and Ishmael, Jacob and Esau, and Joseph's own brothers. Joseph, as it were, picks up the narrative that stretches back to Cain and Abel and provides its long-awaited moment of healing and hope.

But the reason there is a chosen family in the first place, with Joseph as one of its more prominent examples, is that from Genesis 3 to 11 things have taken a disastrous turn. The "fall" of Genesis 3 does not mean that the humans are barred from "heaven." Rather, they are alienated from the garden, their real God-given home, the quite literally *earthly* project whose cultivation had been the primary task for their stewardship, their royal priesthood. But the sorry tale of human evil reaches its peak with humans who really *do* think their task is to climb up to heaven—by building the Tower of Babel (Genesis 11:1–9), completing in a sense the city-building project begun by Cain (Genesis 4:17). This project is, as it were, the opposite of the image-bearing vocation; instead of reflecting God's wise stewardship within creation, the builders were constructing an idolatrous home that focused on their own security and well-being (11:4). The writer makes the point graphically: God *comes down* (11:5) to see what's going on, to judge the human arrogance, and to disrupt it, preventing the humans from establishing a power base that might rival his own, a home in which he would be unwelcome. That sets the context for the very different narrative, which, beginning in

Genesis 12, launches the project of human rescue and, with it, the project of God's intention (despite human unwillingness, rebellion, idolatry, and injustice) to fill the world with his knowledge and glory. Ironically but tellingly, this great moment of transition in the biblical narrative, leading ultimately to God making his home among humans, begins with a childless nomad.

The stories of Abraham, Isaac, and Jacob, and then of Jacob's squabbling, violent, and amoral children, reinforce the point I am making here, which is that these narratives are obviously not about these people "going to heaven when they die," or indeed about them being "heroes of faith." Abraham's great moment of faith, believing that God would give him an uncountable family like the stars in the sky, and a land for them to live in (Genesis 12–15), has often been interpreted in terms of much later ideas about "faith," not least because of the use Paul made of the passage, particularly of the phrase "he reckoned it to him as righteousness" (15:6). I have argued elsewhere that Paul has been misunderstood at this point, with the text being read as though this was the moment when Abraham was "justified" in the sense of being given a "divine righteousness" that, satisfying the demands of a heavenly law court, would enable him to "go to heaven" (not of course that Genesis says anything of the kind). That is simply anachronistic.[4]

What is far more important for our purposes, and actually for Paul's as well in the long argument from Romans 3:21 to the end of chapter 8, is God's promise of *family* and *land*. The human project in Genesis 1 had envisaged humans being "fruitful" and looking after the garden. Abraham is promised that God will make him "exceedingly fruitful," giving him and his offspring the land of Canaan. Abraham puts down markers to that effect, erecting altars where he "invoked the name of YHWH" (e.g., 12:8). In other words, he invokes the presence and power of the creator God to fulfil the promises that, at the time, must have seemed way beyond all human possibilities. Family and land? Abraham, as I just said, was homeless and childless, a nomad with no offspring. Paul sees these promises fulfilled in the creation, through Messiah and spirit, of the ultimate multiethnic family for Abraham, and in the inheritance, not of one strip of territory only, but of the whole world.[5] The Psalmist had already pointed in this direction.[6]

The subsequent meetings between God and Abraham all reinforce the point. God appears to the patriarch in the strange image of the firepot and torch in 15:17, symbolizing the establishment of the covenant. He appears to him again in 17:1, and then again in the image of three travelers (18:1–22). This becomes confusing when, though the strangers have left, Abraham remains "standing before YHWH" (18:22). But the point for our purposes is the initiative of God in visiting Abraham. There is no suggestion that Abraham is thereby being invited to make a return visit, going somewhere else ("heaven"?) to meet God.

The same point can be made in relation to the stories of Isaac and Jacob, with one of the high moments for our present purposes being the "ladder," which Jacob sees in his dream after having run away from his angry brother. The ladder connects heaven and earth (28:12). YHWH stands at the top.[7] It would be easy for Christian interpreters to suppose that the point was to show Jacob the way to heaven, but the text is saying something quite different. The point is, rather, that Jacob is being promised the blessing of heaven on earth—specifically, on *his* bit of earth, the land of promise:

> *I am YHWH, the God of Abraham your father and the God of Isaac; the land on which you lie I will give to you and to your offspring; and your offspring shall be like the dust of the earth, and you shall spread abroad to the west and to the east and to the north and to the south; and all the families of the earth shall be blessed in you and in your offspring. Know that I am with you and will keep you wherever you go, and will bring you back to this land, for I will not leave you until I have done what I have promised you.*[8]

"On earth as in heaven," indeed. When Jacob wakes up, his reaction endorses that view. "Surely YHWH is in this place," he said, "and I did not know it."[9] He calls the place Beth-el, the House of God. The claim of the creator God on the whole world has become focused on the promised land, and the promised land in turn has become focused on one spot. The stone that served as Jacob's pillow is set up, anointed, and given a name—and is remembered in subsequent Israelite tradition. The whole story is about God's homecoming.[10]

There then follows what we might describe as the first great exile. The famine that had brought Joseph to prominence at Pharaoh's court also brought his brothers to Egypt, where the family remained for four generations. But the way the story is told emphasizes that this was not where Abraham's family was supposed to be in perpetuity. Indeed, their long but circumscribed residence there had been part of God's early promise, as in 15:13–16. Not only was Egypt not "the promised land." Egypt was a land of idols, of foreign divinities. It was impossible to worship YHWH properly there, and worshipping YHWH was the Israelites' primary vocation. Moses had to explain that to Pharaoh when giving the reason for the Israelites needing to leave. Slavery was of course a driving reason. Slavery is incompatible with true being-at-home. Additionally, the Israelites wanted to be able to worship their true God in a way that was impossible in Egypt, their pagan slave master.[11]

By contrast with Egypt, Mount Sinai turns out to be "holy ground" (Exodus 3:5). The reader already knows that this is just the start. God has reiterated the promises made to Abraham, Isaac, and Jacob, to give the people the promised land (3:7–10). And so the story unfolds, with Sinai as part of the vital preparation for that homecoming.

The book of Exodus is a powerful narrative of getting the people out of their plight in Egypt and on their way to the Promised Land, supplying them in the process with a stringent moral code. Undergirding this narrative at every turn is its unifying theme: *God coming to dwell with his people.* This major theme of Exodus must be borne in mind all through. Granted that Jesus and his first followers saw Passover and the Exodus as the vital stories that provided the context of meaning for his decisive kingdom-bringing work, we should pay close attention to how the book of Exodus sets up its own climax.

Here there is a problem. Moralistic western Christianity has focused attention on the giving of the Law on Mount Sinai. The Law in turn has been seen as the great ethical standard that all humans break, resulting in a universal condemnation from which one can only be rescued by the work of Jesus. This story has been universalized, particularly in the last two centuries or so, making the Law a kind of overall categorical imperative. But whether in the Reformational retellings of the story (highlighting the problem of law-breaking and the solution provided by the gospel), or in the Kantian or Enlightenment mode in which "Law" stands for all external moral codes, Exodus 20 has loomed too large and Exodus 40 far too small. The construction of the tabernacle, and its filling with the divine glory, have often seemed like an anticlimax, or a side issue. Protestant fear of "religious ritual," not to mention of supposedly sacred buildings, and European fear of Judaism, have conspired to push Exodus chapters 21 to 40 to one side, with attention being then concentrated on the (supposedly universalizable) moral law in chapter 20. This then gets transposed into a general idea of "moral commandments," detached from its original context—moral commandments that are broken by all humans, reinforcing the sinful status of humans as in Genesis 3–11 (and Romans 3:23, a key text in such retellings).

But this is not what the editor of Exodus had in mind. The book unveils what "worshipping God in the desert" was really supposed to be all about, when Moses gave that as the reason for wanting the Israelites to leave Egypt. Israel was called to be the representative nation for the whole of humanity. To that end, the creator God would come to dwell in her midst. This was the point of bringing them out of Egypt in the first place:

> *You have seen what I did to the Egyptians, and how I bore you on eagles' wings and brought you to myself. Now therefore, if you obey my voice and keep my covenant,*

> *you shall be my treasured possession out of all the peoples. Indeed, the whole earth is mine, but you shall be for me a priestly kingdom and a holy nation.*[12]

There we have it again: the worldwide reach of the divine purpose, and the specific vocation of Israel to serve that larger plan (much like the creation of heaven and earth, and the specific vocation of humans to serve that larger intention). Israel has to be prepared for this, made ready to be the Tabernacle-bearing people, the people in whose midst the living God comes to dwell. Hence the gift of the Law: *not to be a legalist's charter for self-salvation, nor to be a threatening voice warning of hellfire and thus driving people to seek salvation elsewhere*, but to form and shape the people in whose midst the Creator would come to make his home. The Law is a charter for that ultimate homemaking. Exodus 20, in other words, is designed to prepare the way for Exodus 40. Here, as elsewhere, our ecclesial traditions over many years have *moralized our anthropology*, assuming that the only thing that really matters is how people behave and what can be done when they get it wrong. Behavior matters enormously. But the larger story of God's purposes includes human behavior within a quite different narrative.[13]

The revelation on Mount Sinai becomes the scene, in Exodus 24, for a remarkable event. Moses and Aaron, Aaron's sons Nadab and Abihu, and seventy elders of Israel are summoned up the mountain to meet God face to face.[14] The scene has long puzzled ancient and modern commentators both Jewish and Christian, granted the normal assumption that nobody can see God and live.[15] Moses is told as much when he asks to see the divine glory; he is only allowed to see God's back.[16]

This is not the place to pursue that puzzle. But it is important to note that the scene cannot be used, as some have tried to use it, as an argument for saying that the ultimate goal in life is to see God. The revival in our day of teaching about the "beatific vision" has looked to passages like this for support, but this will hardly work.[17] The people who go up the holy mountain with Moses cannot be regarded as exemplary saints. Aaron will shortly make the golden calf. Nadab and Abihu, two of Aaron's sons, will later rebel, presuming to create their own style of worship and being destroyed by divine fire as a result.[18] The focus is not on the possibility of humans going up into the presence of God. The story moves forward, driven by God's intention to come down, dangerously it seems, into the midst of Israel.

As with the patriarchal stories, there are—to put it mildly—serious problems and distractions on the way. The tabernacle project is carried forward. But Aaron—the man called to stand at the heart of the Tabernacle, playing Adam at the heart of the new creation—is responsible for the most blatant and potentially disastrous idolatry and wickedness in all Israel's history. During Moses's prolonged absence up the mountain, Aaron makes a golden calf: a ghastly, lifeless parody of the real God who had rescued Israel. The inevitable result is that God announces he will now not come with the people or dwell in their midst. He scornfully declares that, as far as he is concerned, the people now belong, not to him, but merely to Moses. He will send an angel to guide them, but he will not come in person:

> *YHWH said to Moses, "Go, leave this place, you and the people whom you have brought up out of the land of Egypt . . . I will send an angel before you . . . but I will not go up among you, or I would consume you on the way, for you are a stiff-necked people."*[19]

Moses is once more driven to urgent intercession. No, he says; they are *your* people, and *you* brought them out of Egypt; what makes us special is precisely that you dwell in our midst. It's *your* reputation that is at stake. It is *your* homemaking project that is on the line, and homemaking will now require forgiveness.[20] God concedes the point. The covenant is renewed. The tabernacle is constructed. The ark of the covenant, the place where YHWH promised to meet with the people, is placed in the innermost part. Then,

> *The cloud covered the tent of meeting, and the glory of YHWH filled the tabernacle. Moses was not able to enter the tent of meeting because the cloud settled upon it, and the glory of YHWH filled the tabernacle.*[21]

This is where the whole book of Exodus, and actually the whole scriptural narrative from Genesis 3 or even Genesis 1, has been going.[22] God has come to dwell in his new home. This was why he brought the people out of Egypt. Torah had been given to prepare them for this. The point was not to suggest that humans should find their way up to God. The point was to insist that, despite rebellion, idolatry, sin, and hard-heartedness, God in his mercy and grace would come to dwell with his people, to take forward his larger plan for the whole of creation.

The tabernacle, however, is not just the place where God intends to meet with his people. It is a forward-pointing sign to the renewal of all creation. Its construction echoes the creation of the world. Aaron and his sons, despite their sin, function as the image-bearers who, in the absence of any carved "image," stand at the threshold between the dangerous presence of the living God and the awed and reverent human worshippers. The entire book of Leviticus, following at once in Israel's carefully edited scriptures, functions as a kind of "health and safety" code: these are the detailed regulations that will be needed if the living God is truly to dwell among his people.

This, it seems, is the correct way to interpret the Levitical sacrificial system. Despite much misunderstanding down the years, the sacrifices were not designed to punish animals vicariously, allowing sinful humans thereby to escape the fate they might otherwise incur. The only animal that has sins confessed over it is precisely the one that is *not* killed, namely, the scapegoat. The sacrificial system was not, in other words, providing a way for sinners to be forgiven so that they could go to be with God.[23] It was designed to cleanse the tabernacle from the infection of human sin so that God could come to be with them. The blood symbolized God-given life. It was to be used as a moral and cultic disinfectant, to rinse the holy place free from all stain of death, including both sin and every kind of impurity.[24] The purpose of the law was not to enable sinful humans to approach God, but to make it possible for the holy God to live among sinful humans.

From one point of view, this might seem to come to the same thing. God and his people will dwell in fellowship. But whereas Western theology has normally assumed that the vital question is "how to get sinners into God's presence," the scriptural narrative is about God finding the way to live within his creation. The call of Abraham and his family, and their call to be the tabernacle-bearing people, was the vital first move in this plan. The divine glory that now filled the tabernacle was the glory with which God had promised to fill the whole earth. That is what the story is all about.

The narrative that runs from the Exodus to the Exile has several focal points, but for our purposes the key to the story is the temple, which becomes the successor to the wilderness tabernacle.

Once the Israelites had settled in the Promised Land, the tabernacle was "parked" at Shiloh, a town north of Bethel in the hill country of Ephraim. It became the center for Israelite worship. That was where the boy Samuel became assistant to the priest Eli. But when faced with a Philistine invasion, the Israelites tried to use the ark of the covenant as a talisman in battle, hoping that the promise of God being in the midst of his people would secure a victory:

> *Why has YHWH put us to rout today before the Philistines? Let us bring the ark of the covenant of YHWH here from Shiloh, so that he may come among us and save us from the power of our enemies.*[25]

That he may come among us: that is the key. That is what the ark signified. The Philistines recognize it and are afraid, resolving therefore to fight all the harder.[26] But the reader already knows, from the second chapter of 1 Samuel, that Israel as a whole and the house of Eli in particular have been utterly careless of YHWH and his ways. Invoking God's presence when it might be convenient, having ignored it when it wasn't, is a recipe for disaster. The ark is captured. Eli's sons are killed. His daughter-in-law, hearing the news, dies in childbirth, naming her son Ichabod, the Hebrew word for "the glory has departed."

The divine glory was supposed to dwell in the midst of Israel. Now it has gone.[27]

The Israelites may have abused the ark by treating it as a magic symbol, to be invoked only when convenient, but the Philistines discover that it still has potency. Their local god falls down in front of it. They try moving the ark elsewhere, but wherever they take it they find that sickness and death strike the people.[28] So they send the ark back, to the mixed delight and consternation of the Israelites, who are only too aware of danger as well as glory (6:13–7:1). Eventually it is lodged at Kiriath-Jearim, a few miles west of Jerusalem, where it stays during the reign of Saul. When David becomes king—a whole story in itself—he chooses Jerusalem to be his capital. It was easily fortified, and, because until that point it had not been captured by the Israelites, it was now able to serve as a focal point for all the tribes. But for this to make full sense, David had to bring the ark to Jerusalem, not to send it back to Shiloh where it had been before. The underlying theme remains the dwelling of God among his people.

David and the Temple

David's desire to bring the ark to Jerusalem, and to build a permanent dwelling place for it, then precipitates a plan and a prayer that resonate forward into the time of Jesus and are invoked by his first followers to explain what has just happened. This is where, in later Judaean thought and then in a new way among the early Christians, the hope for a coming king merges remarkably with the hope that YHWH will dwell forever in the midst of his people.

David proposes to the prophet Nathan a great project: Why not build a permanent shrine for the ark? Nathan, after an initially favorable response, comes back the next day with a different word from YHWH. David's hope of a permanent dwelling for YHWH will be fulfilled. But the ultimate answer to the royal question is that YHWH will give David a "house"—not a building, but a family:

> *YHWH declares to you that YHWH will make you a house. When your days are fulfilled and you lie down with your ancestors, I will raise up your offspring after you, who shall come forth from your body, and I will establish his kingdom. He shall build a house for my name, and I will establish the throne of his kingdom forever. I will be a father to him, and he shall be a son to me. When he commits iniquity, I will punish him with a rod such as mortals use, with blows inflicted by human beings. But I will not take my steadfast love from him, as I took it from Saul, whom I put away from before you. Your house and your kingdom shall be made sure forever before me; your throne shall be established forever.*[29]

In other words, though Solomon will indeed build the physical house that David has in mind, the ultimate divine answer to the question, How will YHWH dwell with his people? will not focus on a building, or indeed a tent. What will endure will be the house that consists of David's son, adopted as God's own son, and his kingdom and his throne. That will be the mode in which Israel's God will come home to his people once and for all and forever. When we think of the whole sweep of biblical narrative from the perspective both of second-temple

Judaeans (as for instance at Qumran) and the early followers of Jesus, this promise of the coming king, through whom God's purposes will be established, stands out.

The early Christians added an all-important dimension that their second-temple predecessors had not. The coming king would be the one *in whom God's personal presence would forever dwell with them.* "See," says the risen Jesus at the end of Matthew's gospel, "I am with you always, to the end of the world." The Emmanuel promise, quoted in Matthew's first chapter, has come fully true.

As with the stories of Abraham, or the Exodus, this spectacular moment in David's story is swiftly followed by one of the all-time low points: David commits adultery and murder.[30] This introduces the dark note of corruption into David's family, which eventually precipitates his own exile, as his son Absalom rebels and David has to flee Jerusalem. In the larger narrative of Samuel and Kings we see the point: despite all the divine promises, despite times of rescue and reaffirmation, as for instance under Hezekiah (2 Kings 18–19), Israel as a whole will have to do as David did. The people's sin will lead to exile.

But that is to run ahead of ourselves. The medium-term fulfillment of Nathan's oracle is of course the building of the temple by David's son and heir, Solomon. The description of the planning and building of the magnificent structure (1 Kings 5–7) resonates with the instructions for building the tabernacle in Exodus. Both look back, as we have seen, to the creation story in Genesis 1. So, too, the moment when all is completed, and the divine glory comes to dwell in the newly built house, offers a clear echo of Exodus 40:

> *Then the priests brought the ark of the covenant of YHWH to its place, in the inner sanctuary of the house, in the most*

holy place, underneath the wings of the cherubim . . . And when the priests came out of the holy place, a cloud filled the house of YHWH, so that the priests could not stand to minister because of the cloud; for the glory of YHWH filled the house of YHWH.[31]

Solomon's response is to insist that the dense cloud of the divine presence is just what one ought to expect:

YHWH has said that he would dwell in thick darkness. I have built you an exalted house, a place for you to dwell in forever.[32]

He then explains further to the people the sequence of events: David had intended to build a house for YHWH, but the task had devolved onto him. Again, the reference to Exodus is explicit:

I sit on the throne of Israel, as YHWH promised, and have built the house for the name of YHWH, the God of Israel. There I have provided a place for the ark, in which is the covenant of YHWH that he made with our ancestors when he brought them out of the land of Egypt.[33]

This brings Solomon to his great prayer, which we have already noted. It opens with one of the all-time vital biblical questions: "Will God indeed dwell on the earth?" After all, as he says, "heaven and the highest heaven cannot contain you, much less this house that I have built."[34] Here we are at the heart of it all. And this is where the ways divide in subsequent Christian interpretation.

Much of the Christian tradition has recognized the truth of the divine "transcendence," the absolute "otherness" of God, and has rightly rejected easygoing forms of pantheism, in which one ends up blessing the created order as if it were itself divine. But that same tradition has then routinely embraced instead a version of Platonism in which "heaven," a sphere ultimately far removed from "earth," is the real destination at which humans should be aiming. This is not the story scripture is telling. The God whom heaven cannot contain has graciously promised to place his name in this house, so that the Temple will form the perpetual place of overlap between heaven and earth. The apparent incompatibility of heaven and earth leads, not to humans being summoned away from earth, but to the endless grace of God. Solomon prays:

That your eyes may be open night and day towards his house, the place of which you said, "My name shall be there," that you may heed the prayer that your servant prays towards this place. Hear the plea of your servant and of your people Israel when they pray towards this place; O hear in heaven your dwelling-place; heed and forgive.[35]

Solomon continues, envisioning the many situations that might give rise to urgent prayer: false oaths, defeat in battle, drought, famine, blight, imminent war. At each point God's people must pray toward the temple, where God has put his name. Foreigners are to do so as well,

so that all the peoples of the earth may know your name and fear you, as do your people Israel, and so that they may know that your name has been invoked on this house that I have built.[36]

Finally, Solomon foresees the possibility, as predicted in Deuteronomy, that the people will go into exile because of their sin. (Again, we are reading the story as a second-temple Judaean might see it.) From far away they must pray toward the land, the city, and "the house that I have built for your name."[37] Solomon blesses the people, keeping one eye on the larger implications of what is going on. Israel is not simply one people among many, and Israel's God is not simply a local or tribal God. Rather, what this God does in and for Israel, focused now on Jerusalem and its new temple, has worldwide implications:

Let these words of mine, with which I pleaded before YHWH, be near to YHWH our God day and night, and may he maintain the cause of his servant and the cause of his people Israel, as each day requires; so that all the peoples of the earth may know that YHWH is God; there is no other.[38]

The promises come with a warning. If Israel turns away from YHWH, disaster will follow, including the desolation of the temple.[39]

That, of course, is what happens. The rest of 1 and 2 Kings tells a sorry tale in which things steadily fall apart. Solomon organizes gangs of forced labor, not unlike the slavery in Egypt. He gives up some of the promised land in exchange for help from a nearby pagan monarch. And his foreign wives draw his heart away to idols.

The kingdom is then divided under Solomon's successor Rehoboam. The breakaway leader, Jeroboam, becomes king over the northern tribes, leaving only Judah and Benjamin under Davidic rule. With a clear echo of Aaron in Exodus 32, Jeroboam makes not one but two golden calves, placing them at Bethel in the middle of the country and at Dan in the far north. "Here are your gods, O Israel," he says, "who brought you up out of the land of Egypt."[40] The narrative that follows lurches from one wickedness to another, with the people worshipping the Baal (a Canaanite fertility god) and abandoning the moral standards of YHWH.

The prophets, especially Elijah and Elisha, warn of what is to come. Eventually, the northern tribes are carried off as captives by Assyria, and the land is resettled by people from many regions.[41] Then, despite the rallying of Judah under Hezekiah (2 Kings 18–19) and the reforms of Josiah (2 Kings 22–23), the southern kingdom slides back into idolatry and wickedness. Finally Babylon, having tried to make Judaea a client kingdom, loses patience when the puppet king Zedekiah rebels. A disastrous siege follows. The king and his family are captured. The temple is plundered and burned to the ground, along with the king's house and all other great dwellings in the city. The writer of 2 Kings tells the story in detail, but without any of the raw emotion that we find, for instance, in the Lamentations of Jeremiah, or indeed in the relevant Psalms (such as 74 or 137). But one cannot read through 1 and 2 Kings without being shocked by the contrast between the great plans and promises of 1 Kings 8 and the final devastation of the temple in 2 Kings 25. If the temple is the linchpin, the linking point, between heaven and earth, then creation itself has been unmade. The world, said Jeremiah, is going back to *tohu wa-bohu*, being "without form and void" as in the primeval chaos of Genesis 1:2.[42]

The worst of it all was, of course, that the divine glory that had dwelt in the temple was now gone. This is a familiar story. I have explained it more than once before, in other writings. But we need at least to sketch the outline here, because the major point from this whole narrative, looming up above the detail and pointing forward to the early Christian reflection on Jesus and the spirit, is that *the promise of the Creator to fill the whole earth with his glory is now focused on the promise of YHWH to return to Zion.* This follows exactly the logic of the link between creation and temple. And it is these promises, rather than anything to do with a plan to take human souls up to "heaven," that the early Christians eagerly retrieve as they tell the story of Jesus and the spirit.

4

THE DEPARTING AND RETURNING GLORY

The Glory Departs—But Will Return

Ezekiel gives a dramatic account of the departure of the divine glory. The temple has become the focus of corruption and wickedness (Ezekiel 4–8). Judgment is decreed against the idolators (Ezekiel 9). So the divine throne-chariot, on which Israel's God is riding, leaves the temple and the city to its fate (10:1–32; 11:22–25). That sense that "the glory has departed"—a dramatically extended version of 1 Samuel 4:21—haunts the exilic and postexilic periods. Some of the later rabbis, faced with the thought of divine homelessness, speculated that the divine glory had gone to live with the exiles in Babylon. But the prophets of the period seem innocent of that idea. Rather, they insist that the glory will return when the temple is rebuilt at last:

> *Then he brought me to the gate, the gate facing east. And there, the glory of the God of Israel was coming from the east; the sound was like the sound of mighty waters; and the earth shone with his glory . . . As the glory of YHWH entered the temple by the gate facing east, the spirit lifted*

me up, and brought me into the inner court, and the glory of YHWH filled the temple.[1]

The gate through which the divine glory enters the city will then remain shut, except (mysteriously) for the arrival of the "prince," who will come and go that way.[2] Ezekiel thus foresees a "new creation" in which Jerusalem will resonate with the creation story in Genesis 2: living water will flow from the temple to make even the Dead Sea fresh.[3] The book concludes dramatically:

And the name of the city from that time on shall be, YHWH is there.[4]

Ezekiel's prophecy of the return of the divine glory to Jerusalem is woven together with many suggestions that this will be a time not only of Israel's restoration but of the repair of all creation. People will say:

This land that was desolate has become like the garden of Eden; and the waste and desolate and ruined towns are now inhabited and fortified. Then the nations that are left all around you shall know that I, YHWH, have rebuilt the ruined places, and replanted that which was desolate; I, YHWH, have spoken, and I will do it.[5]

This will be the "covenant of peace" promised earlier, with the people finding their true security in God's protection and provision.[6]

The clearest statement of this theme, explicitly linking YHWH's return to Zion with the larger theme of the transformation of all creation, is found in Isaiah, especially chapters 40–55. Those chapters pick up the combination of motifs already announced in chapter 35:

The wilderness and the dry land shall be glad,
The desert shall rejoice and blossom; like the crocus it shall blossom abundantly
And rejoice with joy and singing.
The glory of Lebanon shall be given to it,
The majesty of Carmel and Sharon.
They shall see the glory of YHWH, the majesty of our God.

Strengthen the weak hands, and make firm the feeble knees.
Say to those who are of a fearful heart, "Be strong, do not fear!
Here is your God. He will come with vengeance, with terrible recompense.
He will come and save you."

Then the eyes of the blind shall be opened, and the ears of the deaf unstopped;
Then the lame shall leap like a deer, and the tongue of the speechless sing for joy.
For waters shall break forth in the wilderness, and streams in the desert . . .[7]

Here is your God! In these passages, upon which the early Christians drew so richly to understand Jesus and what he had accomplished, we hear nothing of humans leaving earth and going to heaven. The prophetic hope is not about a far-off world. It is about God coming back to dwell with his people, so that, in the rescue and restoration of the exiled and shamed Israel, creation would be renewed. At every point the text is not speaking about humans in general, or Israel in particular, being saved in the modern Western sense. The prophetic promises envision Israel being rescued from exile and brought back to the land. They see this as the signal for the wholesale renewal of the created order.

Every valley shall be lifted up, and every mountain and hill
be made low;
The uneven ground shall become level, and the rough places
a plain.
Then the glory of YHWH shall be revealed, and all people
shall see it together,
For the mouth of YHWH has spoken . . .

See, the Lord YHWH comes with might, and his arm rules
for him;
His reward is with him, and his recompense before him.
He will feed his flock like a shepherd;
he will gather the lambs in his arms, and carry them in his
bosom,
And gently lead the mother sheep.[8]

Isaiah 40 sets the tone, and advertises the content, of the whole matchless poem we know as chapters 40–55. Everything else here—victory over the Babylonian gods, comfort and encouragement for Israel in distress, and above all the accomplishment of YHWH's servant—is set within this framework. Thus, as the poem reaches its sustained climax with the death and vindication of the servant, the return of YHWH is emphasized, echoing chapter 40 with excited anticipation:

How beautiful upon the mountains
are the feet of the messenger who announces peace,
who brings good news,
who announces salvation,
who says to Zion, "Your God reigns."
Listen! Your sentinels lift up their voices,
together they sing for joy;
for in plain sight
they see the return of YHWH to Zion.
Break forth together into singing,
you ruins of Jerusalem;
for YHWH has comforted his people,
he has redeemed Jerusalem.
YHWH has bared his holy arm
before the eyes of all the nations;
and all the ends of the earth shall see
the salvation of our God.[9]

And, in case anyone should imagine that this "return to Zion" is a private affair for Israel only, unrelated to the vision of new creation in passages such as Psalms 96 and 98, the poem concludes, after the fourth "servant song" (Isaiah 52:13–53:12) and the announcement of covenant renewal (Isaiah chapter 54), with the worldwide invitation to share in the delights of God's redeemed world (Isaiah chapter 55). In the passage we looked at previously in connection with the meaning of the word "heaven," the "word" that, in chapter 40, was the promised agent of new creation ("the grass withers, the flower fades; but the word of our God will stand forever"[10]), will now complete the renewal of the whole earth:

For as the rain and the snow come down from heaven,
and do not return there until they have watered the earth,
making it bring forth and sprout,
giving seed to the sower and bread to the eater,
so shall my word be that goes out from my mouth;
it shall not return to me empty,
but it shall accomplish that which I purpose,
and succeed in the thing for which I sent it.
For you shall go out in joy, and be led back in peace;
the mountains and the hills before you shall burst into song,
and all the trees of the field shall clap their hands.
Instead of the thorn shall come up the cypress;
instead of the brier shall come up the myrtle;
and it shall be to YHWH for a memorial,
for an everlasting sign that shall not be cut off.[11]

With this central poem (chapters 40–55) as its fulcrum, the book we now call "Isaiah" concludes with several oracles all applying the same point. YHWH will come back, and will restore both Zion and all creation. At no point is there any suggestion that God will come to take people to heaven, away from the earth. Rather, YHWH is coming to rescue his people and renew the earth:

YHWH saw it, and it displeased him that there was no justice.

He saw that there was no one,
and was appalled that there was no one to intervene;
so his own arm brought him victory, and his righteousness upheld him . . .
And he will come to Zion as Redeemer,
to those in Jacob who turn from transgression, says YHWH.[12]

Arise, shine, for your light has come,
and the glory of YHWH has risen upon you.
For darkness shall cover the earth, and thick darkness the peoples;
but YHWH will arise upon you, and his glory will appear over you.
Nations shall come to your light, and kings to the brightness of your dawn . . .

The sun shall no longer be your light by day, nor for brightness shall the moon give light to you by night;
but YHWH will be your everlasting light,
and your God will be your glory.[13]

The larger hope, for the total renewal of all creation, comes forward into the present as God's spirit anoints the speaker (the prophet? the coming Messiah?) to bring signs of the future hope even in the present time of distress:

The spirit of the Lord YHWH is upon me,
because YHWH has anointed me;
he has sent me to bring good news to the oppressed,
to bind up the broken-hearted,
to proclaim liberty to the captives, and release to the prisoners;

to proclaim the year of YHWH's favor,
and the day of vengeance of our God;
to comfort all who mourn . . .[14]

This, then, clarifies the mode of YHWH's long-awaited return. It will include the powerful, justice-bringing presence of YHWH's own spirit, enabling the one who is anointed with the spirit (echoing Isaiah 11:2, as well as the "wind of God" brooding over the dark waters in Genesis 1:2) to be YHWH's agent in putting the world to rights.

This future hope is anchored in the memory of the Exodus, when God came in person, and in power, to rescue his people:

It was no messenger or angel, but his presence that saved
them;
in his love and in his pity he redeemed them;
he lifted them up and carried them all the days of old.[15]

The prophet therefore prays, not that YHWH will take his people away from their land or from the earth, to dwell with him in heaven, but that he will come *from* heaven once more:

O that you would tear open the heavens and come down,
so that the mountains would quake at your presence—
as when fire kindles brushwood and the fire causes water
to boil—
to make your name known to your adversaries,
so that the nations might tremble at your presence![16]

The answer comes with the assurance—and the warning—of God's righteous judgment (65:1–16). But this gives way to the promise of "new heavens and new earth," incorporating the vision of the peaceable kingdom from Isaiah 11 (65:17–25). In preparation for that new reality, what will matter is not a rebuilt temple (the prophet raises the same question that Solomon had posed in 1 Kings 8:27, but gives it a rather different answer) but humble, attentive worshippers:

Thus says YHWH: Heaven is my throne, and the earth is
my footstool;
what is the house that you would build for me,
and what is my resting place?
All these things my hand has made,
and so all these things are mine, says YHWH.
But this is the one to whom I will look,
to the humble and contrite in spirit,
who trembles at my word.[17]

God will indeed come back to rule and reign, to rid his world of evil and corruption and to restore his true people:

For YHWH will come in fire,
and his chariots like the whirlwind,
to pay back his anger in fury,
and his rebuke in flames of fire . . .
For as the new heavens and the new earth
which I will make
shall remain before me, says YHWH,
so shall your descendants and your name remain.[18]

Isaiah, then, holds together the twin themes: YHWH, the Creator, will renew his entire creation; YHWH, Israel's covenant

God, will rescue and restore his people, returning to them in person.

Thus the larger promise, that God would fill the whole earth with his glorious presence, has become focused on the specific promise that God will return to Zion; and that this will be accomplished not least through God's anointed, personal agent. These are nested together. God will not take people away to be with him in heaven. The God of heaven will come to act in power, mercy, and judgment on earth.

Isaiah offers the most sustained and developed treatment of these themes, but they are picked up in various other books of the exilic and postexilic periods. We already noted Ezekiel 43. We must now add the last four books of the prophetic canon. Zephaniah echoes Isaiah:

Sing aloud, O daughter Zion; shout, O Israel!
Rejoice and exult with all your heart, O daughter
Jerusalem!
YHWH has taken away the judgments against you,
he has turned away your enemies.
The king of Israel, YHWH, is in your midst;
you shall fear disaster no more.
On that day it shall be said to Jerusalem:
Do not fear, O Zion; do not let your hands grow weak.
YHWH, your God, is in your midst,
a warrior who gives victory;
he will rejoice over you with gladness,
he will renew you in his love . . .[19]

Haggai encourages those who are rebuilding the Temple, assuring them that YHWH's glory will indeed return:

Work, for I am with you, says YHWH of hosts,
according to the promise that I made you when you came out of Egypt.
My spirit abides among you; do not fear.
For thus says YHWH of hosts:
Once again, in a little while,
I will shake the heavens and the earth and the sea and the dry land;
and I will shake all nations, so that the treasure of all nations shall come,
and I will fill this house with splendor, says YHWH of hosts.
The silver is mine, and the gold is mine, says YHWH of hosts.
The latter splendor of this house shall be greater than the former,
says YHWH of hosts;
and in this place I will give prosperity, says YHWH of hosts.[20]

Zechariah, too, promises that YHWH will return to Jerusalem and to the rebuilt Temple:

Therefore (thus says YHWH) I shall return to Jerusalem with compassion,
and my House shall be rebuilt in her.[21]

Sing and rejoice, O daughter Zion!
For lo, I will come and dwell in your midst, says YHWH.
Many nations shall join themselves to YHWH on that day,
and shall be my people;

and I will dwell in your midst.
And you shall know that YHWH of hosts has sent me to you.
YHWH will inherit Judah as his portion in the holy land,
and will again choose Jerusalem.
Be silent, all people, before YHWH;
for he has roused himself from his holy dwelling.[22]

Thus says YHWH of hosts:
I am jealous for Zion with great jealousy,
and I am jealous for her with great wrath.
Thus says YHWH:
I will return to Zion, and will dwell in the midst of Jerusalem;
Jerusalem shall be called the faithful city,
and the mountain of YHWH of hosts
shall be called the holy mountain.[23]

The coming of YHWH, heralded in song by "daughter Zion," is then focused on the arrival of the coming king, whose peaceful rule will extend over the whole earth, echoing the messianic prophecies in the Psalms and elsewhere:

Rejoice greatly, O daughter Zion!
Shout aloud, O daughter Jerusalem!
Lo, your king comes to you;
triumphant and victorious is he,
humble and riding on a donkey, on a colt, the foal of a donkey.
He will cut off the chariot from Ephraim, and the warhorse from Jerusalem;
and the battle-bow shall be cut off,

and he shall command peace to the nations;
his dominion shall be from sea to sea,
and from the River to the ends of the earth . . .
Then YHWH will appear over them . . .[24]

In all these texts three themes are particularly relevant to my present argument. First, YHWH has indeed promised to return to Jerusalem, but there is no suggestion that this has yet happened.[25] Second, once more the whole narrative thrust focuses on the coming of God to his people, not, in other words, on any suggestion that *they* would find their way to *him*. Third, as in passages like Isaiah 11 and Psalm 72, the vision of God's coming peaceable kingdom is firmly tied to the arrival of the ideal king, through whose work, it is implied, this new creation will come about.

Now we must bring in the final prophet. In Malachi's day the temple had been rebuilt after the return of some Judaeans from Babylon. But the priests were bored and careless. They were sacrificing third-rate, polluted animals. And several of the men among the returned exiles—as we see in Ezra 9 and 10—had divorced their Judaean wives and married local, non-Judaean women instead. So Malachi comes with a stern warning, not that they might not, after all, go to heaven when they died, but that they faced imminent judgment when God himself returned as he had promised:

See, I am sending my messenger to prepare the way before me, and the Lord whom you seek will suddenly come to his temple. The messenger of the covenant in whom you delight—indeed, he is coming, says YHWH of hosts. But who can endure the day of his coming, and who can stand when he appears? For he is like a refiner's fire and like fuller's soap; he will sit as a refiner and purifier of silver, and he will purify the descendants of Levi and refine them like gold and silver, until they present offerings to YHWH in righteousness.[26]

The "messenger preparing the way" looks back to the angel in Exodus 23:20, who was to prepare the way before the Israelites as they journeyed, with the strange divine presence in their midst, toward the promised land. More specifically, it invokes the prophet Elijah:

> *Lo, I will send you the prophet Elijah before the great and terrible day of YHWH comes. He will turn the hearts of parents to their children and the hearts of children to their parents, so that I will not come and strike the land with a curse.*[27]

This brings us to the end of the story told in Israel's scriptures. We could amplify various elements by giving the Psalms a more prominent role, but the picture would remain the same. To sum things up one more time: at no point do Israel's scriptures suggest that the aim was for people—some people, all people, devout Judaeans, whoever—to "go to heaven" to be with the creator God. At no point do the scriptures hold out an ultimate hope for devout Israelites to gaze on the creator God in an otherworldly bliss. From Genesis to Malachi (or, in the Hebrew canon, Genesis to Chronicles), the dangerous but life-giving promise is that the creator God will come to dwell with humans. He will fill all creation with his own presence and the knowledge of his glory. In other words, he will do for "all the earth" what he did in filling the tabernacle, and then the temple, with his glory. This cosmic promise becomes increasingly focused on the Zion-specific promise: having abandoned the temple at the time of the Babylonian exile, the glorious divine presence will return, in public and fully visible, and with powerful effect in terms of judging the wicked and establishing the long-awaited kingdom of justice and peace:

> *Here is your God; he will come with vengeance, with terrible recompense; he will come and save you.*[28]

> *The glory of YHWH shall be revealed, and all people shall see it together.*[29]

> *Your sentinels lift up their voices; together they sing for joy; for in plain sight they see the return of YHWH to Zion.*[30]

And this ultimate promised future can be anticipated through the present work of the divine spirit, as for instance in Isaiah 61.

One intertestamental tailpiece to the point that no one at the time thought these promises had yet been fulfilled. In the second chapter of 2 Maccabees[31] the writer reflects on the tradition that, at the time of the Babylonian exile, Jeremiah had hidden the ark and the altar of incense from Solomon's Temple in a cave on Mount Sinai. According to this tradition, Jeremiah had declared that the hiding place would remain unknown

> *until God gathers his people together again and shows his mercy. Then YHWH will disclose these things, and the*

glory of the Lord and the cloud will appear, as they were shown in the case of Moses, and as Solomon asked that the place should be specially consecrated.[32]

But the story that follows, even though it culminates in the Judaean victory over the pagan king Antiochus Epiphanes and the purification of the temple, makes no mention of the glory and the cloud appearing. This absence remains characteristic of the whole period.

Only in Ben-Sirach (c. 200 BC) is there any hint that perhaps YHWH has returned in visible glory. The passage in question (Sirach 50) is a panegyric on the glorious appearance of the high priest Simon son of Onias (c. 219–196 BC). The text hints at the possibility that when people looked at Simon in all his finery they were in fact gazing on the divine glory, that he was somehow the very embodiment of Israel's God. But within a generation this glittering hope had been smashed to pieces. Simon was part of a priestly succession that was swept away a few years later through the Syrian crisis, to be replaced by the Hasmonean dynasty. Few Judaeans after that will have regarded the over-ambitious claims of Ben-Sirach as anything other than an excess of enthusiasm on the part of the author, an aristocratic contemporary of Simon.[33]

On the contrary. It will have been abundantly clear to Jesus's contemporaries in Judaea and Galilee that the great prophecies, and particularly the promise of YHWH's return, had not yet been fulfilled. The Temple in Jerusalem, of course, still carried the powerful memory of its former glory. That's how sacred spaces work. Daily worship and the annual round of festivals continued as normal. Jesus spoke, it seems, of people continuing to bring sacrifices to the holy place.[34] Josephus, in a well-known passage, speaks of angels departing from the Temple before the Romans closed in.[35] But a moment's thought would show that all was not yet well. If YHWH had really returned, to dwell there in glory, the Syrians couldn't have desecrated the Temple in 167 BC. Pompey would not have been able to march straight into the Holy of Holies in 63 BC. In particular, Herod and his family would not now be rebuilding and beautifying the whole structure, as they were doing in the last years BC and the first years AD. Tellingly, when the later Rabbis listed various things that had been in Solomon's Temple but that were missing from the second Temple (including the ark of the covenant), they include the glorious divine presence, the *Shekinah*, in that list.[36]

There was, then, no sense among second-temple Judaeans that the ancient promises of glorious divine return had already been fulfilled. But the themes of an extended exile, and of the delayed promises of YHWH's return, come back regularly in one form or another. Those promises, focused as they were on the restoration of Jerusalem, the recovery of the land, and the liberation of the Judaean people, encapsulated the larger hope of creation's renewal. But that hope, though focal, remained elusive.

It was this hope, rather than some other, that the early Christians declared had been fulfilled in Jesus, however surprisingly, and was being further fulfilled through the spirit.

At the same time, various would-be messianic claimants came and went, with none achieving more than a passing notoriety or a small following.[37] But the promises of YHWH's return, though intertwined as in Isaiah 40–55 with the themes of a mysterious anointed figure, were not brought together in the intertestamental period in the way the early Christians came to see them. YHWH was to come back; some texts spoke of David as active within the new state of things;[38] but the coming of God and the coming of a Messiah were not normally joined together or mutually interlocked. That, too, was more or less an innovation of the earliest followers of Jesus, though they were quick to draw on passages such as 2 Samuel 7, which spoke simultaneously of the building of a dwelling place for God and of the coming of a true Davidic king. Though the texts we have from the period do not fill in the details of how the various long-awaited events might be related to one another, the glorious redemptive and renewing return of YHWH does appear to overlap and interlock with the promises about a coming king. Thus, if the Creator's world of heaven and earth focuses on the person and role of the image-bearing humans, the coming world of new creation appears to pivot on the person and role of David's long-awaited heir.

This focus on YHWH's return to the temple, and on the true Davidic king, does not draw attention away from the larger cosmic perspective. Again, the relevant texts bring all this together. The clearest of the prophetic promises, in Isaiah 40–66, still has the eventual goal of creation's renewal, brought about by the apparently royal servant. The promises made to David are now, indeed, to be shared with all the people, but they are not denied or forgotten.[39] The Psalms, taken as a whole and in many individual cases, do the same.

Hope and Hermeneutics

All this brings into fresh focus the question of biblical hermeneutics. Does a Christian reading of Israel's scriptures require an allegorical view of the Promised Land or Jerusalem as a picture of heaven, the real goal or inheritance? When we move from Israel's scriptures into the early Christian writings, in what sense if any is there a shift of subject, a change of gear? Have Jesus and his disciples spiritualized the whole tradition?

As we have seen, most western Christians have imagined that the answer is Yes. If the point of Christianity is for people to go to heaven when they die, we must find ways of making Israel's scriptures point forward to this, despite their obvious surface meaning. But the evidence is strongly the other way. Again and again, Israel's scriptures show God's purpose to come from heaven and fill the whole earth afresh with his glory, resulting in nothing less than a renewed creation. These promises were focused on the Temple in Jerusalem, whose "filling" with the glorious divine presence was a sign of that larger purpose. And as Israel, the bearer of these promises, suffered devastation and exile, those same promises about the divine glory suffusing all creation were focused ever more sharply on the promise of the personal and visible return of YHWH to Zion. Thus, if these are the promises the early Christians believed were fulfilled in Jesus and the spirit, then either they have been translated into a quite different mode, or much of the Christian tradition has seriously misread the New Testament. I think the latter is the right answer. I shall explore this disturbing possibility further in the Interlude of chapters 8–10.

How then are we to plot continuities and discontinuities? Would it not have been simpler—as much of the church has done de facto, following the explicit lead of Marcion—to put Israel's scriptures to one side as either irrelevant or actually misleading, and to start afresh with Jesus, and with the hope of heaven that he was, supposedly, offering in the gospel?

The early Christians would have been shocked at the very suggestion. The New Testament announces in several interlocking ways that the story it tells, and the salvation it holds out, are to be seen as the *same* story, and the *same* salvation, as the one to which

Israel's scriptures had been pointing. As we shall see in the next chapter, the gospels begin where Israel's scriptures left off: with the promises of Malachi and Isaiah (Mark), with the retelling of the Exodus narrative (Matthew), with echoes of the stories of Samuel and David (Luke), and with the invocation of Genesis and Exodus (John). To say nothing of Paul, Hebrews, and the rest. This rich, multitextured retrieval of the great themes and expectations of Israel's scriptures comes together not least in the interplay, as described in the gospels, between Jesus and the Temple. And it issues in the strange new world, as discussed in Acts and the Epistles, where the God of Israel is said to be powerfully at work through his spirit, coming "home" to dwell, not just *with* Jesus's followers but *within* them. As Jesus promised in John 14, what we are witnessing is *the homecoming of the triune God.* Jesus, the Word made flesh, has come to tabernacle in our midst. The spirit, the Word made breath if you like, has come with the same intent, to enable Jesus's followers to be for the world what he was for Israel.[40]

So when the early Christians say that the events concerning Jesus happened "in accordance with the scriptures" (1 Corinthians 15:3, quoting a widely known early tradition), it looks as though this meant much more than surface-level proof texts. Jesus's first followers really did intend to say that Jesus, and the new life-way that sprang into existence through him, was *the reality to which Israel's scriptures as a whole had been pointing.* And we have seen what that ancient scriptural hope was all about: the coming of God to rescue his people and to restore creation to its intended state of justice and peace. If today's believers were even to glimpse that proposal, let alone to work out what it might mean in practice, it would make an enormous difference to the life and vocation of Jesus's followers as we navigate our way through the strange and often threatening world of the twenty-first century.

5

THE HUMAN FACE OF THE GOD WHO COMES

Introduction

The four canonical gospels—Matthew, Mark, Luke, and John—ask us to do something most readers have found difficult if not impossible. They tell the story of a young man with a short but dazzling public career: quick-witted, shrewd, compassionate, friendly, challenging, funny, alarming, compelling. A healer, a teacher, a campaigner. One who fell afoul of the authorities and came to a horrible end—but who was then, outrageously and improbably, raised from the dead. And the writers of these books ask us, as we listen to their stories, to hold in our minds the overarching rubric: *This is what it looked like when all those biblical promises came true*. The promises, in particular, about YHWH coming back at last. The promise, too, of a long-awaited king. The promises about all creation being filled to overflowing, saturated, with divine glory. This is what God's homecoming looked like.

There are two reasons why it has been difficult to do what the gospel writers ask. First, we have assumed that the story *must* somehow be all about "how we get saved and go to heaven," even though it doesn't say that. In fact, since the stories hardly ever mention the question of what happens after death, we end up misreading passage after passage, twisting them to fit the theory, allegorizing frantically, and usually missing the huge, liberating truth that the evangelists were bursting to tell us.

Second, we have come to the story of Jesus with a fixed view of who God is. In western culture, God has often been seen as high and mighty, a long way off, not only immortal but immoveable, all-powerful, all-knowing, present everywhere, always working toward the good (these are the famous four omni's: omnipotent, omniscient, omnipresent, omnibenevolent). If you come with *that* view of God, which is culled from Greek philosophy rather than from Israel's scriptures, you may perhaps read the gospels in terms of that god merely seeming to be human—at best, an elaborate pretense. Or you may, perhaps, read them in terms of a fully human being who quite obviously was not divine in that sense. Many so-called conservative Christians have gone the first route.[1] Many liberal Christians (and many, if not most, non-Christians) have gone the second.

In the academy, we were all taught various methods (source criticism, form criticism, redaction criticism, "traditio-historical criticism," and sundry other things) that, after a century and more, turn out to be learned and complex ways of avoiding the enormous claim that all four books make. Much academic study of the gospels has not even mentioned—perhaps because it has not even noticed—the multiple ways in which these stories are claiming to describe what it looked like when Israel's scriptures were fulfilled: when God came home at last. What has called itself "historical criticism," in fact, has usually been overly "critical" and not nearly enough "historical."[2] As a general rule, the academic methods have paid little attention to the actual historical setting, the *Judaean* context of the narratives, to the resonances that the gospels set up with the Judaean world of the day, and particularly the hope for God's kingdom "on earth as in heaven." This is part of the de-Judaizing of early Christianity about which we shall have more to say in due course.[3]

There are, no doubt, various reasons for this. But the net result has been a failure to glimpse what all four books, in their interestingly distinctive ways, were wanting to say: that we should understand the kingdom-bringing work of Jesus, in life, death, resurrection, and ascension, in terms of the ancient Israelite and Judaean hope of YHWH's return to renew both covenant and creation.

Within academic study, the gospels have fragmented into small glimpses of the early church's self-understanding and self-expression. This failure of reading, led particularly by Rudolf Bultmann, had deep roots in German idealism and similar movements.[4] But the fragmentation of the gospels has also been helped on its way by the normal expectation that Jesus must have been teaching people how to avoid going to hell and how to get to heaven instead. In order to arrive at that reading, you have to scour the gospel stories for small hints, ignoring Jesus's constant claim that God's kingdom was arriving on earth as in heaven. We have thus strained out the "gnats" (arguing over small historical details) and swallowed the "camel" of a platonic inversion of the biblical message. Thus Jesus's "powerful works" have just become miscellaneous "miracles," perhaps designed to prove his "divinity" as part of a modernist apologetic against Deism, without any sense of how a first-century Judaean might see them. We have ignored the way in which the gospel stories draw on older, scriptural traditions, providing at point after point a shocking, radical, but also deeply satisfying answer to the unanswered Judaean questions about God's return in glory.

Those unanswered questions are indeed the starting point for all four gospels, though in quite different ways. The writers take for granted the world we have been looking at, the world of the scriptures, the Judaean world that was waiting, hoping, and praying for YHWH to return to his temple, to overthrow pagan rule, to establish justice and peace in the world, and finally to fill all creation, saturating it with his glory. They set the story of John the Baptist, and then particularly the story of Jesus, within that world. That, and nowhere else, is where it makes the sense it makes.[5]

Mark

Mark opens (1:2–3) with two of the most obvious prophetic passages in our earlier survey (Malachi and Isaiah), and an echo of a third. Here is Malachi 3:1, promising that God will send a messenger ahead of him, to get things ready for his own arrival. And then here is Mark, telling the story of John the Baptist preparing the way for Jesus. The extra echo here is of Exodus 23:20: YHWH will send an angel ahead of Israel, into the promised land, to get things ready—and then he himself, dwelling in the movable tabernacle in the desert, will come in due time, will come to dwell in the midst of his people. Then here is Isaiah 40:3, speaking of the voice that calls out in the desert, getting everything ready for YHWH, for his glory to be revealed so that everyone will see it. How much clearer could Mark make it? John the Baptist is the advance messenger, the voice in the desert. *The one who comes after him can be none other than YHWH himself.* For John, this is a moment of hope—and also great danger:

> *"Someone a lot stronger than me is coming close behind," John used to tell them. "I don't deserve to squat down and undo his sandals. I've plunged you in the water; he's going to plunge you in the holy spirit."*[6]

Within Mark's story, and within his evocation of Israel's story, he can only be referring to Israel's God. But what happens next indicates that Mark has in mind a dramatic combination of scriptural themes. What in one passage will be accomplished by Israel's God might elsewhere be achieved through the coming king, exercising authority delegated from God. But these themes do not seem to be combined in texts of the second-temple period. That is not to say they couldn't have been, or that they never were (perhaps in texts now lost to us), merely that we have no evidence for such a combination.

Here in Mark, however, the two themes are woven tightly together. Having been told in no uncertain terms that John the Baptist is preparing the way for the arrival of Israel's God, we are introduced to Jesus, heralded through the voice from heaven:

> *Then there came a voice out of the heavens: "You are my son! You are the one I love! You make me very glad."*[7]

This text echoes, and combines, Psalm 2 (the king who will be God's "son" and ruler of the whole world) and Isaiah 42 (the "servant" through whom God's saving plan for Israel, and God's consequent plan for all creation, will be effected). The wide, flowing river of scriptural promise comes rushing together into a narrow crack in the rock of time, producing the powerful torrent of fulfillment that Mark is about to describe. We are invited to view the whole fast-paced story that follows in terms of passages like Isaiah 11. Perhaps, Mark's reader ought to be thinking, this is what it looks like for the spirit to equip Israel's Messiah to bring about a new era of wisdom and peace, judging wickedness, rescuing the poor, and filling the world with the knowledge of YHWH.

We ought not then to be surprised when Mark's story leads Jesus to confrontation with the temple in Jerusalem. The biblical conjunction of temple and creation is now focused on the human being at the heart of the divine plan. Mark has instructed us to read his story of Jesus in those terms. Jesus, not the temple, is now filled with the divine glory, as the sign and means of God's plan for the world. That becomes momentarily visible at the "transfiguration."[8] When Mark later draws attention to Jesus's sayings about the destruction of the temple and the vindication of the "son of man," those sayings resonate within the acoustic chamber precisely of biblical expectation.

Let's put this argument the other way around. Supposing Mark, aware of Israel's traditions about "the coming of God" and the consequent rescue and transformation of Israel and all creation, had wanted to say, "Well, those were interesting ideas, but of course with Jesus we have the key to something very different, namely how we can leave earth and go to heaven." If that had been Mark's aim, he has made an embarrassing blunder by displaying Jesus in the way he has, both at the start of his gospel and then in its climactic scenes. No: Mark is insisting that we see Jesus through the lens of *those* scriptural expectations, not in some other way.

Jesus's contemporaries, after all, had various points of view. The Pharisees, the Essenes, the supporters of the Herodian dynasty, the various revolutionary groups, and many "ordinary Judaeans" (a deliberately vague category!), all had their own understandings of what it *ought* to look like if and when God came back in person, or indeed if that turned out to be simply a vivid metaphor for some kind of upturn in Judaean fortunes.[9] Jesus affirmed the prevailing hope for scripture to be fulfilled and carved out new ways of imagining what that might look like. That is what his parables were designed to do. That is how Mark presents them. Mark's story of YHWH's return is deliberately dramatic and subversive. But of one thing we may be sure: he is *not* saying, "Forget that Judaean expectation about God coming back to set up his rule on earth; Jesus, instead, is showing us the way to leave earth and go to heaven."

Matthew

If you are going to tell your readers that someone called Jesus has come to show the way to heaven, it is more than a little misleading to begin with a genealogy running from Abraham, through David, to the Babylonian exile, and then to a child who arrives after three groupings of fourteen generations. If there have been six "sevens" up to now, it looks as though we are beginning the seventh seven, the climax of the sequence—not, in other words, starting a quite different narrative. Matthew must intend his readers to see Jesus as the culmination, not the denial, of that long and often puzzling history. Nor is this about "progressive revelation," with the light steadily getting brighter as in some evolutionary scheme.

On the contrary, the best-known characters in the story come early on (not least Abraham, Isaac, and Jacob, and then David and Solomon). What little we know of subsequent ancestors is not particularly impressive; certainly not a crescendo toward a goal. But this, typical of many biblical schemes of promise and fulfillment, reveals a standard pattern: the long sequence of history, providential though puzzling, arrives all of a sudden at the unexpected, even shocking, fulfillment. "Covenant" and "apocalyptic" come together. And the "apocalypse" in this case, unveiling the fulfillment of the covenant promises, is the naming of the child who comes last in the genealogical sequence. He will be the "Emmanuel," "God with us," picking up the royal prophecy of Isaiah 7:14.[10]

Matthew reinforces this at the very end of his story. "Look," declares the risen Jesus to his friends, "*I am with you*" (Matthew 28:20). Not, "wait awhile and *you* will be with *me*"; rather, "*I* am with *you*." And, referring to Daniel 7, he claims "all authority in heaven and on earth."[11] Matthew clearly intends this as the fulfillment of the entire scriptural train of thought. Jesus is the Lord of *this* world, not of some other. The Gentile mission, for which the disciples are here authorized as his representatives, follows from this. Jesus is not pointing away to some allegorical reading in which Israel's story refers to the Neoplatonic goal of heavenly ascent and "beatific vision," with the disciples being commanded to tell the nations of this new possibility and to invite them to seek it.

All this demands, of Matthew's readers, a total change of perspective on such obvious passages as the Sermon on the Mount. Here we meet one of the best-known misunderstandings in the whole New Testament. Matthew almost always has Jesus refer, not to "the kingdom of God," as in the other gospels, but to "the kingdom of *heaven*." Since many readers quite naturally begin with Matthew, and probably assume that the point of Christianity is "to go to heaven," they routinely suppose that this is what Matthew (or Matthew's Jesus) is talking about when he says things like, "Unless your covenant behavior is superior to that of the scribes and Pharisees, you will never get into the kingdom of heaven" (5:20). The famous list of "beatitudes" ("Blessed are the meek" and so on, in Matthew 5:3–12) will then be read as a list of moral qualifications. Match up to these, Jesus seems to be saying, and you'll get into heaven; but if you fail, you'll miss out. But this is entirely wrong. Actually, as I have explained elsewhere, that whole approach does lasting damage to many ideas about God and salvation.[12]

The phrase "kingdom of God," or (in reverent periphrasis) "kingdom of heaven," was in fact a well-known slogan in Jesus's day.[13] It referred to the hoped-for time when Israel's God would come back at last to rule and reign over Israel and the world. It referred neither to "going to heaven" nor (as some in the twentieth century have proposed) "the end of the world" in some literal sense.[14] It was a way of gathering up the threads of biblical expectation and winding them together into a strong, tight cable of hope. Hope for the coming of God. For the *homecoming* of God.

Jesus was reaffirming that expectation—and redefining it. But the redefinition was not, as mainstream Christianity has often supposed (and as I grew up believing), a way of saying, "Well, the Judaeans have held a this-worldly hope, but I have come to tell you about an otherworldly, heavenly one instead." His fresh proclamation made no change to the idea of Israel's God ruling the whole creation (not just Israel) in a reign of justice and peace.

Matthew highlights two particular ways in which Jesus redefined the scriptural hope. The first redefinition had to do with Jesus himself being the kingdom-bringer. He would take Israel's role on himself; Matthew tells Jesus's story in terms of Israel's story, arranging his narrative into five great blocks of teaching to correspond to Israel's Torah. In particular, Jesus would embrace the dark strand of scriptural prophecy in which Israel's sufferings and ongoing "exile" would come to be concentrated on one spot, either on a small group of martyrs (as in Daniel and 2 Maccabees) or, in the case of Isaiah 40–55, on the "servant of YHWH."[15] In Isaiah's vision, the suffering and death of the "servant" (52:13–53:12) appears to be the mode in which YHWH "bares his holy arm before the eyes of the nations" (Isaiah 52:10), appearing at last in visible glory (Isaiah 52:7–8). That is how the covenant and the creation are to be renewed, with the open invitation going out to anyone and everyone who wants to benefit from it (Isaiah 55:1–9).

We have no evidence for any Judaean readers of scripture prior to Jesus expounding such a notion. Nobody expected a *Messiah* to die at the hands of the pagans; far less the returning God, YHWH himself. There is every reason to suppose that this radical innovation in the kingdom-of-God tradition goes back to Jesus, and that Matthew, like Mark, has displayed it appropriately.

The second main redefinition, which then opens up an entire strand of our investigation, is found in the role that Jesus appears to give his followers within his kingdom-project. Insofar as kingdom-movements in Jesus's day envisaged a group of people (like, for instance, the followers of Simeon ben Kosiba in the AD 130s), such a group would almost certainly consist of what we would call "freedom-fighters": revolutionaries, "zealots," ready to use violence to get rid of the hated pagans and usher in the new day. The hardline Pharisees (people like Saul of Tarsus!) would have agreed. The more moderate Pharisees, including ironically Saul's teacher Gamaliel, might have said that the key was for Israel to keep Torah properly and wait for God to act. In both cases, the arrival of the kingdom would involve at least some participation by loyal Judaeans. For Jesus, the kingdom would arrive in a dramatic way through his death and resurrection. But the way it would be implemented—a task that was to begin already during the course of his short public career—would be through his followers living in a different way, a way of humility and hope, hungry for justice, grieving over the wickedness and pain of the world, living by the rule of mercy, purity, and peace rather than by the way of violence. Such people, the "meek," would "inherit the earth," rather than the platonic dream of "going to heaven." The Sermon on the Mount showcases Jesus's own prayer, which highlights precisely the divine intention to establish his paradoxical earthly reign. It is astonishing, and tragic, to reflect on how many Christians have prayed that prayer while failing to realize that it meant what it said.

Once we see that Matthew really does intend to show how Jesus was fulfilling the scriptural promises we have examined in our previous three chapters, a whole new perspective opens up on Jesus's powerful works, both of healing and of multiplying food. We are still, unfortunately, heirs to the wrongly perceived eighteenth-century standoff between (a) followers of the philosopher David Hume, who declared that "miracles" were impossible, and (b) those who have felt under obligation to insist that God can and does "intervene," doing things that normally seem out of the question. The controversy has usually been badly framed. Both sides have regularly assumed either a Deist or an Epicurean view of a "distant" God. The skeptics would insist that such a "god" would never "reach in" and do extraordinary, "supernatural" things. The traditionalists would claim that he might indeed do such things from time to time, whether to prove his supernatural power or, more specifically, to demonstrate the "divinity" of Jesus. (This argument, advanced by nervous "orthodox" Christians in the last two centuries in particular, ignores the fact that the biblical resonances of Jesus's powerful deeds, particularly in terms of Elijah and Elisha, do not indicate unaided "divine" action or incarnation but rather the work of prophets.)[16]

Once we pay attention to Matthew's way of setting things out, we discover that he is well aware of the biblical prophecies about *new creation* and wants to highlight the fact that Jesus referred to them to explain what he had been doing. When the imprisoned John the Baptist sends messengers to Jesus to ask whether he really is "the one who is coming," Jesus in reply echoes Isaiah 35:

> *Go and tell John what you've seen and heard. Blind people are seeing! Lame people are walking! People with virulent skin diseases are being cleansed! Deaf people can hear again! The dead are being raised to life! And the poor are hearing the good news! And God bless you if you're not upset by what I'm doing.*[17]

Jesus's powerful actions, in other words, are not an alien invasion into the supposedly closed system of the present world. They reveal the world's Creator, active within his own world, to mend it, to put it right, to do, close up and personal, what the Creator has long promised to do for the whole creation. So too with the multiplication of loaves and fishes, and even with Jesus's walking on water. These are not miscellaneous "miracles" designed to "prove his divinity" in a Deist world where "supernatural" events might be supposed to carry that significance. They are the signs—again, picking up biblical expectations—of the divine spirit at work in a new way.[18] Signs, in fact, of God's homecoming.

In particular, they are the signs that the biblical expectations are being fulfilled, not translated into a different philosophical or metaphysical mode. Matthew's vision of God's kingdom stands firmly within the framework of scriptural expectation. Insofar as Matthew offers something new within that tradition, as he obviously does, it isn't a matter of pushing scriptural hopes to one side and replacing them with something radically different. As Matthew's Jesus says in the Sermon on the Mount (5:17), the point is not to destroy but to fulfill.

When Jesus appears deliberately to flout the Sabbath rules, this isn't a matter of rejecting the biblical hope and going in a different direction altogether. Jesus's actions have nothing to do with the Judaeans being "legalists" and him being a "libertarian," or using this as a test case for "living by grace rather than law." Those massively anachronistic (though still widespread) abstract analyses miss the point. For many Judaeans, every Sabbath was an anticipation of the Age to Come, the time when God would indeed become king on earth as in heaven.[19]

That was why not only rest from work, but also peace between all species, was mandatory. Isaiah 11 was arriving in the present, however fleetingly. But, for Jesus, Isaiah 11, and 35, and 40–55, and 56–66, were indeed arriving in the present, in and through his own work. The God of hope was arriving to take charge, however unexpectedly.

Matthew draws especial attention to this in the answer that Jesus sends to his anxious cousin in Herod's prison. Isaiah 35 is being fulfilled at last, even though not in the ways most people were expecting.[20] And this is because John was indeed the coming Elijah—which means, again, that Jesus was to be seen as the returning YHWH.[21] In Jesus, God has come home, and he is now offering the "rest" which that homecoming was always meant to produce.[22]

Luke

The biblical theme of God's coming is expressed in Luke's writings equally emphatically, even if in a different register. He opens his gospel with the surprising conception and birth of John the Baptist, woven together with the conception and birth of Jesus. The two run in parallel. Luke tells the story in such a way as to awaken echoes of the birth of Samuel, and then of Samuel's role in anointing David to be king in place of Saul.

For Luke, clearly, Jesus is to be the new David. Granted, the angel's announcement to Mary is at one level about the coming of God into the world ("the Holy One who is born from you will be called God's son," 1:35), but this is to be expressed in the Davidic work and rule of Jesus as Israel's Messiah ("he'll be called the son of the Most High; the Lord God will give him the throne of David his father," 1:32). The promises to Abraham and to David will be fulfilled through him (1:68–79). Luke makes more precise what was left as a hint in Mark 5:20. There, Jesus tells the healed demoniac in Gadara to "go and tell how much the Lord has done for you," whereupon he goes and tells everybody what Jesus has done for him. Mark leaves it ambiguous who "the Lord" actually is. Luke has no such reticence:

> *"Go back to your home," [Jesus] said, "and tell them what God has done for you." And he went off around every town, declaring what Jesus had done for him.*[23]

Like all the gospels, Luke highlights Jesus's confrontation with the temple in Jerusalem. Again making explicit what seems implicit elsewhere (and in parallel with John's very different way of making the same point), Luke sees Jesus's extended journey to Jerusalem as precisely the long-awaited return of YHWH to Zion. That is what is at stake in the often-misunderstood parable of the nobleman who goes away to be given royal authority and then returns (Luke 19:11–29). Jesus told the parable, says Luke, because they were getting close to Jerusalem after their long pilgrimage, "and they thought that the kingdom of God was going to appear at any moment" (19:11). Some have suggested that the excitement of the crowds was precipitated particularly by the remarkable behavior of Zacchaeus in Jericho, though that remains speculation.

But what does the story mean? More explicitly than in the Matthean parallel (25:14–30), Luke indicates that Jesus intends this story to be about Israel's God going away at the time of the exile, leaving Israel with tasks to perform, and now coming back to call his people to account. Jesus's response has often been read as saying, in effect, "No—it won't be at once; there will be a long wait while I myself go away and return." But, as verse 44 makes clear, Jesus's challenge to the crowd's expectations is not about postponement. The time of divine visitation has arrived. The people believe it; Jesus is reaffirming it. But his challenge is to the popular expectation that "the kingdom of God" would bless, vindicate, and validate the political hopes of the Judaean people. Instead, the imminent arrival of God's kingdom will mean judgment.[24] As Jesus, in tears, then rides down the slope of the Mount of Olives, he sobs out a devastating oracle of judgment:

> *"If only you'd known," he said, "on this day—even you—what peace meant. But now it's hidden and you can't see it. Yes, the days are coming upon you when your enemies will build up earthworks all around you, and encircle you, and squeeze you in from every direction. They will bring you crashing to the ground, you and your children within you. They won't leave one single stone on another, because you didn't know the moment when God was visiting you."*[25]

This was that moment of God's tragic homecoming, but they couldn't see it. This is exactly cognate with Jesus's rebuke to the two disciples on the road to Emmaus. The Messiah's crucifixion and resurrection was what Israel's scriptures had been pointing to all along, but even Jesus's own followers—and how much more his unbelieving contemporaries!—were "senseless" and "slow in your hearts to believe all the things the prophets said to you."[26] Luke, like Mark and Matthew, strongly endorses the scriptural hope, even while explaining that its fulfillment had come about in a way nobody had imagined. Nobody, that is, except apparently for Jesus. When the angels in Acts 1 tell the disciples to stop looking up into heaven, generations of interpreters should perhaps have taken the hint. And when Luke describes the coming of the spirit in Acts 2 we should pick up the resonances with the divine glory filling the tabernacle and temple.[27]

John

Of all the gospel writers, John is the one who most obviously evokes the scriptural promises of Israel's God returning to dwell with his people, as in the tabernacle or the temple. Like the other writers, John fuses this together with the recognition that Jesus is Israel's Messiah. This twin theme is framed by the famous Prologue in terms of a new Genesis: "In the beginning" (1:1) says it all. And, as with the biblical narrative that runs from the creation of the cosmos in Genesis 1 to the creation of the microcosmos—the tabernacle—in Exodus 40, the Prologue runs from the divine Word as the agent of creation to the divine Word as "becoming flesh" and *tabernacling in our midst*. The Greek here is striking (*ho logos sarx egeneto kai eskēnōsen en hēmin* (1:14), with *eskēnōsen* echoing the Greek *skēnē*, "tent"). In case of any remaining doubt, John adds—as a kind of running head for all that is to come—"we gazed upon his glory." The glorious divine presence that had filled both the wilderness tabernacle and the Jerusalem temple had returned at last, in plain sight as promised in Isaiah 52:8. And this—this Jesus!—was what it looked like. "Anyone who has seen me," declared Jesus later, "has seen the father."[28] If you want to gaze on God's glory, John is saying, don't imagine that your soul needs to go on a platonic journey to the heights of heaven. Just read this story and gaze at its central character.

Approaching the Fourth Gospel from this perspective opens up one of John's main themes: Jesus is the *replacement for the temple.* He speaks of himself in terms of Jacob's ladder, an obvious temple-symbol, linking heaven and earth in the time-honored manner (1:51). When he expels the traders from the shrine in chapter 2, he explains his action with the cryptic word about destroying and rebuilding the temple—a saying that, in Mark's trial narrative, comes back to haunt him.[29] John comments, tellingly: "He was speaking about the 'temple' of his body."[30] The human being Jesus is now the place where heaven and earth meet. There is a straight line from that point to the moment when the empty tomb is discovered, with an angel at either end of where Jesus's body had been lying—just as the seraphim stood guard at either side of the mercy-seat in the innermost shrine of the Temple.[31] All through, John is telling us (sometimes obviously, but more often with a measure of subtlety) that Jesus is the ultimate reality toward which the tabernacle and temple had been pointing all along.

We should not therefore be surprised when, after what had seemed to be the climax of the narrative with Jesus arriving triumphantly if dangerously in Jerusalem in chapter 12, we are taken aside from the excited crowds into an upper room, in private, where Jesus is giving the disciples their final instructions. These "farewell discourses" emphasize the forthcoming gift of the spirit, up to now mentioned only briefly.[32] The language of mutual indwelling, with which Jesus describes the gift of the spirit to his followers, is best explained in terms of his constituting them as, corporately and individually, the new shrine, the new Temple.

The key passages begin with John 14:15–20:

> *If you love me, you will keep my commands. Then I will ask the father, and he will give you another helper, to be with you forever. This other helper is the spirit of truth. The world can't receive him, because it doesn't see him or know him. But you know him, because he lives with you, and will be in you. I'm not going to leave you bereft. I am coming to you. Not long from now, the world won't see me anymore; but you will see me. Because I live, you will live too. On that day you will know that I am in my father, and you in me, and I in you.*

This prepares the way for the specific work the spirit will do in and through Jesus's followers. They are to be *witnesses*, and in that capacity to hold the world to account:

> *When the helper comes—the one I shall send you from the father, the spirit of truth who comes from the father—he will give evidence about me. And you will give evidence as well, because you have been with me from the start . . .*
>
> *It's better for you that I should go away. If I don't go away, you see, the helper won't come to you. But if I go away, I will send him to you. When he comes, he will prove the world to be in the wrong on three counts: sin, justice, and judgment. In relation to sin—because they don't believe in me. In relation to justice—because I'm going to the father, and you won't see me anymore. In*

relation to judgment—because the ruler of this world is judged.

There are many things I still have to say to you, but you're not yet strong enough to take them. When the spirit of truth comes, though, he will guide you in all the truth. He won't speak on his own account, you see, but he will speak whatever he hears. He will announce to you what's to come. He will glorify me, because he will take what belongs to me and will announce it to you. Everything that the father has is mine. That's why I said that he would take what is mine and announce it to you.[33]

Such passages, at first reading, may appear dense and forbidding. But at their heart, they are about Jesus's followers being equipped to carry forward into the wider world the work that he had been doing. They were to be for the world, in fact, what he had been for Israel.

People have often objected to this, citing John 18:36 (in the King James version, "My kingdom is not of this world"). But the Greek there is *ek tou kosmou toutou*, "*from* this world," as the end of the verse makes clear (in the King James, "now is my kingdom not from hence"). The kingdom is not, then, "from" the present world—Jesus's kingship is given from above—but it is certainly *for* this world, and is now to be implemented as such through the gift of the spirit:

"Peace be with you," Jesus said to them again. "As the father has sent me, so I'm sending you."

With that, he breathed on them.

"Receive the holy spirit," he said. "If you forgive anyone's sins, they are forgiven. If you retain anyone's sins, they are retained."[34]

John's resurrection narratives are all about new creation. The gift of Jesus's own spirit to his followers takes us back to passages where scripture had spoken of the divine spirit as the one who had dwelt in the tabernacle or temple.[35] The disciples are now to *be* that shrine. They are to be the sign, set up in the midst of the wider world, that God the Creator has won the victory over the powers of the world (as in John 12:30–33), and that he is even now renewing the cosmos. The mission of Jesus's followers is to be the advance sign of the ultimate new creation, summoning the world to forsake lifeless idols and worship the creator God.

John, in other words, like the other three, does not offer a reversal of the scriptural promises. He is not suggesting that Jesus has come to take people away from "earth" so that they can go to "heaven." John is disclosing the fulfillment of the scriptural heaven-and-earth narrative, focused on the ancient promise of the homecoming of God. Israel's God has returned to his people in the person of Jesus, *and now in the presence and power of his spirit.* Jesus's followers, equipped with this strange, new, powerful divine presence, are charged with living and speaking in such a way as to declare the news of judgment and mercy to the whole creation. John writes the resurrection story so as to say that new creation has indeed begun. Jesus's own risen body is the beginning. He is rightly mistaken for the gardener.[36] The rest will follow. God's own powerful presence will guarantee it.

The Fourfold Gospel

The fourfold gospel, then, was not designed to tell people how Jesus would take them to heaven. It was designed to tell them that, in Jesus, the creator God had kept his promise to come back, both to Israel and to the whole creation; to come *home* to the world he had made for himself. It was further designed—explicitly in John, implicitly in a few hints in the others—to explain that God was also "coming back" in a new and largely unexpected way: in the spirit, the mysterious but powerful breath that came to inhabit Jesus's followers. Thus the scripture-fulfilling work that needs to be done—the work of Isaiah 11, of Psalm 72, of the whole sweep of Isaiah 40–55 in its cosmic unfolding—is to be done, on earth as in heaven, by God the Creator, having come home to dwell with his people, working in and through the spirit to put into practice what Jesus, the appropriate human face of the one true God, has decisively accomplished. He has won the victory over the forces of evil, and launched God's kingdom on earth as in heaven. The spirit, working through his followers, will take the project forward from there. Then—though the four gospels say very little about this—Jesus will return, to complete the establishment of God's kingdom. That remains vital, of course, but too much focus on that ultimate hope has often led to these main gospel themes being ignored. As far as the gospels are concerned, the central theme of much western Christianity (the going-to-heaven story) is simply not on the radar.

But by this time many readers will have been saying "But what about . . . ?" There are indeed passages in the New Testament that appear to offer obvious exceptions to this rule. For them, we need a brief explanatory chapter.

6

THE APPARENT EXCEPTIONS

Today in Paradise

Whenever I have tried to explain the New Testament's reaffirmation of the Old Testament promises, people regularly come up with one or more of nine well-known apparent exceptions. It will be good to examine these more closely. When we do that, they strengthen the basic point rather than undermining it.[1]

We find our first example in the crucifixion narrative at the climax of Luke's gospel. Luke has one of the brigands crucified alongside Jesus saying, "Remember me when you finally become king"; or, in the well-known King James version, "Remember me when thou comest into thy kingdom."[2] This is, of course, ironic: it is failed Messiahs who end up on crosses. Any thought of Jesus being the true "king of the Judaeans" (as on the placard above his head) is out of the question. Jesus's response, however, has regularly been taken as an assurance of the usual going-to-heaven story: "I'm telling you the truth: you'll be with me in paradise, this very day."[3] The normal reading envisages Jesus saying, in effect, "Yes, you and I will be together in heaven."

But this runs into problems. As Luke's reader knows, or

will shortly, Jesus will not be staying in paradise for long. Insofar as we have any idea what paradise might mean to a first-century Judaean, it would most likely refer to some kind of intermediate state. The rare term "paradise" is in fact an old Persian word denoting a blissful garden or park, a place of peace and rest. It does not in itself convey any sense of "going to be with God," though Jesus does affirm that the brigand will at least be with *him*.[4] The word is rare in the New Testament, but its occasional other uses seem to confirm that it was a general term (gesturing back, perhaps, to the Garden of Eden) for a pure, transcendent realm, without being any more precise.[5] In the Judaean world of Luke's day, where the Pharisaic hope of eventual resurrection for all God's people was widely believed, the term might be used, as the word "today" strongly suggests, not to indicate a *final* postmortem state, but to denote the otherwise hard-to-describe "intermediate" state. By the time of Tertullian, "paradise" referred to the blissful resting place of the great saints, while the remainder of the faithful departed would enjoy a less exalted but still pleasant wait in the refreshment of a *refrigerium*.[6] Once again we remind ourselves that symbols like this are signposts pointing into a fog, not detailed photographic representations.

This interpretation is reinforced by the larger context. For Luke, obviously, wherever Jesus "was" immediately after his death, he was certainly alive again, in a quite new though definitely bodily sense, on the third day. One cannot, therefore, take Jesus's words to the brigand as an indication that, despite all the signs to the contrary, Luke supposed that "salvation" meant the going-to-heaven story. The saying then has a triple emphasis. First, Jesus is endorsing the strange idea that he really is "becoming king." Second, the effect of this (as with the parable in Luke 19) is immediate, not pushed ahead to a long-distance future: "Today"! Third, the promise of being with Jesus in "paradise" is not a promise of eventual resurrection, but it strongly implies it.

Room in My Father's House

The second apparent exception, widely quoted, is John 14:1–4:

> *"Don't let your hearts be troubled," Jesus continued. "Trust God—and trust me, too! There is plenty of room to live in my father's house. If that wasn't the case, I'd have told you, wouldn't I? I'm going to get a place ready for you! And if I do go and get a place ready for you, I will come back and take you to be with me, so that you can be there, where I am. And as to where I'm going—you know the way!"*

In the customary reading of this passage, Jesus is promising (a) that "heaven" is the ultimate destination of his followers, and that it has plenty of room for them, and (b) that he will eventually return (in the "second coming," presumably) to take them to be with him there.

If the passage has this meaning, it is unique in the New Testament, and certainly in John's gospel. But there are signs that Jesus is pointing to something different, something more in tune with John's larger themes. These may initially appear complex, but this is largely because our default mode has been so firmly set in the normal western tradition.

The overall thrust of John 14 is the challenge to the disciples to believe in Jesus, to trust him, and through the gift of the spirit, to do in the world the works that will continue and develop the work that Jesus has been doing. The basic homecoming here, stated at the climax of the chapter, will be that of both the father and the son, coming in the spirit to dwell with believers:

> *If anyone loves me they will keep my word. My father will love them, and we will come to them and make our home with them.*[7]

The chapter as a whole thus suggests a quite different understanding of the opening verses. There seem to be at least three overlapping points.

First, if the "home" where both father and son will come to dwell is the community of believers, then the phrase "in my father's house" can be read as referring to the father's *household*, the "house" or family within which there is plenty of room for all.

Second (this can seem confusing, but John's gospel is full of this kind of double meaning), the phrase "my father's house" clearly refers to the temple, a major theme throughout John. But the temple is the heaven-and-earth building, not simply an image of "heaven" itself. And, as we saw, ever since 1:14 and 2:21, Jesus has been designated as the ultimate reality to which the Jerusalem temple was an advance signpost. In belonging to him, the disciples are being given their places in this new temple.

This is presumably why, third, he goes on to explain that he is the "way" to the final destination (14:6). If there is also a long-range glance to the ultimate future, this is how it must work. John's reader already knows, from John 5:28–29, that Jesus promises his followers bodily resurrection, which implies the wider context of a whole new creation. Here he promises that, in between their own death and that final new reality, the God of heaven and earth will look after them, equipping them for their Jesus-like "works" in the present and, if there is also a glance at life beyond death, looking after them prior to their resurrection.

The key term here, which I have translated as "room to live," is actually in the plural: *pollai monai*, "many places to live." The word *monē* has a clear and regular meaning in Greek, and it is neither the King James version "mansions" nor any other sense of a permanent dwelling. A *monē* is not a final dwelling place. It refers, rather, to a place to stay for a while, perhaps a resting place on a journey.

This, I have discovered, is controversial. We had better consider some evidence.[8] The modern version of Arndt and Gingrich's *Lexicon*, though intending to suggest parallels for the sense of "dwelling-place," "room," or "abode," actually provides several passages that undermine this, suggesting rather that the word cannot mean a permanent residence. In Chariton's novel *Callirhoe* (1.12.1) the pirate chief Theron, having abducted the heroine, gets his men to land a few miles from Miletus in order to remain undetected while he decides what to do. He tells his men to "construct a shelter" (*monēn poiein*) for Callirhoe, not (of course) intending that she will live there forever, but only hoping to keep her safe overnight while further plans are hatched. Pausanias (10.31.7), cited for the same meaning, actually refers to a "stopping place" or "station," a temporary pause on a journey.[9] Josephus, retelling the story of Elijah running away to Mount Sinai, says that he found a cave where he "made his abode for some time" (*poioumenos en autō tēn monēn*); he had no intention of living there permanently. Other examples (cited, for instance, in the *Brill Dictionary of Ancient Greek*, which translates *monē* as "act of staying behind, rest, pause"), include a rest on a journey (Thucydides), a break on a march (Xenophon), a pause in a dance (Plutarch), or a staging post on the way (Clement[10]). Not until later Christian usage, where the word can denote a monastery, and may intend an echo of the present passage, does it refer to a permanent dwelling.

The sense of a *temporary* resting place, then, is the natural Greek meaning of Jesus's promise. Ahead of the final resurrection, any of Jesus's followers who die will be looked after until that great day. By the same token, the promise in John 14:23, where the word is used for the dwelling of the father and Jesus with those who keep Jesus's word, indicates that this, too, is in advance of the final restoration of all things.

In particular, then, the promise that Jesus will "come back and take you to be with me" is, to say the least, ambiguous in this context. The customary reading has been that Jesus will return at the "second coming" and take his followers to be with him in "heaven." But in the same passage the "coming again" of Jesus refers, not (or not primarily) to the "second coming," but to the "coming" of Jesus *in the form of the holy spirit*. Thus in John 14:18 he promises:

> *I'm not going to leave you bereft. I am coming to you . . .*
> *Because I live, you will live too. On that day you will*

know that I am in my father, and you in me, and I in you . . . Anyone who loves me will be loved by my father, and I will love them and show myself to them . . . If anyone loves me, they will keep my word. My father will love them, and we will come to them and make our home with them . . . I've said all this to you while I'm here with you. But the helper, the holy spirit, the one the father will send in my name, he will teach you everything . . . You heard that I said to you, "I'm going away, and I'm coming back to you."[11]

The promise is not that Jesus, at his own "second coming," will take his people to heaven. It is, rather, that when the spirit comes there will be a new kind of mutual indwelling. Believers will dwell in Jesus; Jesus will dwell in the father; Jesus-and-the-father will together dwell, by the spirit, in the believer—and they will be *at home* there. This state of affairs will be partial and incomplete until the final new creation and resurrection. But we have said enough to indicate that John 14:1–3 is best read as an assurance of Jesus's presence with his people in the new creation, presently inaugurated but not yet complete, rather than as a promise about going to heaven, specially not about heaven as a final destination.[12] John 20, describing Jesus's resurrection and his gift of the holy spirit, must be seen as part of the fulfillment of this promise, though there remains the haunting promise of Jesus's personal return in 21:22–23 ("If it's my intention that he should remain here until I come, what's that got to do with you?").

It thus appears that the gospels endorse the vision of Israel's scriptures, while narrating the shocking and unexpected mode of their fulfillment. God the Creator had made promises to

Israel and to all creation, promises shaped in advance by his coming to dwell in the wilderness tabernacle and then the Jerusalem temple. These strands of promise were concentrated on the divine intention to return to Zion after Israel's prolonged exile. The gospel writers, in their different ways, insist that God's promise to come home to his people and his world has been fulfilled in Jesus, and that it is being fulfilled, and will be fulfilled, by the spirit.

At Home with the Lord

The third apparent exception is the tricky little passage in 2 Corinthians 5:1–10. Taken out of context, what Paul says appears to reinforce the popular perception of Christian hope: he wants to be "away from the body and at home with the Lord" (2 Corinthians 5:8). But the wider context shows that Paul was certainly not talking about a permanent state of (a) disembodiment and (b) "going home" to be with Jesus. Chapter 5 verses 1–10 are explicitly, if complicatedly, about awaiting the resurrection.[13] He speaks of the ultimate state in terms of clothing: we do not want to be *un*clothed but to be *more fully* clothed (verse 4), so that the present physical body may be swallowed up by a life anticipated in the present by the spirit. The links with passages like Romans 8:9–11 (not to mention 1 Corinthians chapter 15!) are obvious. This should make it clear that "being at home with the Lord" designates, not a final disembodied existence, but the temporary state of being with Jesus while awaiting the resurrection. Paul, in any case, is writing out of a time of considerable suffering, making it the more understandable that, though he would indeed long for the final putting on of the resurrection body, he would look ahead with an almost equal desire to a time of being with Jesus and no longer undergoing physical tribulation.

Depart and Be with the Messiah

A similar train of thought is evident, fourthly, in a famous passage in the first chapter of Philippians. Facing the possibility of imminent death, Paul declares that in all sorts of ways he would prefer that: it would, he says, be "far better" to "depart and be with the Messiah," even though his sense of vocation indicates to him that he still has work to do for which that eventuality will have to be postponed. This passage, like the previous one, can indeed be used with integrity for the comfort and encouragement of those facing death, whether their own or that of one they love. But we should note what Paul does *not* say. He does not mention the going-to-heaven story. He does not say that the "soul" will then be "at home with the Lord" or "with the Messiah." There were, after all, many speculations about "life after death" in Judaean writings of the period. This makes Paul's cautious restraint all the more remarkable. He does not want to stir up speculation about a topic that was not central to the gospel.

In any case, the next passage to be considered will make it quite clear that Paul's hope in Philippians was not simply "dying and going to be with Jesus," but that the far more glorious reality would dawn.

Citizens of Heaven

The fifth apparent exception, also in Philippians, is the popular reading of 3:20–21:

> *We are citizens of heaven, you see, and we're eagerly waiting for the savior, the Lord, Messiah Jesus, who is going to come from there. Our present body is a shabby old thing, but he's going to transform it so that it's just like his glorious body. And he's going to do this by the power which makes him able to bring everything into line under his authority.*

The phrase "citizens of heaven" is both the reason for the misunderstanding and the clue to the correct reading. Commentators and preachers have regularly had Paul agreeing with Plutarch and other pagan thinkers who said that heaven is our home and that we're looking forward to going back there. This has often been combined with a view of the "rapture": Jesus will come again to take his people back with him to heaven.[14]

But that's not how "citizenship" works. Some residents of Philippi were Roman citizens. Rome had founded colonies in Philippi and elsewhere, after the civil wars in the previous century, because Rome did *not* want military veterans returning "home." Rome already had a problem with overcrowding and food shortages. The task of a Roman citizen in Philippi was to represent and advance Roman civilization right there. Paul's first hearers would not have made the mistake that many still make in reading Philippians 3.

Eternal Life

The phrase "eternal life," *zōē aiōnios*, which is regularly read in a platonic sense, invokes instead the traditional Judaean view of "two ages," the present age and the age to come. This is our sixth apparent "exception." The "age to come," *ha-ōlam ha-ba*, was not the non-spatio-temporal philosophers' heaven, but the Judaean view of *a world put right at last*, the Isaianic new-creation vision with the wolf and the lamb lying down together and the earth being filled with "knowing-YHWH" as the waters cover the sea. When Paul looks ahead to God being "all in all," this is the sort of thing he has in mind.[15] "Eternal life" is therefore "the life—the resurrection life—of the coming age." Unfortunately the phrase is now so widely taken in a platonic sense that one needs to paraphrase it and say something like "the life of the coming age." As in Romans 8 and elsewhere, this will be the new creation of what we would call the material world of space, time, and matter: like the present world, only with its beauty enhanced, its problems (particularly death) eliminated, and God's presence and glory glinting from every corner.

Treasure in Heaven

So, too, seventh, the promise of "treasure in heaven" (Matthew 19:21 and parallels, together with the references in Paul and First Peter to salvation being "kept in heaven"), doesn't mean that you have to "go to heaven" to get it.[16] To adapt a regular illustration, if a friend comes to stay and I tell him that his bath towel is in the cupboard, that doesn't mean he has to get into the cupboard in order to get dry. The polyvalent word "heaven" is used here, as often in Judaean writings, to denote *the unseen dimension in which God's future purposes are stored up*, ready to be brought out into the world of humans, either simply on the present earth or on the combined, and renewed, "new heaven and new earth" of Isaiah and the New Testament. "Salvation" is already present in God's world, God's sphere. When that world combines with our world (heaven coming to earth) the gift of God's rescue will be one of its main features. The use of "treasure" or "salvation" in heaven belongs in the same world of belief as Jesus's claim in John 18:36 that his kingdom is "not from this world." God's future purposes—kingdom, salvation, treasure—are stored up safely until their appropriate time. Heaven is not, after all, a place to be differentiated spatially from earth. It is the (normally hidden) dimension of God's world that will one day be joined with earth in visible splendor.

In Abraham's Bosom

The eighth puzzling text takes us back to Luke. In chapter 16, within a section warning his hearers about the dangers of relying on ordinary wealth and ignoring the needs of the poor, Jesus tells the story now known as "the parable of the rich man and Lazarus."[17] However, even those who know it by that name regularly forget that it is precisely a *parable*, not an attempted description of a permanent "life after death." To be sure, it does assume a future life, and that choices and actions in the present have ongoing postmortem consequences. But as a *parable*, rather than as a piece of eschatological/moral exhortation, it no more intends to give a precise description of life after death than the parable of the sower intends to give advice to Galilean farmers. It looks as though Jesus was making use of a well-known folktale in which a recently deceased person, realizing his own earlier folly, asks to go back and warn others. In other versions of this tale, the request might well be granted. But Jesus—and Luke, in his placement of this teaching—have other ideas. In the previous chapter, the resurrection of the younger son ("this your brother was dead and is alive again") is the clinching argument used by the father to change the mind of the older son. Here, though, the warning is stark: if they don't listen to Moses and the prophets, neither will they believe (and presumably change their behavior) even if someone were to rise from the dead. We note in passing that the ancient Judaean idea of "Abraham's bosom" is another way of gesturing toward a promised future, after death but before resurrection.[18]

Till We Cast Our Crowns Before Thee

Revelation 4 and 5 are often invoked unthinkingly as pictures of the *final* heaven, when in fact they are visions of *heaven as it is presently.*[19] This is our ninth and final apparent exception to the case made in the previous chapters.

The normal understanding is emphasized in Charles Wesley's hymn "Love Divine, All Loves Excelling," which finishes with the stanza:

Changed from glory into glory
Till in heaven we take our place;
Till we cast our crowns before thee
Lost in wonder, love and praise.

This is the more remarkable in that the whole hymn, up to that point, has resonated with the true biblical story about God coming to dwell with his people:

Love divine, all loves excelling,
Joy of heaven, to earth come down;
Fix in us thy humble dwelling,
All thy faithful mercies crown.
Jesu, thou art all compassion,
Pure unbounded love thou art:
Visit us with thy salvation,
Enter every trembling heart.

Come, Almighty to deliver
Let us all thy life receive:
Suddenly return, and never,
Never more thy temples leave.
Thee we would be always blessing
Serve thee as thy hosts above:
Pray, and praise thee, without ceasing,
Glory in thy perfect love.

Up to this point, the whole poem has been in tune with the great biblical story of God coming, coming back, coming to dwell in and with his people. I do not know whether Wesley scholars have noticed this puzzle, or discussed it.

Of course, the idea of "changed from glory into glory" is an echo of 2 Corinthians 3:18. But the two glories there are not the glory of the present world and the glory of heaven. And the final three lines of the hymn (about casting crowns before the throne) allude to Revelation 4 and 5; but as we see in Revelation 21 and

22, heaven and earth are to be renewed and combined, with the new Jerusalem "*coming down from heaven*," so that the dwelling of God is with humans. Revelation 4 and 5 are not a vision of the ultimate state when God's people have finally been taken up into heaven. They are an essentially Judaean vision of the *present* heavenly reality in which all creation is already worshipping God.

There are other well-known misunderstandings, but these stand out in my experience as key texts that many have relied on to perpetuate the western understanding of going-to-heaven against otherwise compelling evidence that early Christians all believed God's kingdom would come to earth, through Jesus and the spirit.

The extraordinary claim we find in the gospels is filled in by the rest of the New Testament, celebrating what *has* been accomplished in Jesus, looking ahead to what *will* be accomplished at his final return, and in the meantime exploring what *must now* be done in the power of the spirit, to build on the first and to anticipate the second. At each point the theme is broadly the same. God the Creator, the covenant God of Israel, comes home to dwell with his people. That is the reality behind Christian faith. It is the object of Christian hope. It is the impetus for Christian love.

7

THE HOMECOMING OF GOD: FILLED WITH THE SPIRIT

The Promise of the Spirit

The gospels' vision of heaven coming to earth, as foretold in Israel's scriptures, is brought to a fine point in the opening of Acts, where the disciples are firmly told not to gaze up into heaven, as if that is their final destination. Jesus will come back in the same way that they saw him go. For the moment, we are given to understand, he is indeed in heaven, that is, in God's dimension of reality. But that is only for a time. He will be back. There is work to do in the interim, work to be done by Jesus's spirit through his followers. For that to happen, the one God will come "home" in a further sense: coming to dwell not only with but also within Jesus's followers. That is the main theme of this present chapter.

The idea of God's spirit at work in the present is framed by the completed work of Jesus on the one hand and, on the other, the coming time of "restoration," as promised by the prophets of old:

> *So now repent [says Peter to the crowd], and turn back, so that your sins may be blotted out, so that times of*

refreshment may come from the presence of the Lord, and so that he will send you Jesus, the one he chose and appointed to be his Messiah. He must be received in heaven, you see, until the time which God spoke about through the mouth of his holy prophets from ancient days, the time when God will restore all things [achri chronōn apokatastaseōs pantōn]. (Acts 3:19–21)

There we have it. The eventual aim is the long-prophesied "restoration of all things," the new creation. This can only mean the vision of Isaiah 11 and its several cognates. We find the same theme in the unusual remark of Jesus in Matthew 19:28, referring to the *palingenesia*, the "regeneration," "God's great new world" as I have translated it. Matthew's Jesus apparently takes it for granted that there will be such a coming great event, the time when "the son of man sits on his glorious throne," the time of ultimate judgment. Jesus's first followers found themselves poised between the decisive events of his death and resurrection and this coming final age.

But the final time, according to the biblical promises to which the early Christians clearly looked back, was when the whole earth would be filled with the knowledge or the glory of God, "as the waters cover the sea." This is one of the two great promises about the coming of God. I have suggested that the promise that Israel's God would return in person is the best context for the claims that the gospel writers make about Jesus. But the other promise—the repeated assurance that God, the Creator, would fill all creation with his glorious presence, in the same way that his glory had filled the wilderness tabernacle and the Jerusalem temple—is fulfilled, not completely but in anticipation, by the filling of the church with the divine spirit. This is what I now want to propose, in a way that I have not seen done elsewhere, though the work of Jürgen Moltmann is pointing in this direction. Some at least of what the New Testament says about the coming of the holy spirit is designed to indicate that the filling of the church with God's spirit in the present time, with God "coming home" in this new way, is to be understood as the anticipation of the final filling of all creation.

In both cases—Christology and pneumatology—we are thus faced with inaugurated eschatology. During his public career, Jesus was embodying the return of YHWH to Zion; he will return to complete his work by making all things subject to himself. The spirit's present task is to fill and energize the church for its vocation of implementing Jesus's victory and new creation, against the day when what God does by the spirit in the world, not least through the church, will be matched by what God will do in and for the whole creation. The final "coming of God" will be the moment spoken of in Romans 8:18–25, 1 Corinthians 15:20–28, Philippians 3:20–21, and 1 Thessalonians 1:10. It will be when, as promised in Acts 1:11 and 3:20, Jesus will return as the crowning glory of God's renewal of all things. But this ultimate "coming" is decisively anticipated in the gospel events that constitute the "homecoming" of God: the coming of Jesus, and the gift of the spirit.

God's Homecoming in the Spirit: Paul

It is hard to overstate the dramatic reversal of perception that is involved in trying to reconsider the coming of the spirit in terms of God's homecoming. So much talk about the work of the holy spirit in recent years has focused on the "spiritual experience" of individuals and churches. Building on the earlier Pentecostal movements, the various "charismatic" movements of the last generation have fostered new depths of experience, new fervency in prayer, new energy in love for God and for the world. This has brought much-needed new life to many traditional or "formal" church contexts, and to many individuals who were either on the fringe of the church or outside it altogether. All that is granted, and very welcome.

But the New Testament, by its evocation of scriptural promises, makes a much larger claim. The gift of the spirit is not simply about followers of Jesus receiving extra energy in their discipleship and mission. The gift of the spirit is about *God himself coming at last to fill his creation*—in the representative persons of Jesus's followers, and ultimately in the whole world. It is about God coming to "be at home" in his creation in a whole new way. As with much of what I am arguing in this book, the work of the spirit is not simply about "us" and what happens to us. It is about God—and the fulfillment, in anticipation, of the desire God the Creator had from the very start, that he would dwell within, and flood with his love, his whole beautiful and powerful world. God's homecoming to tabernacle and temple is to be fulfilled in his homecoming to the whole creation. As the sign, foretaste, and energizing power of that future, God has come home to dwell on the earth by dwelling in, and filling, his church.[1]

The link between God's holy spirit and the tabernacling presence in the wilderness (and then in the temple) is already made in Israel's scriptures. Isaiah 63 foresees the people, after a time of rebellion, asking themselves:

> *Where is the one who brought them up out of the sea, with the shepherds of his flock? Where is the one who put within them his holy spirit, who caused his glorious arm to march at the right hand of Moses, who divided the waters before them, to make for himself an everlasting name, who led them through the depths? . . . Like cattle that go down into the valley, the spirit of YHWH gave them rest. Thus you led your people, to make for yourself a glorious name.*[2]

In the same way, Haggai assures the postexilic community of God's presence and strength in their work of rebuilding:

> *Take courage . . . for I am with you, says YHWH of hosts, according to the promise that I made you when you came out of Egypt. My spirit abides among you; do not fear.*[3]

The *present* indwelling of the spirit assures the people of the *future* "shaking of heaven and earth" through which the new temple will be built, and through which God will give prosperity.[4]

The great prayer of Nehemiah chapter 9 looks back similarly to the time of God's presence in the wilderness:

> *You in your great mercies did not forsake them in the wilderness: the pillar of cloud that led them in the way did not leave them by day, nor the pillar of fire by night that gave them light on the way by which they should go. You gave your good spirit to instruct them, and did not withhold your manna from their mouths, and gave them water for their thirst . . .*[5]

All this provides clear precedent for the way, in Galatians and Romans, Paul retells the story of the Exodus with the holy spirit playing the role of the divine glory in the tabernacle, leading the people to their inheritance. This is for Paul neither the narrowly circumscribed "promised land" nor the platonic dream of "heaven." It is *the whole world*, over which Jesus already rules as Lord, and in which he is to be proclaimed as such in the dangerous and subversive gospel.[6] When Paul speaks of the spirit he is indicating that what Israel's God did, coming to dwell in the tabernacle to lead the people to their inheritance, is now fulfilled in the indwelling of the spirit within the church. Paul's development of this theme, particularly his focusing on the rescue and renewal of the cosmos in Romans 8:18–30, goes closely with the biblical theme of the rescue and renewal of all creation, whether in Psalms like 96 and 98 or in the promises of restoration under the rule of the coming spirit-anointed king in Isaiah 11 or Psalm 72. In Romans 8 the spirit enables the church to be in prayer, connected intimately with "the heart-searcher" (God the father) at the place where creation is "groaning together, going through labor pains together."[7] This prayer thus enables Jesus's people to share in the messianic work of rescue and renewal. In a paradox matching that of the gospels' passion narratives, the wordless groaning of the spirit within the church becomes the moment when, and the means by which, the redeeming purposes of God are put into effect. In both, God appears weak, defeated, hopeless—but for Paul and the gospel writers this is the moment of victory.

Paul describes this in terms of the church "having the first fruits of the spirit's life within us."[8] Again, we see that the *present* "filling" of the church with the spirit anticipates the *future* time when, through the spirit, Jesus's followers are given their resurrection bodies (8:9–11; 8:23) to share in the larger reality in which "creation itself [will] be freed from its slavery to decay, to enjoy the freedom that comes when God's children are glorified."[9] The divine glory that dwelt in tabernacle and temple is already dwelling within Jesus's followers. It will in the end reach out, as in Isaiah 11, to fill the whole creation.

Isaiah 11, in fact, is Paul's text of choice to round off the entire theological argument of this great letter. As we shall see later, in chapter 13, in Romans 15:7–13 Paul pulls together the careful and sensitive discussion he began in Romans 14, and indeed the argument of the whole letter. His flurry of biblical quotations indicates that the life of the church fulfills the ancient promises, rather than deflecting them into a new mode. He concludes with Isaiah 11:

> *There shall be the root of Jesse; the one who rises up to rule the nations; the nations shall hope in him.*[10]

By emphasizing the Messiah's "rising up" to rule the nations, Paul is circling right back to the letter's introduction, in which Jesus, the Davidic Messiah, has been marked out powerfully as God's son through the resurrection of the dead (Romans 1:3–4).

But Isaiah 11 has one more secret to reveal. The verse before the one Paul quotes is the passage where the prophet announces the coming "filling" of all creation with the knowledge of YHWH:

> *They will not hurt or destroy on all my holy mountain; for the earth will be full of the knowledge of YHWH as the waters cover the sea.*[11]

The church is to be "filled" with God's spirit in the present time, as evidenced in being "filled with all joy and peace in believing." They are thus to "overflow with hope by the power of the holy spirit" (Romans 15:13). The present *filling* of the church with the spirit points forward to the ultimate *hope* of the *filling* of all creation, as in Romans 8 or the promise in 1 Corinthians 15:28 that God will be "all in all." The present unity of the church, *glorifying* the one God "with one mind and one mouth" (Romans 15:6), is then the sign, both to the church itself and to the world around, that Israel's God, the Creator, has inaugurated his long-term purposes of filling all creation with his powerful and glorious presence. God *has* come home; God *will* come home.

Another way of saying all this would be to point out that the church is designed as the new temple, and that the temple was the physical building that was filled with the divine glory, pointing ahead to the coming time when God would fill all creation. Paul, of course, is thoroughly familiar with the new temple theme, as we see in 1 Corinthians 3:16 (the whole church as "temple") and 6:19 (the body of the individual Christian as "temple"), with 2 Corinthians 6:16 picking up the former. And in 2 Corinthians 3:12–4:6 Paul offers a complicated exegesis of the scene in Exodus 34 in which the divine glory, which came to dwell in the wilderness tabernacle, is now to be seen by individual Christians as they gaze at one another as in a mirror. The claim at the end of that dense section echoes once more the promises of Isaiah and the rest, about the earth being filled with the knowledge of the glory of YHWH, even though for the moment it is the hearts of believers that are filled in anticipation:

> *The God who said "let light shine out of darkness" has shone in our hearts, to produce the light of the knowledge of the glory of God in the face of Jesus the Messiah.*[12]

The letter that expounds all this most fully is Ephesians, as we shall see in chapter 13.

God's Homecoming in the Spirit: Acts

Acts displays the spirit at work throughout, though not usually providing an explicit theological framework within which to understand what's going on. Except, that is, in the opening spirit-scene, the day of Pentecost in Acts 2.

There have been endless discussions on the "baptism in/of the holy spirit," on whether this is a near synonym for conversion itself, on whether it is a decisive second stage in Christian pilgrimage, on whether the gift of tongues is a crucial sign of all this having happened, and so on. These questions, however, do not seem to me to be raised by Acts itself. They arise from within the basically modern western Christian culture in which questions about assurance have become ever more refined (assurance that one has indeed been "born again"; assurance that one is going to heaven; assurance that one has received the spirit, or has moved into a new mode of Christian experience). Some of these questions have been posed very sharply. Some have divided churches.

But in the middle of it all something is going on that these discussions seem to ignore. The stages that matter are not successive individual spiritual experiences, which might, or might not, lead up from one floor of Christian spirituality to the next. The stages that matter for Luke are the public career of Jesus, leading to his death and resurrection, then the short period of waiting, including the drama of Jesus's ascension, and then the filling of the disciples with God's spirit. What matters is that in Acts 1 there is now one part of earth, namely, Jesus's human body, in heaven; and what matters in Acts 2 is that the breath of heaven, the powerful wind of the spirit, has now come to animate Jesus's followers on earth. Ascension and spirit together thus constitute Jesus and his people as the new temple, *signaling God's intention to reach out to the whole world with the gospel*, as heaven comes to earth. After this, it is no surprise that most of the controversies in Acts focus on temples, starting and ending with Jerusalem but taking in the great pagan shrines of Athens and Ephesus in particular.

Once we appreciate the significance of the biblical promises about the whole creation being filled with God's tabernacling presence, Luke's language about the filling of the church is very striking. The day of Pentecost had, he says, been fulfilled: the Greek *symplērousthai*, applied here to the day itself, incorporates the root *plēroō*, "fill." In my own translation the word appears as "finally arrived," but ideally one would note the theme of "filling" as well, since it's an unusual way of speaking and Luke seems to employ it deliberately.[13] The point is that when the powerful wind arrived, finding the disciples all together in the house, that wind "filled the whole house where they were sitting" (Acts 2:2), whereupon the disciples "were all filled with the holy spirit" and began to speak in other languages. Anyone familiar with Exodus 40, or 1 Kings 8, or Isaiah 6, or indeed Genesis 1:2, should pick up the overtones at once. What is happening to the house, and to the disciples, is what happened to the tabernacle and the temple when the glorious divine presence came to dwell there, and, behind that, what happened to the primal waters when the divine *ruach* brooded over them at the beginning.

Acts 2 is thus the story of God's homecoming, of the Creator coming in the presence and power of the holy spirit to dwell in and with the followers of Jesus and to equip them for their worldwide mission, symbolized in the tongues that enabled them to speak at once to a multilingual audience.

There are indeed subsequent moments when this or that person is said to be specially "filled with the spirit." But the scene in Acts 2 is primary. It determines how we are to understand everything that follows. Of course there is still a future dimension. Jesus will come again (1:11; 3:21)—at which point, Acts wants us to understand, the final fulfillment of the new creation will take place, as in Paul or Revelation. But the present "fillings" of Jesus's followers are pointing forward to that ultimate fulfillment of the scriptural promises.[14]

The Work of the Spirit in John

To understand the significance of the spirit in John's gospel, it will be as well to return to the dramatic words of 20:21–23 and see them in context. Jesus's commission to his followers ("As the father has sent me, so I'm sending you.") is as weighty as anything in the whole gospel. Jesus's mission into the world, more specifically his mission to Israel, is to be the model for the disciples' mission to the wider world. The clear implication is that, just as Jesus performed "signs" through which the divine glory was to be glimpsed, so his followers will now do and say things that will reveal that same glory to the world. As Jesus said in 14:12:

> *Anyone who trusts in me will also do the works that I am doing. In fact, they will do greater works than these, because I am going to the father.*

For this, they will of course need to be equipped, and that is precisely what is promised in the rest of chapter 14. The "helper" (the *paraklētos*, the "advocate," "counsellor," "comforter," or something that combines all of these) will come from the father. This will be the mode in which the great promise of God's homecoming will be further fulfilled.

Why "further"? Because this is in addition to, and is generated by, the basic "homecoming" that is the incarnation, as with the Word becoming flesh in 1:14:

> *"If anyone loves me," Jesus replied, "they will keep my word. My father will love them, and we will come to them and make our home with them. Anyone who doesn't love me won't keep my word. And the word which you hear isn't mine. It comes from the father, who sent me."*[15]

When we put this together with Jesus's simple but profound act of breathing on the disciples in chapter 20, we understand. When father and son together come to "make their home" with the disciples, this is not static, but missional. The spirit comes so that the whole divine presence and power may be with Jesus's followers in going out into the world to live and preach the gospel. When God comes home, the rule of the household is love: the outgoing love that overflows into the world in new creation.

John 20 understands this fresh in-breathing within the context of this *new creation*. The repeated "first day of the week" in verses 1 and 19 says it all: chapter 20 answers to "in the beginning" in 1:1, declaring that this is indeed a new Genesis. Jesus has "finished" the work the father had given him to do, as he said in 17:4. That, we presume, is the primary meaning of his final word, *tetelestai*, "It's all done," in 19:30. This in turn answers to Genesis 2:1–3, where the Creator "finished" his work and rested on the seventh day. In John, the seventh day sees Jesus dead and buried, resting in the tomb, and at 20:1 new creation is launched, "on the first day of the week": the eighth day, one might say, of creation. It is still dark when Mary comes to the tomb. But soon the light shines.

Many have seen the link between Jesus's breathing on the disciples and Genesis 2:7. There the Creator breathed the breath of life (Hebrew *nishmath hayyim*; Septuagint *pnoē zōēs*) into the human nostrils, "and the man became a living being." What is not so often noticed is that the gift of the spirit, interpreted in the light of John's striking comments earlier in the gospel, becomes the new-creational equivalent of the rivers flowing out of Eden to refresh the world (Genesis 2:10–14). This connection is made, in typically Johannine allusive style, by the comment at the feast of Tabernacles:

> *On the last day of the festival, the great final celebration, Jesus stood up and shouted out, "If anybody's thirsty, they should come to me and have a drink! Anyone who*

believes in me will have rivers of living water flowing out of their heart, just like the Bible says!"

John comments,

He said this about the spirit, which people who believed in him were to receive. The spirit wasn't available yet, because Jesus was not yet glorified.[16]

The biblical reference most commentators highlight is Ezekiel 47, where the river flows out from the restored temple to make even the Dead Sea fresh. But behind Ezekiel 47 stands Genesis 2, with the river flowing out of Eden and dividing into its four branches (Pishon, Gihon, Tigris, and Euphrates). So, putting John 7 together with John 20, we can suggest that the work of the spirit is to be understood as God's irrigation of the new-made world. The newly commissioned disciples are to become agents of the new creation that began with Jesus's resurrection. Just as Ezekiel's new river flows out of the temple, so the disciples' work flows from the heaven-and-earth accomplishment of Jesus, the one in whom the Word "tabernacled in our midst"; the one who "spoke of the temple of his body."[17] As the temple pointed to the promise of new creation, so now the new creation provides the outflowing "rivers of living water."[18]

The other cryptic note in 7:39, where the spirit was not available during Jesus's ministry because Jesus had not yet been "glorified," is quite dramatic. Throughout John, the glorification of Jesus focuses particularly on his crucifixion. John seems to take it for granted that the spirit could not be given without Jesus's victory on the cross. This strongly implies some view of the atoning and cleansing work of Jesus's death. Until the dark powers had been overthrown, even those closest to Jesus were not ready to receive his spirit. Just as Jesus's resurrection indicates that his cross won the victory over death, so the gift of the spirit indicates that this victory included the cleansing of the disciples. Now, as with the consecrated tabernacle or temple, the divine glory could come and dwell within them.

This is the fuller reality of John 1:14. The Word became flesh and tabernacled in our midst; now, the Word has become spirit, poured out on, and then through, the disciples. This sequence—first Jesus's death, then the mission to the world—is echoed in the equally dramatic passage in chapter 12, where some Greeks seek access to Jesus and Jesus, in effect, replies that they must wait until he has been "lifted up," whereupon he will then "draw all people" to himself.[19]

This opens the way to the initially strange commission about not only forgiving sins but "retaining" them (John 20:23). If we read the whole chapter with Genesis 1 and 2 in mind, a line of thought opens up that belongs with Jesus's prediction about the work of the spirit in chapter 16. In Genesis 2 we find two trees: the tree of life, and the tree of the knowledge of good and evil. Here in John 20, "life" is promised lavishly by the newly alive Jesus, and also by the evangelist himself. Those who believe that the Messiah, God's son, is none other than Jesus will have "life in his name."[20] But the commission to forgive or retain sins might be seen as a Johannine allusion to the other tree in Eden. Now at last, with the gift of the divine spirit, humans can, without arrogance, "know good and evil" and declare it where appropriate. This is, at one level, a royal prerogative,[21] but it seems to have a *priestly* and *prophetic* function as well. It is not basically about interpersonal relationships, as in the discussion of forgiveness in Matthew 18. It is about the spirit-given task of the church to hold the world and its rulers to account. This has already been articulated in chapter 16:

> *When [the spirit] comes, he will prove the world to be in the wrong on three counts: sin, justice, and judgment. In relation to sin—because they don't believe in me. In relation to justice—because I'm going to the father, and you won't see me anymore. In relation to judgment—because the ruler of this world is judged.*[22]

This is once more dense and cryptic. One way to discern the meaning is through the third statement, which goes with Jesus's announcement that his crucifixion will be the means of God winning the victory over the dark power that has usurped his rule over the world:

> *Now comes the judgment of this world! Now this world's ruler is going to be thrown out!*[23]

Seen in that light, the announcement of the spirit's work in John 16:11 must mean that, through the spirit, Jesus's followers will apply the victory of the cross to the critique of those in power. The Judaean and early Christian traditions were clear that God the Creator wanted his world to be run by human beings. That is part of what it means to be made in the divine image, to reflect God's wise authority into the world. But the corollary is that rulers will then bear responsibility for their decisions and actions. Jesus said more or less exactly this in addressing Pilate: Pilate had a God-given authority over him, but the one who handed Jesus over to the governor—Caiaphas, perhaps?—was "guilty of a greater sin" (John 19:11). This, I suggest, is a model of what "retaining sins" might look like. The spirit will enable Jesus's followers to hold the world and its official rulers to account. We see Paul and the others doing just this in Acts.[24]

If that is the right way to read John 16:11, perhaps we can read verses 9 and 10 similarly. The spirit, working through Jesus's followers, can, will, and must "retain sin" when people do not believe in Jesus. That is, the disciples must be guided by the spirit to demonstrate and articulate to the world that the only way to be genuinely human is to follow Jesus, and that to fail there is to miss the mark of God's best will for his image-bearing creatures. That is verse 9. Then the point of 16:10 would be that the vindication of Jesus, in his resurrection and ascension, his enthronement at the father's right hand, is the ultimate model of justice. The world tries in vain to "do justice," to put things right. Jesus's vindication shows up those attempts and holds rulers and judges to account. The church, in the power of the spirit, is tasked with making that clear.

This, I think, is what is meant by "forgiving and retaining" sins in John 20:23. The spirit is to guide Jesus's followers into the knowledge of good and evil, not just for themselves and their own behavior—though, to be sure, that matters vitally as well!—but in relation to the wider world.

If there were any doubt about this, it ought to be dispelled by the scene in chapters 18 and 19 where Jesus is arguing with Pontius Pilate about kingdom, truth, and power. The church's public stance, in the power of the spirit, will have the same features. That is part of what it means to say, "*as* the father has sent me, *so* I'm sending you." The church, as the people of the new Eden, the new creation, is equipped by the spirit to confront the old world with the truth of the new. This is part of the meaning of God's homecoming. God comes in the person of the spirit, to dwell within the world and to shine the light of new creation into its remaining dark places.

All this flows directly from the ancient biblical tradition according to which God will come back to hold the world to account, as part of the larger project of filling all creation with his knowledge and glory. This is what I mean when I say that the filling of the church with the spirit is the present mode of the promised future reality, the moment when God will judge the world, holding it to account, dealing finally with all evil, and filling all creation (by then set free from corruption and decay) with God's powerful and healing glory. The church, as the small working model of new creation, is to play the role, in the present time, of anticipating every aspect of that coming and filling. We are to be "filled with all God's fullness" because that is God's purpose for the whole of creation. The church is called to live as the advance guard and foretaste of that glorious coming reality.

What this will mean is the subject of the second main part of the present book. But before we can get there we must face, however briefly, the question I have routinely been asked when I have lectured through these remarkable biblical themes. How has today's church, in large part, managed to miss the point? How did Plato come to elbow the Bible out of center stage?

Interlude

HOW DID WE MISS THE POINT?

8

SWITCHING THE SCRIPT? THE BIBLE AND THE CHRISTIAN TRADITION

Changing the Story

If the Bible, read as a whole in the way I have indicated, tells the story of the creator God coming to be at home with humans in the renewed creation, how and why did followers of Jesus come to tell the story the other way up? This question is regularly posed when I (and others) have tried to articulate the biblical narrative and to show how different it is from today's popular belief. How did the original story become so overlaid with other ideas as to be all but forgotten? And how did that alternative reading become the mainstream Christian viewpoint?

One easy way of answering this question has been to say that it was actually Jesus and the early Christians who changed the storyline. That is how many, perhaps most, Christians see things today, insofar as they reflect on the matter at all. The explanation, or at least the assumption, would go like this. The ancient Judaeans did indeed believe in a this-worldly salvation. But Jesus and his first followers rejected or at least relativized all that, and grasped the more important truth, which was about saving people's souls for an otherworldly heaven. This goes closely with the other assumed either/or, which became popular later on: that ancient Judaeans believed in doing good works (in the "material" world) to earn God's favor, but the early Christians believed in free grace (operating in the "spiritual" world). This maps salvation onto a platonic cosmology (heaven having priority over earth), anthropology (the soul or spirit as more important than the body), and eschatology (souls leaving earth to go to heaven).

That antithesis (worldly Judaeans, otherworldly Christians) would explain, one might suppose, why Israel's scriptures had remarkably little to say about "life after death." After all, if the going-to-heaven story is the real message of the Bible, much of the Old Testament is, to put it kindly, irrelevant padding. And where the New Testament does seem to pick up the Old Testament's this-worldly message, such as the emphasis on a Davidic Messiah, or the fulfillment of the covenant with Abraham, this has often been sidelined as a vestigial remainder from the Judaean background and context, to be swept away in the radical discontinuity introduced by the supposedly apocalyptic gospel. Anyway, in terms of life after death, there are one or two passages in the Old Testament that hint at God's love for his people extending beyond their death. A few passages even promise resurrection.[1] So (a reader of this type might say) the message of life after death, and hence the going-to-heaven story, was after all the real message of the scriptures, even if it was in effect hidden, or even disguised, behind the predominantly this-worldly message offered by Law, Prophets, and Writings. One would then have to read the Old Testament as a book of "figures," to be decoded if one was to get at the real meaning hiding underneath the text's unpromising surface. That way of reading Israel's scriptures has, to put it mildly, retained great popularity.[2]

Let's be quite clear: Israel's scriptures do indeed offer what we might call a predominantly this-worldly message. The great overarching story told by Law, Prophets, and Writings is manifestly to do with the promises of family and land, focused on Abraham's descendants, and then on David and his kingdom, looking particularly to Jerusalem and the temple as the place where the God of creation and covenant had promised to be present with his people. But the story is not *merely* this-worldly. It embodies a metaphysical assumption about the overlap of God's realm and the human realm, heaven and earth. That is what the temple was all about. But the focus remained on what the creator God was going to do in and for the present world, not on how people could escape it for another one.

The need for salvation in that context looked back to the earlier rescue from slavery, and from the dominion of foreign gods, in Egypt. In the time of the Judges and the early monarchy, salvation routinely meant that God was delivering his people from traditional enemies such as the Philistines. But the central Old Testament message of salvation arose from the destruction of the temple, from the victory of Babylon and its gods over the Israelites and their God, and from the resultant exile. Even after some Judaeans had returned from Babylon and rebuilt the temple, all was not well. The heirs of David failed either to rebuild the temple satisfactorily—the Herods were still trying to do it in Jesus's day—or to provide the long-promised time of restoration, justice, and peace. Pagan rulers were still in charge.[3] Salvation, throughout this long story, had nothing to do with people being snatched away from the space-time world into a different or "supernatural" sphere. It was about God doing once again, fully and forever, what he had done at the original Exodus. This time he would rescue his people from Babylon and its gods, and/or from the subsequent world empires that appeared (as monsters emerging from the dark sea of chaos) in the nightmare vision of Daniel 7. In that dream, "one like a son of man" is exalted to reign over the monsters. That promise is interpreted by the text itself in terms of the righteous Judaean remnant being exalted to reign over the world, sharing the authority of Israel's God.

That point alone should cause the average modern western reader of the Bible to pause. Daniel 7, after all, plays an important role in the New Testament, especially with the reference to the exaltation of "one like a son of man." Were the early Christians reading it wrong? Did *Jesus* read it wrong? Were they all misinterpreting the real story? Did they "spiritualize" a message that was originally about a this-worldly kingdom, about the coming time when the monstrous pagan empires would be called to account by the true God and his Judaean representative?

These were my own questions as I grew up and began to try to think such things through for myself. As a young man I, like many others, was firmly taught that the whole Bible was "authoritative," and that God had given it as the special book for his people. But the great bulk of the Bible—somewhere around a thousand pages of Israel's scriptures, as opposed to the modest 300 or so of the first Christian writings—didn't seem to have much to do with the "salvation" that the churches were talking about. The Christian fellowships in which I was nurtured taught that, when people came to believe in Jesus, when they said a prayer of commitment and then began, however stumblingly, to try to follow Jesus, they were assured of a "salvation," which meant going to heaven. (I remember being shocked when I noticed that in Luke Jesus sometimes refers to physical healing as "being saved."[4]) But much of the Bible—so it seemed—was not about that at all. So one was led to assume that there had indeed been a great shift, a major transition, from the Old Testament to the New, from the this-worldly salvation that was the obvious, surface meaning of the Old Testament to the otherworldly salvation supposedly spoken of in the New. (Again, the supposed Judaean concentration on "works" and the Pauline focus on "faith" was mapped on to this same either/or.) That then raised the question: Does the phrase "the authority of the Bible" really mean "the authority of the New Testament, plus a few out-of-context proof texts from Israel's scriptures"? Were we then to say that (what I now know to be) the platonic traditions of scriptural interpretation, from at least the fourth century onward, were a more important guide to the meaning of Jesus and his gospel than the great bulk of the Old Testament? Were we, in fact, *saying* "the authority of scripture" but *meaning* "the authority of some later philosophically shaped traditions of interpreting the New Testament, over against the Old"?

That, indeed, seemed to be how we were invited to think, though it wasn't usually put in that stark form. I grew up in the 1950s and '60s, and my early Christian education was not very different from that of many other western Christians across many traditions. We were given a picture of Jesus in which he was setting aside the beliefs and hopes of his Judaean contemporaries and offering something quite different. He was, so it appeared, claiming to teach, and to launch, a new vision of "God's kingdom" as a different realm altogether, something barely dreamed of in the scriptures of his day except for a small handful of passages that might be read as distant hints of the otherworldly salvation he now had in mind. Thus some interpreters strangely suggested that the Judaeans of Jesus's day thought of their God as remote, and that Jesus was telling them to see him instead as the "father" who was "near them" in a whole new way.

This way of understanding Jesus's teaching, making it focus on a personal relationship with an otherwise distant God in the present, and on the soul going to heaven in the future, went with a reading of Paul in which the great Apostle had opposed the Judaean world of his day by speaking of the way to heaven in terms of faith rather than works of the law. Here again the implication was of an intimate relationship rather than a detached legalism, a spiritual belief rather than the performance of works—which in any case all took place within the world of space, time, and matter, and were thus the focus of suspicion for a platonically minded believer. That provides a clue to one aspect of what has been going on in western Christian thought over the last two or three hundred years, a clue whose dark overtones remained unimagined by many of us when we heard this kind of teaching in our young days. *"The Judaeans"* (so it was implied) *"had been getting it wrong, looking for a this-worldly salvation achieved by 'works,' but the Christians were now getting it right with their otherworldly hope attained by 'faith.'"* This offered a popular, supposedly historical account: Jesus taught about God's love and grace, and about the going-to-heaven story, but "the Judaeans" opposed this because they believed in legalism, in "works" (which involved relentlessly material things like food and human bodies), in a do-it-yourself moralistic justification, in a this-worldly salvation, and in a militaristic or nationalistic Messiah. So the apparently sharp distinction between Old and New Testaments was explained by saying that "the Judaeans," of course, believed in a this-worldly salvation, but that "the Christians" had discovered the true otherworldly one. And that Jesus had died and risen again to make it possible.

And of course we didn't say "the Judaeans." We said, or thought, that "the Jews" were basically wrong and "the Christians" were basically right. But a half-truth masquerading as a whole truth becomes an untruth, and in this case a horribly dangerous one.

This apparent contrast between Old and New Testaments, and the meaning of "salvation" in each, struck me particularly in the summer of 1979, when for the first time I sat down and read the works of the Judaean historian Flavius Josephus. Josephus, to be sure, is a strange and in some ways unattractive character. *But he was there*. He was in Jerusalem, mixing with his fellow aristocrats and the leading priests. He was in Galilee at the start of the revolution against Rome in AD 66. He was in Jerusalem again in the latter stages of the revolt, having switched sides and now acting as adviser to Titus, the Roman general (and subsequently emperor). And what struck me forcibly as I read page after page about the plotting, the revolutionary schemes, the hopes, the prayers, the aspirations of the various groups and factions of Judaeans at the time, is that *none of them was concerned with whether they would go to heaven when they died*. That was not the subject of their discussions. Their sometimes furious debates were not about an otherworldly kingdom. They were focused on the immediate, the concrete, the questions to which two thousand years of covenant history and prophecy had led them: *How was Israel's God going to be faithful to his promise to rescue his people from the wicked pagans?* And, not least, who among the present Judaeans was going about their present responsibilities in the right way? How could you tell, even now, who would be vindicated, be shown to be in the right, a true covenant member, when Israel's God acted dramatically at last to save his people from their enemies? How were the promises of Daniel, not to mention Isaiah, Jeremiah, and the rest, to be fulfilled?

Now my reading of Josephus might indeed have served simply to reinforce my earlier assumptions. Josephus and his friends were, after all, first-century Judaeans, ignorant of the new Jesus-message that had so recently burst on the scene: so of course they were still talking about a this-worldly salvation, rather than the otherworldly one supposedly taught by Jesus. But they were not, as it were, secularists, this-worldly thinkers looking for this-worldly solutions. *They were talking about what Israel's God was going to do in history*. They were heaven-on-earth activists. And by the time I read Josephus I had been studying Paul intensively for several years, and had come to the view that Paul, too, was precisely concerned with the same question, of how Israel's God was going to be, and indeed had already been, faithful to his promises. What did those promises mean, and to whom did they now apply?

Equally, I had begun serious work on "historical Jesus" questions, learning from scholars like Ben F. Meyer to see the gospels within the Judaean world of Qumran, the early Rabbis, and yes, Josephus.[5] The great divide I had assumed was a fiction. The New Testament, at point after point, insisted that what had happened in Jesus, and what was happening through the fresh work of God's spirit, was the real, if startling, fulfillment of the ancient promises. The message of both Jesus and Paul offered a focused, polemical alternative to the aspirations of the time, not a change of subject.

That, after all, was why Jerusalem broke out in riot when Paul came back after his missionary travels and tried to explain to a suspicious crowd what he had been doing and why. If he had been saying, "No, no, that's not the question; the question is how we go to heaven after we die," he would have been a minor irrelevance. Neither the Sanhedrin, nor the Roman governor, nor (especially) the mob, would have bothered with him. But if he was saying that *this*, this cataclysmic, apocalyptic, messianic truth about Jesus of Nazareth and his death and resurrection, was how Israel's God had been faithful to his promises, this would (and did) cause riots. If he was saying that the events to do with Jesus of Nazareth have saved God's people from the real enemies, the dark powers that had usurped God's rule over the world, he would appear a traitor. If he was saying that the way to tell, even now, who was a true member of Abraham's covenant family was through their believing allegiance to this Jesus, and that this meant opening up God's people to include all Messiah-believers, not least Gentiles, then this would be sharply relevant, and shockingly disruptive.

All this would of course include the assurance of ultimate resurrection, which the Pharisees believed anyway. But the word "resurrection" had never referred to the going-to-heaven story. It always referred to a new bodily life at some future moment, after whatever intermediate state there might be.[6] And here was Paul presenting that hope as *both* the fulfillment of Israel's scriptures *and* the direct result of Jesus's messianic achievement, particularly in his death and resurrection.[7]

Josephus and his contemporaries were not being obtuse. They were not radically distorting the message of their own scriptures. After all, many Judaean thinkers, ancient and modern, have pointed out that what most Christians have meant by "salvation" (souls going to heaven) is not a basically Judaean concept (though some philosophically minded Judaeans, such as Philo of Alexandria, went in that direction). It is not the teaching of any part of Israel's scriptures, in the way that it is the plain teaching of Plato and his many followers in the first century and later. Some Judaean thinkers have even distinguished sharply between "the Christian Messiah" and "the Jewish Messiah."[8] That idea contrasts the later Christian idea of Jesus, seen as the one who rescues people from this world so that their souls can go to be with God somewhere else, and the supposedly authentic (Judaean/Jewish) Messiah, yet to appear, who will do what Israel's scriptures said he would do, bringing about the wise, just, and healing restoration of the present creation and of God's people within it. Think of Psalm 2, or of Isaiah 11. And reflect that the early Christians treasured those passages, and quoted them in relation to Jesus.

So we must put the question the other way around. Did the early Christians really teach something so very different from what one might find in Israel's scriptures? The early centuries—in which many Christian thinkers engaged in dialogue with many Judaean thinkers—show no evidence of such a split between two different kinds of Messiah. When we look beyond the New Testament to second- and third-century figures like Justin Martyr, Irenaeus, Tertullian, and Cyprian, it is quite clear: Jesus of Nazareth had been vindicated as the scripturally promised Messiah, who would bring about the just, peaceful, and wisely ordered new creation.[9] The "Christian" Messiah simply *was* Israel's true Messiah, who had fulfilled the promises set out in the scriptures, not least in his conquering of the ultimate enemy, death. This is at the heart of Jesus's explanation to the two puzzled disciples on the road to Emmaus.[10]

We are presented, then, with a puzzle at the level of *method* as well as *content*. Do we believe in one Bible or two? And, in the last analysis, do we go with the Bible or with the traditions of the later church? If there is a significant difference between what Israel's scriptures teach and what the fourth-century church taught, when did the shift come, and why? And what should we do about it? Does the New Testament really belong with the Old, or does it stand at the head of quite a different vision, the one developed by some Christian writers from the third century onward?

Re-Reading the Texts

One way of resolving this dilemma was that of Marcion, a native of Turkey who taught in Rome in the second century. He drove a clear wedge between the Testaments and their views of God, anticipating the views of many Christians in the modern period who, shocked at the violence displayed in some parts of the Old Testament, had been eager to distance themselves from such barbarism. Marcion rejected Israel's scriptures and those early Christian writings that drew most obviously on them, preferring the gospel of Luke that, he thought, could be read in a non-Judaean way. Many today have been taught a position not unlike Marcion's, though few would come out and say that in so many words.[11] But I recall from my teens and twenties hearing more than one teacher, faced with puzzled questions about the place of the Old Testament in the liturgy and in Christian theology, quoting with a smile Paul's line, "Christ is the end of the law" (Romans 10:4) as a way of dismissing the question. It's been settled. That old legalistic book—that old *Jewish* book—can be safely put back on the shelf.[12]

This should now be seen as a reductio ad absurdum. When

Paul wrote Romans 10:4, the one thing he certainly did not mean was that Jesus, as Messiah, was abolishing the Old Testament.[13] One of the darkest results of all this prejudice was of course the ease with which a whole swathe of "Christian" Europe became persuaded that "the Jews" were a dangerous menace politically as well as theologically. Recognizing this has been, for me and for many, one of the starting points for fresh study of Jesus and the early Christians within their first-century Judaean context.[14]

So what was one to do with Israel's scriptures, granted that, officially at least, the church both ancient and modern has known it could not abandon them? Well, a tradition at least as old as Christianity had already become very good at *allegorizing*. The Judaean philosopher Philo, a near-contemporary of Paul, had worked through large swathes of the scriptures, providing allegorical explanations and meanings, not least in terms of the soul's cultivation of virtue. So, too, another near-contemporary, the pagan priest and philosopher Plutarch, had re-read his Homer in such a way as to show that of course the *true* gods were not to be thought of as the amoral egotists who rampaged through the *Iliad* or the *Odyssey*. (How could a sensible, thoughtful, up-to-date first-century Greek really believe that the gods could behave in the irresponsible way Homer suggests?) The much-revered texts could still be held in high honor. But sophisticated readers would have to learn how to look beneath the surface for the real meaning.

Many early Christians, from at least the third century onward, tried their hands at similar re-readings. Paul's contrast of the "letter" and the "spirit" was seized on as the clue: "the letter kills, but the spirit gives life."[15] The letter of the law, of the Judaean world, of the Old Testament, would take you in the wrong direction, getting you to focus on this-worldly realities, perhaps encouraging you to suppose that you could please God by your good moral works, and so go to heaven that way. But the supposedly spiritual meaning could be discerned behind, or perhaps within, the apparently this-worldly meanings, and it was the spiritual meaning that would give life. Thus one could read a Psalm about "going up to Jerusalem" and interpret it as an allegory for the going-to-heaven story, and so on. By the Middle Ages a vast, complex system of figural readings had been developed, a sophisticated method for including the Old Testament within a world of thought that neither Moses nor the prophets would have recognized. The church developed ways of making the Bible say what it ought to have said instead of what it in fact said.

The word "spiritual," so often used to denote this "true" reading, carried its own rhetorical force. What devout Christian would want to opt for an "*un*spiritual" meaning? And if the true meaning was "spiritual," this would correlate with the sense many Christians have always had (not least, one might add, in passages like the Psalms or Isaiah!) of being confronted in their innermost depths with the reality of God's love, forgiveness, and promises, regardless of the outward this-worldly circumstances of one's life. That sense of being addressed by God's own spirit in the quiet of our hearts as we read the sacred text, whether or not we understand it in exactly the way the writers may have intended, is part of what we might call normal Christian life. Thus teachers such as Clement and Origen, at the start of the third century, offered a way out of the problem of interpretation. When one read Israel's scriptures "spiritually" in this sense, one might by this means detect the same "inner" experience, and otherworldly hope, that one was learning to find in the New

Testament, explaining the "devotional" impact the text was having but directing attention away from its surface meaning. The wise Christian reader had to learn to decode the this-worldly biblical themes with which the "real" message had come to be clothed.

There is an obvious problem with this way of reading the overall picture, with the Old Testament being worldly and unspiritual while the New Testament is otherworldly and spiritual. The problem is that, as we have seen, the New Testament declares, one way or another, that the story the early Christians are telling and interpreting is the *fulfillment* of Israel's scriptures. And fulfillment here is a lot more, and a lot deeper, than simply finding a few proof texts in the Old Testament that might appear to offer long-range and decontextualized prophesies of this or that feature of Jesus and his achievement. Fulfillment here indicates strong *continuity*: a great story, dark and winding, is arriving in a strange and unexpected place, but discovering it to be what the story had actually been about all along. And, after all, a good deal of Jesus's teaching is sharply practical in relation to life in the present world.

Not that Jesus simply fit into existing ideas. There were indeed shocks to the system. Jesus scandalized many of his contemporaries. He said and did things that could not sit comfortably alongside the interpretations of Israel's traditions that had become popular in his day. His crucifixion, above all, appeared to put paid to any claim he might have had to be God's Messiah. The Messiah was supposed (by those who thought about such things) to be defeating the pagan enemies, not dying at their hands. Jesus's first followers, telling his story and doing their best to live by it, continued to be, as Paul put it, a scandal to Judaeans and foolishness to Gentiles.[16] But when the shocks are absorbed and taken on board it becomes clear, above all, through Jesus's resurrection, that this was where the original story was meant to end up, dark pathways and twisted narratives notwithstanding. It would not be putting it too strongly to say that the entire New Testament claims to be describing, and working out the implications of, the completion, the fulfillment, the accomplishment of the story told in many different but convergent ways in Israel's scriptures. This whole question maps on to the current (and often confused) debate about the meaning of "apocalyptic" among Jesus's first followers.[17]

Think again of the two disciples who met Jesus, incognito, on the road to Emmaus. The crucifixion had dashed their hopes that Jesus had been Israel's long-awaited redeemer. But everything changed when Jesus explained to them that, according to the scriptures, this was how it had to be.[18] We may puzzle over what exactly Jesus meant when Luke says that he explained things "beginning with Moses and all the prophets."[19] But we can be sure that he did *not* mean "forgetting Moses, and highlighting three or four isolated texts snatched from prophetic books that were otherwise talking about something quite different." But that is how many readers, in many traditions, have in effect treated the claim.

Considering the Options

The dilemma we then face looks like this. We seem to have two radically different conceptions of God's purpose for humans and the world. The first, it appears, is taught by the

Old Testament, and the second by many at least in the later church. There is a great gulf between them:

Old Testament ———/ /——— Later Church
(land, family, coming of God) (otherworldly "kingdom"; souls in heaven)

So what can we say about that great gulf? The New Testament, including the message of Jesus, which it claims to display, appears to be perched uncomfortably in the middle. At one level, the early Christian writings form, for the most part, a thoroughly Judaean set of books, rooted in the Old Testament, insisting that its message is "in accordance with the scriptures." At another level, it contains passages that have regularly been understood as promising a kingdom "not of this world," a "citizenship in heaven," a "dwelling place" within the house of Jesus's father, and so on. All this has caused many Christian readers, from quite early days, to conclude that Jesus was indeed launching a movement different from anything envisioned by the devout Judaean communities of his day. That would mean that Jesus and his first followers were responsible for the decisive break, the all-important shift:

Old Testament, Judaean World ———/ /——— Jesus, NT and Later Church
(this-worldly hope) (souls going to heavenly "kingdom")

This is, more or less, the solution proposed by Marcion. Marcion was firmly rejected by the main church teachers in the second and third centuries. The sense of Christian faith being rooted in Israel's scriptures was too strong to be abandoned, even if it was not always obvious how the picture joined up. That is where teachers like Origen, steeped in platonic thought, hung on to the scriptures by means of relentless allegorization, a tradition that developed into the complex methods of the Middle Ages.

Of course, there really are radically new features in the message *of* Jesus and the message *about* Jesus. The contrasts in the Sermon on the Mount ("you have heard that it was said . . . but I say to you . . .") are not accidental.[20] There are comprehensible reasons why riots broke out around Paul and his preaching, even though Acts does its best to explain that these were actually unwarranted. The question is, do these discontinuities between Old and New Testaments consist of the contrast between a this-worldly Old Testament and an otherworldly New Testament? Or is there something else going on?

The answer is emphatically "something else." There are at least five ways in which the Old and New Testaments appear to be pulling in different directions. But in no case is this a matter of swapping a this-worldly perspective for an otherworldly one.

First, the temple in Jerusalem has come under divine judgment, announced by Jesus in a tradition going back at least to Jeremiah. The temple had been the focus of Israel's prayer, pilgrimage, and lament for a thousand years, looking back even earlier to the wilderness tabernacle. Paul and Peter pick up from Jesus's denunciation of the temple by writing boldly about the church as constituting a new, worldwide temple, which as we have seen is part of the theological foundation of Acts.[21] But the "new temple" they all pictured was not an otherworldly or invisible community. It was the this-worldly reality of a transethnic community, with real flesh-and-blood humans indwelt by the spirit.

Second, the Sabbath, mandatory in Law and Prophets alike, becomes at best optional.[22] Paul argues in Romans 14 that one may, but need not, observe holy days, and that those who do and those who don't should not judge one another. Strikingly, whenever Jesus and the New Testament writers list the commandments, the sabbath is missing. Jesus seems to have taught and implied that the "age to come," to which the sabbath had pointed forward, had now actually arrived: "the time is fulfilled."[23] The signs of this, again, were actual space-time events, not least his remarkable healings. This has nothing to do with Judaeans being "legalists" and Jesus believing in "grace not law," or with Judaeans being "worldly" and Jesus being "spiritual." It has everything to do with the transformative fulfillment of ancient promises.

Third, the people of God are expanded to include believing Gentiles. Many came from east and west, as Jesus (and Israel's scriptures) had said they would, to sit down within the people of Abraham.[24] This was basic to Paul's understanding of the church as an actual community, in which literal, visible table-fellowship, not merely invisible or "spiritual" kinship, displayed and demonstrated the meaning of Jesus's crucifixion.[25]

Fourth, the food laws, one of the obvious markers of the ancient separation between Judaean and Gentile, have themselves also become optional.[26] This debate rumbles on in Acts, Galatians, 1 Corinthians, and Romans, along with the telltale line in Mark 7 about all foods now being regarded as "clean."[27] Again, this is not about a distinction between spiritual and material. It is about actual food and actual behavior.

Fifth, and perhaps most significant, we should note the

peaceable nature of the kingdom of God, as expounded by Jesus in the Sermon on the Mount and elsewhere, and as applied by the various New Testament writers. This is the more remarkable in that some of the early Christians' favorite biblical texts (like Psalms 2 and 110, and indeed Daniel 7) speak of the future king exercising a violent, punitive judgment on the wicked nations of the world. This shows up in a striking contrast between the early Christians and their Judaean context: the rejection of revenge. We might compare the threats and imprecations called down by the martyrs in 2 Maccabees 7 with Jesus's prayer for his killers in Luke 23, and Stephen's for his murderers in Acts 8. Paul insists in Romans 12 that vengeance belongs to God alone.[28] We should perhaps see this as a corollary of the third element above. Jesus's followers are to form a real this-worldly community in which the prophecies about the wolf and the lamb lying down together will at last be fulfilled.[29]

These five significant differences between Old and New Testaments should not, then, be mistaken for a shift from a this-worldly salvation to an otherworldly one. As far as the New Testament writers are concerned, they mark *the shift between two vital stages of the same story.* As Jesus insisted in his parables and his practice, as in his response to the imprisoned John the Baptist, the scriptural promises were coming true, even if not in the way, or with the results, that people had expected.

Towering above even these five highly significant features, and invoked by the early Christians to explain them all and the new direction in which the kingdom-promises were now being taken, is the position of the Messiah. One later rabbinic commentary on the "suffering servant" passage in Isaiah 53 transferred the "suffering" from the prophesied Messiah to the enemies he was supposed to be defeating.[30] The early Christians seem to have made the opposite move, regarding the sufferings of Jesus as somehow absorbing and overcoming the hatred, enmity, violence, and human degradation of the whole world, and winning the victory over the dark powers that stood behind it all. The violent defeat of enemies we find prophesied in Israel's scriptures seems to have been turned back on to the king himself, seen shockingly as the human embodiment of Israel's redeeming God. Following hints from Jesus, the early Christians sometimes spoke of God winning the ultimate victory, through Jesus's crucifixion—not over the normal this-worldly enemies (whether Rome or anyone else), but over the dark satanic forces that stood behind them and operated through them.[31]

These various major transitions, as we have already suggested, stand behind the puzzlement of the two disciples on the road to Emmaus. Their vision of a Messiah—"one who was going to redeem Israel" (Luke 24:21)—was of one who would execute God's judgment on the wicked, not die at their hands. But this does not mean that, once they had grasped the astonishing new reality, the early Christians shifted from a this-worldly salvation to an otherworldly one, from a Judaean reading of the scriptural promises to a platonic one. The stories of Jesus's resurrection and ascension are not saying, "Jesus has gone into the other world, the nonphysical one, and is showing you how to follow him there." Anything but. Such a proposal would, at a stroke, collapse Jesus's bodily resurrection into a platonic going-to-heaven story and distance the early church from its Judaean context. These have both been familiar tactics within certain strands of "liberal" thought over many years.[32]

No: the resurrection means that God's new creation has

been launched; the ascension means that Jesus is now the world's true Lord. The Gentile mission of the early church is about putting this new creation, and this worldwide rule, into effect in actual communities, not about showing people how to escape the material world either in detached present spirituality or future otherworldly hope. After all, the "principalities and powers" had exercised their malign dominion over the space-time world. Their defeat meant that the world, the good creation, was in principle set free from their deadly rule, and was ready in consequence, again at least in principle, to acknowledge a different god, a different "Lord." To suppose that the victory spoken of in the New Testament meant that humans could now leave the world of space, time, and matter and go somewhere else would leave the rule of the "powers" untouched, just as a would-be Christian eschatology about dying and going to heaven would leave the rule of death unaffected. The Platonist, ultimately, has to make peace with death, not seek its overthrow. For that philosophical tradition, death is not *defeated*, but rather welcomed: it releases the soul from the prison-house of an earthly body.[33] But for the early Christians death was the last enemy. It would be destroyed in the final outworking of Jesus's victory.[34]

If Jesus's messianic death provides a major discontinuity with first-century Judaean expectations, the same is obviously true with his resurrection and ascension. Each element here is vital. Those Judaeans (the Pharisees in particular) who taught a future resurrection foresaw the future bodily resurrection of *all* God's people at the *end* of time, not of one (a representative?) in the *middle* of time.[35] Those who hoped for a Messiah to conquer the world, as for instance in Psalms of Solomon 18, envisioned (as it appears did James and John in Mark 10) the same kind of victory and rule that seems to have been in the mind of Bar Kochba and his supporters in the final revolt of AD 132–35.[36] Acts indicates in its first chapter that the risen and ascended Jesus is indeed now enthroned as the world's true Lord, as Israel's Messiah was expected to be, but that the form his rule is to take will be very different from what most contemporaries had been expecting. The five elements of discontinuity already noted are contained within that radical redefinition.

The question I am posing in the present book, then, can be brought into focus by concluding that all this apparent discontinuity was nothing to do with Judaeans being focused on this-worldly matters and early Christians being focused on otherworldly matters. Both believed strongly in the overlap of heaven and earth. But they construed this in radically different ways, with the radical difference embodied in Jesus's redefinition of the messianic vocation. We can see the difference already in the transformation of the zealous persecutor Saul of Tarsus into the zealous reconciler Paul the apostle.[37] Jesus's redefinitions of God's kingdom coming on earth as in heaven were not about switching from the present world to a nonmaterial heaven. They were deepening the world-transforming hope, and radically clarifying the means by which it was to come.

Nor did the early Christians suppose that the problem with the first-century Judaean worldview was that it was too this-worldly. Paul's charge against those who were now in the position he had been in was that they had "a zeal for God" but that this was "not based on knowledge."[38] It wasn't that they were forgetting God and concentrating only on the present world, as though they were first-century versions of today's secularists. On the contrary. They believed in the scriptural promises, that *the one true God would come to dwell with his people on earth, thereby to establish his wise, sovereign rule*. The problem was that Paul's Judaean contemporaries, and indeed Paul himself until his moment on the Damascus Road, had thought themselves into a position where they could not recognize that, in Jesus, these promises of God's homecoming had come true and were coming true.

Thus the platonic reinterpretation of the message of Jesus and his first followers was a more subtle version of Marcionism. The all-important break came, it seemed, not between the Old and the New Testaments, but between the biblical story of Israel, Jesus, and the church on the one hand and the reinterpretations of that story that began to emerge from the third century onward.

To see how this played out, we must offer a brief sketch of some lines of development in Christian reflection down the years. This will lead, in chapter 10, to a somewhat more extended examination of two themes that have become prominent in the going-to-heaven narrative: the question of a final "beatific vision" and the proposal for an intermediate "purgatory."

9

GOD'S ARRIVAL ON EARTH OR THE SOUL'S ARRIVAL IN HEAVEN?

The Bible and the Church

So how did we get to the point where, despite the deep continuities between Old and New Testaments, most Christians today assume that the early Christian message was about "souls" going to "heaven"? How did we get from what the Bible actually says to what most Christians today assume it says? We must now focus in on some specific lines of thought that have been advanced in answer to this question.

To begin with, we must rule out one popular way of describing the transition. Adolf von Harnack (1851–1930), in his magisterial *History of Dogma*, offered what has come to be known as the Hellenization thesis.[1] Harnack was a brilliant historian, but, as most now realize, his proposal was a long way wide of the mark. He drew sharp distinctions between the Judaean world and Jesus *and* between Jesus (and his first followers) and the developed dogmatic tradition. On the first: he did his best to rehabilitate Marcion, producing a "Jesus" who was only tangentially related to the Judaean world. On the second: he argued that the simple message of Jesus ("the fatherhood of God and the brotherhood of man") had been corrupted by later Greek philosophical thought, producing dogmas that distorted, and possibly even falsified, Jesus's core message. When people think of Harnack, they associate him particularly with his theory of the distortions supposedly introduced by Hellenistic philosophy into the pure message of Jesus. But he was if anything even more emphatic about the deep gulf, as he saw it, between Israel's scriptures (and the whole Judaean world) on the one hand and Jesus and his first followers on the other. This has, perhaps, received less attention, because so many in the centuries after Harnack have shared this view, at least in softer versions.[2]

Harnack's proposal involves clean breaks between the three elements:

Old Testament and Judaean World		Jesus (and Some New Testament)		Later Church Philosophical Teaching
This-worldly Judaean hope		Simple teaching of Jesus		Trinity, Incarnation, etc.
Legalistic moralism		Personal religion		Philosophical dogma; souls going to heaven

It is important to be clear how different my proposal is from all this. We have just noted interesting shifts from the Old Testament, and its Judaean retrievals, to the message of, and the message about, Jesus. And of course I agree that there are significant developments between the New Testament and the theological writings of the third and fourth centuries. But Harnack's central idea, of the simple, lofty teaching of Jesus rising like a noble mountain peak between the dusty plains of legalistic Judaism on the one hand and the tangled landscape of dogmatic theology on the other, simply will not do. The truth is more complex and more interesting. And more challenging for the church of today and tomorrow.

Harnack's picture encapsulated what we now see as the impossible naivety of German liberal theology at the start of the twentieth century, holding that the simple, universal (and by implication non-Jewish) message of Jesus—now being rediscovered by nineteenth-century liberalism!—had been muddled up by the early Fathers with their philosophical complexities. For Harnack, this meant that the central doctrines of developed Christianity, including the Trinity and the Incarnation, were mere later inventions, pulling and squashing the original message out of shape.

In reaction to Harnack, it has now become fashionable for thinkers to offer a polar opposite: that the Bible offers random, scattered bits and pieces of true belief, providing a puzzling jigsaw that was finally reduced into a coherent picture by the great theologians of the fourth and fifth centuries. Many theologians today claim that the best place to start theological investigation is with the Nicene-Constantinopolitan Creed (AD 325, revised 381) and the Chalcedonian Definition (AD 451), where all that earlier biblical muddle got sorted out. (Some of the problem, I suspect, arises from the way many theologians were taught biblical studies at university, being plunged into speculative and atomistic so-called historical criticism before escaping into the more coherent and satisfying teaching of later theologians.[3])

Harnack's first break, between the Judaean world and Jesus, was a caricature in both parts. First-century Judaean thought and practice was not the dark, gloomy legalism that many nineteenth-century liberal Lutherans liked to imagine. And Jesus's message and achievement was not the de-Judaized "fatherhood and brotherhood" of Harnack's idealized universal religion. I have written elsewhere about Jesus's message in its first-century Judaean context, making the case for Jesus's accomplishment as the *transformative fulfillment* of the scripture-fueled expectations of his day.[4] Many of Jesus's contemporaries were indeed expecting the arrival of God's kingdom on earth as in heaven; Jesus affirmed that expectation, but he constantly and dangerously subverted the normal view of how that kingdom would come about and what it would mean in practice. But that subversion had nothing to do with replacing a this-worldly Judaean expectation with a generalized spirituality and ethic. It involved a fresh reading, and a fresh proposed fulfillment, of Israel's scriptures. It meant what it meant within the metaphysical world of those scriptures. It focused, as did the scriptures, on the heaven/earth creation symbolized in the temple, and on the interplay of the present age and the age to come. Jesus, as a matter of vocational obedience, drew it all on to himself. The creator God was coming home at last, inaugurating his reign on earth as in heaven.

The second break that Harnack postulated was between the teaching of Jesus and the dogmas of the fourth- and fifth-century church, with its philosophically shaped doctrines of incarnation, trinity, and the rest. These, Harnack insisted, were foreign to the ideas of Jesus and represented a decline into Hellenism. He was undoubtedly right to note the influence of Hellenistic philosophy, particularly Neoplatonism. But he was wrong to suggest that the actual content of notions like "incarnation" and "trinity" was foreign to Jesus and the New Testament. The key theologians of the third, fourth, and fifth centuries were, I believe, doing their best to articulate things that really were there in the New Testament and to do so in language that their contemporaries might understand.

Thus the fact that the New Testament does not use the explicit language of "trinity," or words like "person" or "nature" (in their later technical meanings), is not nearly as important as some have imagined. Any developing tradition may claim the right to offer fresh summaries, succinct shorthand, or technical terms, to refer to complex issues for ease of discussion. The question is whether such summaries really do express the heart of what had been said already, or whether they introduce distortions. I suggest that the notions of trinity and incarnation were *both* thoroughly appropriate as summaries of what was already there in Jesus and the early church *and* potentially misleading in drawing attention to themselves rather than to the actual mission of Jesus and his first followers—in other words, to the earthly inauguration of God's kingdom. The major dogmatic formulations of the fourth and fifth centuries were articulating *the key in which the music is set* rather than *the tune that is being played.* And since the "tune" was God's homecoming, the paradoxical arrival of God as king on earth as in heaven, the fact that the Fathers then focused attention on the "key" for this music (trinity, incarnation, and so on) suggested a different "tune." The way was open for the substitution of platonic theories about God, and about the going-to-heaven story, for the biblical vision of the triune God arriving to take charge on earth as in heaven.

My proposal, in short, is that the observable "breaks"—between the Old and New Testaments, and between the early Christians and the more platonic teachers of several centuries later—are both important. They need to be investigated historically. But that creates a double dilemma. What happens to the remarkably "earthly" promises of the Old Testament when we move to the New? And when, as in this book so far, we discern that they are fulfilled, albeit with significant modifications, what then happens to the later church story about going to heaven?

To repeat: to challenge the latter narrative is not to say, with Harnack, that all developed doctrine from the second century onward constitutes an overintellectualized distortion of the original faith. Far from it. From Paul onward, the great theologians have done their best to love God with their minds, to "take every thought prisoner and make it obey the Messiah."[5] At the same time, it will not do to cite Jesus's promise of the continuing guidance of the holy spirit, leading people into all truth (John 16:13), as though this might validate any and every subsequent teaching, and by implication rule out any critique of later dogma. It would be ridiculous to suggest that the church, over the course of two thousand years and in many different geographical and cultural contexts, has never made mistakes; just as it would be naive and shallow to suggest that it had *always* got things wrong, and that the solution was to pretend that we could "go back to the first disciples" and, with a kind of second naivety, try to reproduce their faith and their ways of expressing it.

If the first dilemma is resolved in the way I have suggested (the "earthly" promises of Israel's scriptures being fulfilled in Jesus's launching of God's kingdom), what about the second one, the move from the Jesus-shaped kingdom of God to the idea of "souls" going to "heaven"?

At the theoretical level, this brings us to the old question about scripture and tradition: Do we give priority to what scripture actually says, or do we say that the Bible means what the later traditions said it meant? This question in turn awakens echoes of the sixteenth-century debates in which the protestant reformers claimed to base their views on scripture, resisting what they saw as unscriptural church traditions.[6]

As often, we must beware of a false either/or. I happily affirm the fourth- and fifth-century creedal statements. But I resist any suggestion that they contain the heart of the matter, or that they can or should provide a starting point for Christian thought, *over against the Bible*. As I have tried to show, the earliest Christian writers regularly articulated a view of the creator God, of Jesus, and of God's newly outpoured spirit, which compelled their hearers to think of the One True God of Israel's scriptures in three interlocking ways, whatever language one uses to say such a thing. But, to repeat, if that was the key for the music, the tune being played was the inauguration of God's kingdom on earth as in heaven.

In particular, then, the first Christians were telling the *story* of what the One God had done. Paul, faced with theological backsliding on the part of his Galatian converts, declared that they had a choice. You must either have the God who sent the son and then the spirit of the son, or else some kind of paganism.[7] To that extent, the later Fathers were spot on. But, though you can understand how one might get from the New Testament's picture of God, Jesus, and the spirit to the later formulas, it's well-nigh impossible to go in the other direction. One would never guess, from the great Creeds and the Chalcedonian definition, that the Jesus of whom they speak with such rich philosophical subtlety was the friendly, challenging, alarming, warm, welcoming, authoritative, shrewd, stern, tender-hearted, self-giving young man portrayed so vividly in the four gospels.[8] That should give us pause for thought, at least.

No: the contrast I am drawing is not between a Judaean world incapable of containing the emerging Christian belief and a Greek world now at last happily articulating it. The contrast I see is between (a) the biblically rooted view of creation as God-given, to be redeemed and reestablished through the coming of God to be at home, and to set up his wise, sovereign rule on earth as in heaven, and (b) some variety of Greek thought in which the material world was at best a secondary, and at worst a dangerous, place from which the wise would naturally want to escape. There are of course many varieties of ancient Judaean thought, and still more of ancient Greek thought and practice. I have written at length about all that elsewhere.[9] (There are also significant overlaps, such as in Philo of Alexandria, who did his best to interpret the traditions of Israel through the lens of platonic philosophy, and, to a lesser extent, the Wisdom of Solomon.) But, when all that is said, there is still a fundamental contrast. Are we hoping to "go home" to God, or is he promising to come and be at home with us?

To map these stages of development properly would take a much longer book. But a brief sketch may be offered. Specialists will undoubtedly see many flaws and gaps. But if the question is, "How did we get from what the Bible *actually* says to what most Christians today *assume* the Bible says?" these may at least be signposts on the way.

Stages of Development

Certain key moments stand out to my nonspecialist eye. First, *the transition in the third century.* Chronological markers are seldom neat. But one vital moment was the failure of the Bar Kochba rebellion (AD 135). Bar Kochba (the name means "son of the star," alluding to the prophecy of Numbers 24:17), was hailed by some as Messiah and led an initially successful revolt against Rome, establishing a three-year independent Judaean ministate, until the Romans wiped it out. His movement embodied what until then had been one standard Judaean way of interpreting the scriptural promises: God's kingdom would indeed come on earth as in heaven, with the true Son of David leading the way into the new world. He would defeat the pagans, rebuild the temple, and establish a free and everlasting Judaean state. That hope, which in today's jargon would be both "apocalyptic" and "political," and of course "covenantal" in its retrieval of long-term scriptural promises, was what had driven the earlier revolt of AD 66–73, and now precipitated the briefly successful, and then utterly disastrous, movement of AD 132–35.

This debacle led many Judaeans to assume that such revolutions, and the kingdom-dreams that fueled them, were category mistakes, and that the wisest course now was the devout study and practice of Torah, rather than any attempt to impose God's rule on the world.[10] The compilers of the Mishnah, in the late second and early third century, were emphatically of the Hillelite school, content to live and let live, rather than the Shammaite school, committed to "zeal," that is, to the establishment of God's kingdom by force. Though this point might seem to concern the Judaean world rather than the early Christians, it becomes highly relevant because, when theologians of the third and subsequent centuries conversed in dialogue with their Judaean contemporaries, the latter were among those who had more or less abandoned the hope for God's kingdom on earth as in heaven. This was the time, after all, when some Judaean thinkers, appalled at the way the biblical promises appeared to have led to disaster, stood everything on its head and embraced forms of Gnosticism. It was against that kind of movement, influencing some Christian circles, that Irenaeus and Tertullian wrote so strongly in the second and early third centuries, insisting that the promises of creation's renewal, and of God's homecoming, meant what they said. But at the same time Clement of Alexandria and Origen were drawing on platonic ideas to explain and defend Christianity, inevitably giving less weight to the biblical promises of creation's renewal. It is with Origen in particular that the strain of platonic piety, aiming above all at the soul's vision of God, came for the first time into the bloodstream of Christian tradition.[11]

The ancient roots of our contemporary confusions have been explored by one of the leading historians of our day, Peter Brown, in his recent book *The Ransom of the Soul.* He contrasts Tertullian (AD 160–240) and Cyprian of Carthage (AD ?–258) with various later writers. Tertullian and Cyprian already thought in terms of the soul, which we shall soon want to question. But the point is that they focused on new creation and resurrection, not an immortal soul going to heaven:

> *For Tertullian, the average Christian soul was a strangely subdued thing . . . The trajectory of the individual soul after death was not important to him. The notion of the afterlife was dwarfed, in Tertullian's thought, by the idea of the transformation of the entire universe associated with the Christian doctrine of the Resurrection . . . Tertullian imagined [this] to be so majestic, so radical, and so total as to make the interval between death and the Resurrection of the dead seem short and empty of significance.*[12]

For Tertullian, Christian martyrs passed directly into paradise, a kind of inner chamber within God's palace, though they still had to wait there for the final renewal. For ordinary Christians, the waiting period was not so splendid, but still perfectly pleasant. This was the *refrigerium*, described by Brown as "a refreshing period of rest in the other world, as delightful as the taste of cool water and of food shared, in shady bowers, with boon companions."[13] When we remember that Tertullian lived in what is now Tunisia, in north Africa, the idea of a cool resting place makes a lot of sense and offers real comfort.

Anyway, as Brown describes it, a great change was coming over Christian teaching in the third century, moving away from the New Testament's vision of the renewal of creation and the bodily resurrection and instead using ideas from popular paganism and philosophical theorizing. What we find from Origen (AD c. 185–253) onward is that the souls of the departed were not waiting for resurrection. They were on an upward journey:

> *A high-pitched, Platonic notion of the soul . . . had begun to spread in Christian circles at the expense of earlier notions of the waiting of souls. Heaven was the true "fatherland" of the soul.*[14]

It wasn't just Platonists. Most philosophers of the time simply assumed that humans had immortal souls whose proper home, and at least possible destiny, was somewhere one might call heaven. Only the Epicureans would have disagreed.[15]

This third-century transition worked its way through later thought. As Christian thought developed, Tertullian's view of a robust physical new world struggled with the going-to-heaven narrative of Augustine and his successors, like the twins in Rebecca's womb. It was the younger theory—the platonic story—that eventually stole the birthright from the older vision of cosmic renewal and resurrection. By Augustine's day (linked, as Brown explains, to shifting social and also economic attitudes and beliefs) the idea of "resurrection," though still present, has been pushed further forward, almost out of sight. What mattered was the soul reaching for the heights, not God coming to establish his kingdom on earth as in heaven.

The question then became: How does one get to heaven? The saints, it was assumed, would go there directly. But most Christians, still for the most part distressingly unholy, would have to take a more tortuous route. Then, cutting very short the long story told by various historians, we arrive at Thomas Aquinas and his faithful poet Dante.[16] For them, the resurrection was still affirmed—as it was bound to be, granted not only scripture but the church's ecumenical creeds—but the whole idea of the renewal of creation, and of the anticipation of that renewal in the present time, had ceased to resonate. It no longer provided the larger frame within which other beliefs about the future made the sense they make in scripture (which then, as we saw, had to be read allegorically). Rather, it had given way to the full medieval scheme of heaven and hell, with souls bound for one or the other, and most souls even of the redeemed (except for the greatest saints) having to spend time in purgatory before they arrived at the "beatific vision." And it is this picture, rather than that of Tertullian or Cyprian, or even Augustine, that set the parameters for the confused western debates in the sixteenth and subsequent centuries.

A second stage in the shift away from the biblical hope is the remarkable transition of the church in the fourth century from persecution to state sponsorship. That story has been told often enough. The pros and cons of Christianity becoming established have been endlessly debated.[17] But the main thing for our purposes is this: the dogmatic statements of the fourth and fifth centuries, so often now cited as the truly authoritative doctrinal statements over against the Bible, were produced at a time when the overriding imperative was to hold the sprawling Roman empire together. The church's internal agreement on its faith was perceived as one vital element in that ambition.

What then had happened to the first-century vision of God's kingdom coming "on earth as in heaven"? There was a spectrum of views. At one extreme, the conversion of the empire could be hailed as the coming of God's kingdom on earth, with the bishops sitting down to dinner with the emperor. At the other, the whole thing appeared a hollow sham, compelling those who saw it that way to retreat to the desert and pray—and to replace the vision of God's kingdom on earth with the hope for the postmortem redemption of the soul. Thus, in Henry Chadwick's memorable summary, the Christian world divided between those who wanted to rule the world and those who wanted to renounce it.

When, in that setting, theologians tried to hammer out "creeds," and other agreed doctrinal statements that might hold together both church and empire, they regularly invoked particular biblical texts. But they by no means always reflected on the larger contexts of those texts, or of the actual overall narrative of the Bible. And the absence of those larger contexts, including the great themes of God's homecoming, allowed the message to be systematically distorted.

I have already hinted at the third stage, which requires brief notice: the medieval development. The Neoplatonism of Augustine, who had drawn deeply on Plotinus, was joined with the more recently discovered Aristotelian texts in the magnificent synthesis of Thomas Aquinas (c. 1225–1274). From my perspective, this is bound to seem like the substitution of a grand, Greek metaphysical vision for the one the Bible offers (the overlap of heaven and earth, and of the present age and the age to come). The Bible then becomes a loose collection of scattered godly teachings, requiring a metaphysical framework—which would need to be drawn from elsewhere.

This emerges not least when we consider the ultimate hope.

Aquinas of course affirmed bodily resurrection. But it is an open question whether he succeeded in integrating this with the Neoplatonic dream of the "beatific vision." That question is also addressed to one of Aquinas's greatest expositors, the poet Dante, and also to the many today who see a retrieval of Aquinas as the clue to a fresh contemporary exposition of the faith. Even if you manage somehow to affirm the primacy of the upward ascent of the soul to the vision of God while at the same time affirming the eventual bodily resurrection into the renewed creation as in (say) Romans 8 or Revelation 21, we ought to inquire, among other things, not only how these two work together but how it is that one (the resurrection) is so emphatically biblical while the other (the beatific vision) is not.[18] And whether that matters. We will look at this more closely, along with its companion "doctrine" of "purgatory," later on.

But certainly, by the time Michelangelo painted the famous Sistine Chapel (1508–12), the implicit narrative had become clear. By contrast (for instance) with earlier frescoes, which, with Ezekiel 37 in mind, had depicted the saints emerging from their tombs, with bones first, then flesh, and then breath, Michelangelo's work told the story of the soul arriving before Christ for judgment and being sent either to heaven or to hell.[19] The popularity of this painting is a strong reason why most Christians, at least in the west, assume that this is how the story works.

A fourth stage came with the sixteenth-century protestant reformers. Their emphasis on a supposedly Pauline doctrine of "justification by faith" focused on the contrast of "works" (the supposed "Jewish" view) and "faith" (the supposed "Christian" view), thus further underlining the implied platonic divide between present, earthly things, and "spiritual" truths and realities. Martin Luther, albeit not the most internally consistent of writers, saw the Law of Moses as part of the problem, inciting people to a self-help (but doomed) attempt to earn salvation by good works. His alignment of supposedly ancient Judaean thought with his perception of medieval Catholicism has been the focal point of attack in Pauline scholarship for half a century.[20] Even Calvin, with a much more positive view of the Law and of the story of ancient Israel, remained a definite Platonist. In terms of theological method, the Reformers did their best to insist on "going back to the Bible" over against the developed church tradition, especially on matters like Purgatory and the Mass. But they retained what was arguably the most distorted part of the western medieval synthesis, namely, the idea of heaven as the destiny of the Christian soul. Their dispute was about how the soul might get there, not about whether that was what the biblical narrative was actually about.

At the same time, not only Calvin in Geneva but also the radical Reformers in Germany, and in their different ways Tyndale and the later English reformers, all recognized the importance of a "reformation" not only of theology but of society. The this-worldly meaning of God's kingdom was not forgotten. But the impression we gain reading them today, despite their careful and patient learning and attention to original languages, is of the attempt *to use the Bible to answer the medieval questions*, rather than allowing the Bible to raise its very different questions. We might think, for instance, of the treatment (or nontreatment) of Romans 8:18–28, the great passage about creation's renewal through the wise and lamenting work of spirit-led humans. The fact that the famous King James version makes the passage virtually unreadable, and certainly incomprehensible, tells its own story: the reformers regularly appealed to Romans as their principal authority, but the actual climax of Paul's argument was not relevant to their controversies.[21] Creation's renewal was not high on the agenda for sixteenth-century teachers anxiously concerned about how to get to heaven without encountering purgatory on the way.

The fifth stage in this short glance at "how we got here" comes when the Protestant rejection of "Jewish works-righteousness" teamed up, in the Enlightenment philosophy of eighteenth-century Europe, with the philosophically Idealist split of matter and spirit. Thus Hegel could regard Judaism as the archetypally wrong sort of religion, focused as it was on land and family (a heavily ironic charge in view of subsequent developments in Germany). That kind of approach, inheriting various aspects of medieval anti-Judaism, positively *wanted* to escape from the Jewish world and to make Christianity something quite different. We know where that has led.

An extra impetus toward a platonic reading of Christianity has come in the last two centuries from the perceived problem of what some call Secularism, but which I prefer to think of as a modern form of Epicureanism.[22] As secular agendas have advanced, many Christian apologists have looked to Plato for help. A good example is C. S. Lewis in his book *Miracles*. He contrasts "Naturalism" with "Supernaturalism," which turn out to be, in effect, Epicureanism and Platonism. Later in the book Lewis gives a fine account of the resurrection, and of "new creation." But, as we saw earlier, he never allows the biblical worldview, so different from that of Plato, more than a walk-on part.[23]

Lewis was in this respect typical of many in the nineteenth and twentieth centuries. We should not be surprised that Nietzsche was able, contemptuously, to refer to Christianity as "Platonism for the masses." That is what it had effectively become. The biblical story of God coming to be at home in his creation, with, in, and through his human creatures—of God the Creator coming in the person of the son and then in the person of the spirit, not to take people away from this world but to renew them and the world together—this story has not been rejected. It has not been known or even imagined. Most western Christians, including many self-styled Bible Christians, have never heard it.

The going-to-heaven story of which they have heard, by contrast, includes two elements: the postmortem ascent of the soul to the beatific vision of God, and the intermediate state of purgatory. These medieval developments have been important and influential. What happens when we look at them in the light of the biblical theme of "God's homecoming"? This double question requires a further chapter.

10

THE IMAGINED GOAL AND THE UNNECESSARY JOURNEY

The Vision of God

The high point, if we can call it that, of the great medieval development of the Christian story was the idea not simply of going to heaven but of the beatific vision: the anticipated moment of seeing God face-to-face at last. The redeemed soul was to find its way, perhaps through dark pathways, until it arrived at the vision of God. Since the Bible does occasionally talk about "seeing God," this has a superficial plausibility. We have, of course, already argued that this stands the actual biblical narrative on its head. But since the idea of seeing God as the ultimate goal has been so popular in Christian tradition, it is important to substantiate the charge that it gets things the wrong way around. And this will bring us to consider as well the very popular doctrine of "purgatory."

The well-known theologian Hans Boersma has recently written a book insisting that the way to understand the Bible is through the lens of Plato.[1] We should not, then, be surprised when he also writes a fascinating book on the "Beatific Vision." Without engaging in any detail, in what follows I summarize what I believe to be the appropriate response. (A full treatment would of course require a much wider range of reference, but that is not appropriate or possible in a book of the present kind.[2])

The first and sharpest thing to say is that Jesus and the earliest Christians appear to be innocent of the whole platonic construct:

(1) They assume final resurrection, and only occasionally glance at "what happens to people immediately after they die."

(2) They do not use the word "heaven" to denote either the ultimate destination of believers or their possible interim state.

(3) With the exception of two passages in Revelation, they do not use the word *psychē* (normally translated "soul") to denote the immortal core of a human being that will continue after death. The apparent exceptions prove the rule.

The picture should then be clear. Jesus taught that God's kingdom was arriving on earth. Paul taught that Jesus, already enthroned as Lord, would return to rule and reign over the ultimate transformed creation. In John's account, Jesus taught that the real "homecoming" would be the coming of the triune God to humans, not the other way around.

What should we say, then, about the renewed popularity of the Beatific Vision, the supposedly Christian equivalent of the platonic heavenward ascent?

The New Testament does indeed speak, here and there, of "seeing God." This is a striking promise, granted the biblical context in which the seraphim veil their faces, and even Moses is only allowed to see God's back.[3] The pure in heart will see God, says Jesus in the fifth beatitude (Matthew 5:8). The inhabitants of the new Jerusalem will see God's face (Revelation 22:4). Hebrews 12:14 assumes that "seeing the Lord" is the goal for which the pursuit of holiness is the necessary preparation. John implies the same thing (1 John 3:2): we will be like him, because we shall see him as he is. All this is clear.

But it is striking—though you would not realize this from writers like Boersma, who insist repeatedly that the much later tradition as found in Aquinas and elsewhere is "what the Bible teaches"—that in the New Testament this idea is, at the very most, marginal. The passages I have just noted are the *only* relevant references. In fact, even they are not all that relevant: Hebrews and 1 John seem to be referring, not to seeing the father, but to seeing the Lord, Jesus himself. These references are in any case almost incidental, a by-product of the much larger reality that the New Testament writers are expounding. One might notice, for instance, that the beatitude about the pure in heart seeing God is the fifth in a much longer list, neither the first, nor the last, nor the climax. Why should one not equally highlight the beatitude about the meek inheriting the earth—something that might prove very awkward for the platonic vision?

Another passage frequently cited is 1 Corinthians 13:12 ("For at the moment all that we can see are puzzling reflections in a mirror; then, face to face.") But this passage doesn't suggest that "face to face" here means the human face seeing God's face. That is a possible reading, but it's more likely that, just as "through a glass darkly" is a vivid metaphor for partial understanding of all reality, so "face to face" is a general metaphor for the "full knowledge" referred to in the rest of the verse. If we'd asked Paul whether that included seeing God face to face, I suspect he would have said yes. But it's interesting that neither here nor elsewhere does he actually come out and say so.

Similar remarks could be made about 2 Corinthians 5:7, "we live our lives by faith, not by sight." Paul is there talking, not about the future "sight" of God—though again that would not be denied—but the future sight of the ultimate future state, including the promised resurrection body. Yes, the context speaks of being "at home with the Lord," which goes with Philippians 1:23, the passage about departing and being with the Messiah. If Paul had wanted to emphasize the "beatific vision" in the way the later (avowedly platonic) tradition would have wanted, he had every opportunity to do so, but he did not. Both Philippians 1:23 and 2 Corinthians 5:6–8 are referring, quite explicitly in their wider contexts, to the "intermediate" state, prior to final bodily resurrection.

In particular, one cannot defend the notion of the "beatific vision" by referring to 2 Corinthians 12:1–7. There Paul describes, with teasing irony, being caught up into the third heaven, and seeing things he can't now talk about. The reference to the *third* heaven may well intend a contrast with the *seventh*, where more serious or ardent heavenly travelers might have hoped to arrive.[4] In any case, even in that passage Paul talks about having *heard* things he cannot relate. He doesn't mention *seeing* things, and certainly not seeing God. What is more, Paul has clearly been driven by his opponents to speak of this strange experience.[5] It isn't a subject he would have raised himself, had he not been challenged. So far from providing any kind of biblical bedrock for understanding the "beatific vision" as the ultimate goal of the Christian life, Paul's rhetorical thrust goes in the opposite direction. In 2 Corinthians 11 Paul was mocking his opponents, caricaturing their desire for his apostolic credentials. Here he is doing the same with their desire to hear about his superspiritual experiences. To use this passage as a would-be "biblical" foundation for the medieval doctrine of the "beatific vision" is to build on sand.

I suspect, in fact, that those who advocate the "beatific vision" as the ultimate goal—one way of expressing the supposedly master narrative of Christianity that the present book is aiming to turn the other way up—are reacting, quite understandably, against a "secular" vision that would focus all Christian hope simply on the present world. Their countermove is to stress the ultimate goal of human life, our telos, as being elsewhere altogether. Hence the imagined goal of the vision of God, anticipated in the present by the sacramental and contemplative life.

But in the New Testament the telos of human life is not simply—in fact, not normally at all—spoken of in terms of vision.[6] The New Testament, in line with Israel's scriptures, sees the human goal in terms of the royal priesthood. That is the purpose for which humans are rescued, according to the heavenly vision in Revelation 5.[7] Of course, worship and adoration are part of the "priestly" vocation. And of course the biblical vision of the ultimate goal is not "earthly" *as opposed to* "heavenly." It is about the combined "new heavens and new earth," which as we have seen is anticipated in the person of Jesus and the work of the spirit. The "royal" element of "royal priesthood" is equally important, as we saw in passages like Romans 5:17 or Revelation 5:10. The "reign" of God's people—modeled on the humble self-giving rule of Jesus, as in Mark 10:35–45—is properly anticipated in the present life, not by substituting a "secular" vocation for a "spiritual" one but by discovering that God's coming in the person of the spirit results in the church's mission within the created world, bringing about signs of renewal and hope. This is both the outflowing of God's arrival in Jesus and the anticipation of Jesus's final arrival at his second coming.

This outflanks the proposals of those who see the practical work of the church as an accidental spin-off, or even a potential distraction, from the contemplative vocation.[8] Some followers of Jesus are, indeed, called to that demanding way of life. But the New Testament offers an inaugurated eschatology in which the ultimate union of heaven and earth is anticipated in the present. I suspect that most true contemplatives realize this very well. This anticipation comes, to be sure, in worship and especially the sacraments. But it also comes in the unity of the church, and precisely by that practical kingdom-work, the present work of new creation: in the church's traditional tasks of caring for the poor, of education and medicine, and celebrating beauty through art and campaigning for justice, all of which point ahead to the ultimate reality "on earth as in heaven."[9]

So What About Purgatory?

Those who have seen the heavenly ascent of the soul to God as the main narrative of the Christian faith have run into a problem. One central feature of the developing picture, a telltale symptom of wrong decisions being made at various stages, has been the proposal of a "purgatory" in which the souls of the faithful—all except for very great saints—are made ready after bodily death for their arrival in God's full presence. Once the imagined goal had been expressed in terms of the soul's vision of God (rather than in the biblical terms of royal priesthood), theology was driven to articulate the notion of what I have argued elsewhere is an unnecessary journey. If the soul was to be made fit for God's presence, it would have to pass through the fire. This has been so important that we must take a few pages to explain what is wrong with it.[10]

By the late fifteenth century the medieval idea of purgatory had come to dominate the imagination of western Christianity.[11] The rich built "chantries," providing for monks to sing, to pray, and above all to say Mass, to ease the passage of the departed through purgatory and up to heaven. All sorts of abuses grew up around the doctrine, of which the most notorious was the sale of "indulgences," a kind of get-out-of-jail-free certificate available (supposedly) from the Pope. That was one of several issues against which Martin Luther directed his initial protest. But he and his successors were not concerned simply with theologically unwarranted fundraising techniques, playing on popular fears and superstition. They were concerned with justification by faith, and behind that with debunking the whole vision of an angry God making it hard for people to find their way up to him, rather than with the God of scripture who had revealed his grace and mercy in the gospel of Jesus. Their protests struck, not at a few offshoots of "purgatory," but at the foundations of the doctrine. Any suggestion that people still needed to be punished for their sins was ruled out; Jesus had taken the whole punishment on the cross. And any suggestion that people still needed to be purified was likewise ruled out; bodily death, as Paul insisted, completed the process of purification and "mortification" that the holy spirit had been accomplishing during the course of a Christian life.

The Council of Trent (1545–63) did its best to pull back from what were widely seen (and not only by protestants) as unjustified and unhelpful practices.[12] It still affirmed what have been called "the fundamental commitments" of the doctrine, while distancing itself from "speculative understandings of its inessentials." But its reaffirmation of the doctrine did not address the real problems. Nor do today's purgatory apologists.[13] The cautious approach of Trent had no effect at the level of ordinary teaching, belief, liturgy, and practice, where the powerful vision of Aquinas, Dante, and Michelangelo retained its massive grip on spirituality and popular culture. Lurid speculation continued, producing such masterpieces as John Henry Newman's *Dream of Gerontius*.

All this has now "landed" in Anglican as well as Roman liturgy, with the adoption of the medieval All Souls Day (invented in AD 993), whose liturgy, the day after the joyful All Saints Day, plunges churches back into quasi-pagan gloom, far removed from the sure and certain hope of the resurrection. In a bizarre reversal, many churches now seem to make All Souls far more important than All Saints. At the same time, two major Roman theologians of the last generation—Karl Rahner and Pope Benedict—have proposed important revisions to the traditional doctrine.[14] When faced with that, apologists for the traditional doctrine will simply say, "But the official teaching has not changed"—even if many priests, having read Rahner or Ratzinger, follow them rather than Trent, let alone Dante, in their teaching.

The Reformers, having rejected the whole doctrine of purgatory on solid biblical grounds, were left with their own version of the problem. What can and should be said about the faithful departed prior to the general resurrection? As we have seen, this remains one of the questions most commonly asked by anxious faithful folk to this day, and naturally so; as I revise this chapter, I have just attended, albeit online, the funeral in another country of a beloved family member. One possible answer might of course be to treat "resurrection" as a synonym for the going-to-heaven story, and then to declare that at death all believers would arrive there at once. But for those in the sixteenth century who understood that "resurrection" meant a far more material new-creational existence than had yet come about, there was then the usual question of the gap between bodily death and bodily resurrection. If one accepted the dualist anthropology of "body and soul," as most did at that time, this became a question simply of the "soul" and its postmortem state. Was the soul asleep, as might be implied by Paul's metaphor, echoing Daniel 12?[15] Or was it awake, and if so in what condition? Was it on some kind of a heaven-bound pilgrimage, perhaps toward the beatific vision?

All this was a matter of unresolved controversy among the reformers, as in the debate between William Tyndale (c. 1494–1536) and his fellow translator George Joye (1495–1553). Joye, aware that bodily resurrection within the ultimate new creation strongly implied an intermediate state, altered some passages in Tyndale's translation with the intention of allowing for this. Tyndale, anxious to allow no loophole through which purgatory could be smuggled back in, hotly rejected the suggestion.[16] The same questions are addressed by other sixteenth-century writers, notably John Calvin in his early work of 1534, *Psychopannychia*, aiming to refute the idea of "soul-sleep."

In any case, the deeper-level problem was not addressed by the sixteenth-century reformers. They broadly shared the medieval view that the aim of Christianity was for the soul to get to heaven. They simply (though sharply) disagreed on the means by which that could happen, insisting that, having got rid of purgatory, there was nothing to prevent the soul reaching its rightful destination at once. To this day, the reformers' successors in the protestant and evangelical churches have been much more inclined to think of going to heaven immediately on death, rather than speculating about any kind of intermediate state. But if we follow the New Testament in insisting on bodily resurrection, and if we reject the body-soul dualism as unbiblical, then the question is bound to come back.

The present confusion, whose earlier roots I have been sketching, has sometimes in my experience focused on the use (and abuse) of the Bible. For the exegete, these debates can be frustrating. Theologians are wont to toss random lines from scripture into the mix. This seems to assume either that the Bible was addressing the questions at issue (which it usually is not), or that any biblical text, regardless of its original meaning, could be cited in support of new developments a thousand years later. When biblical scholars raise this methodological objection (for instance, at interdisciplinary conferences) the answer is usually, "Don't give us historical reconstructions of original Bible meanings. Augustine and Aquinas were great Bible scholars, and if this is how they read the texts, that's good enough for us. When we read them we *are* reading the Bible."

This rather shocking response may come, as I hinted earlier, from the theologians' having been taught biblical studies in a negative and nit-picking mode. I understand that reaction. But it can easily result in a flight from history, inoculating the theologian against ever hearing anything new from scriptural exegesis. In particular, it prevents people from ever hearing anything *Jewish*, rooted in Israel's scriptures, that might undermine the Platonism that, as Brown indicates, was already making early inroads into Christian teaching.[17] From that point of view, instead of Paul declaring that he was determined to "take every thought prisoner and make it obey the Messiah," we would seem to be saying that we must take every biblical thought prisoner and make it obey Plato.[18]

There is a fundamental question of allegiance here, as well as authority.

Meanwhile, orthodox theologians have learned to distrust anything reminiscent of Adolf von Harnack, for whom, as we have seen, Jesus's simple message had been muddled up by the Fathers' philosophical speculations. That is certainly not my position; nor is it Brown's. The Judaean eschatology of Irenaeus and Tertullian, conjuring up the renewal of the cosmos, and the resurrection of Jesus's followers within that, is very different from Harnack's "simple teaching of Jesus." The whole New Testament, not least in its retrieval and affirmation of Israel's scriptures, is solidly on the side of Irenaeus, Tertullian, Cyprian, and others, in this respect at least. The renewed popularity of medieval eschatology is the result of would-be orthodox thinkers, faced with rampant secularism, going for help to Plato rather than to the Bible, and thereby turning the story upside down. It is time to call a halt to such an abdication of Christian responsibility.

So what can we say, what must we say, about the naggingly persistent proposal of "purgatory"? Or, more positively, what must we say, in obedience to the biblical narrative, which is about God's coming to us rather than ours to him, about the "intermediate state" between the Christian's bodily death and bodily resurrection?[19]

As I said from the start of this book, the platonic idea of the soul, common to all parties in the late medieval and reformation periods, is thoroughly misleading if we want to understand scripture. The Bible nowhere suggests that humans possess an immortal interior identity that predated their bodily conception and will continue into an immortal future. According to 1 Timothy 6:16, only Jesus "possesses immortality." All others who share his new life receive it as a gift from him, not as part of their automatic, inalienable human capacity. The powerful and prevalent philosophical idea of the soul has ousted from the Christian imagination the more subtle but far more biblical idea of the *spirit*: the human spirit, which through God's grace in the gospel is joined to the divine spirit. In the light of our earlier suggestion that the holy spirit is to be seen as "coming" to the believer, and to the world, as one aspect of "God's homecoming," this may provide us with a way forward.

To explore this will take a further chapter, specifically chapter 14 below. But before we can offer a positive account of how the early Christians may have envisioned those who are poised between bodily death and bodily resurrection, we must first clear out of the way the question: Do such beings, after all, need to go through a postmortem purgatory before their resurrection? Is there, in other words, any explicit or even implicit biblical basis for such an idea?

The supposed biblical roots of the medieval doctrine are so slight as to be almost nonexistent. People have regularly referred in this connection to 2 Maccabees 12:39–45, which describes how some Judaeans who had died in battle were found to have had pagan idols under their clothes. Judas Maccabaeus and his colleagues concluded that this was the reason why they had been killed. But Judas then took up a collection, to send money to Jerusalem for a sin offering on their behalf, "taking account of the resurrection" (v. 43). The author explains that Judas "was looking to the splendid reward that is laid up for those who fall asleep in godliness," and so "made atonement for the dead, so that they might be delivered from their sin" (v. 45). The use (and abuse) of this text in the much later debates about purgatory is a classic example of people looking rather frantically for a text, any text, that might offer anything that might seem to point forward to the developed doctrine, as though to claim that the earlier text really did have the later idea in mind.

That would strain credulity. Second Maccabees never mentions the going-to-heaven story. It says nothing about the soul. There is no sense of postmortem punishment or purgation. It looks as if, without the atoning sacrifice, the dead soldiers would be assumed to have forfeited the resurrection itself. In other words, the *only* way in which this passage anticipates the much later invention of purgatory is in the (biblical) thought of an interval between bodily death and final destination, and in the (not explicitly biblical) idea that it might be possible, or even desirable, to pray for those in that intermediate state. But in the classic purgatory doctrine the dead are assured of heaven; here in 2 Maccabees they are not. Their impenitent idolatry might have been their complete undoing. Only at the most superficial level, then, can this passage provide more than a distant and partial analogy to one aspect of the later doctrine. This passage has, inevitably but misleadingly, colored debates about the extent of the canon of scripture, as though by including the Apocrypha in the Bible one might be striking a telling blow for purgatory—or as though, by excluding it, one would be striking a blow against. This, as Ecclesiastes might say, is vanity and a striving after wind.

One might, however, raise the further question about Paul's reference to being baptized on behalf of the dead.[20] Might that relate to a view comparable to that of the Maccabees? As commentators wearily point out, the practice seems to have died out very early, and we simply don't know what problems it was hoping to solve. The practice does indeed seem to be, as in 2 Maccabees, a way of ensuring that the people concerned will be raised from the dead. But Paul doesn't say whether they are believers who hadn't yet been baptized, or unconverted idolaters, or something else altogether. Again, even if that turned out to be the proper interpretation of a notoriously difficult passage, at the most it indicates the propriety, in view of the resurrection (not in view of "getting into heaven"!), of some kind of intercession for the departed. It says nothing about the major aspects of purgatory, that is, punishment for sin, purification of the soul, prayers for the departed, and so on.

The parable of the Rich Man and Lazarus (Luke 16:19–31) has often, unsurprisingly, been cited in connection with speculation about life beyond death. But, even if it is a kind of morality tale rather than, as I believe, a parable (that point was argued variously in the Middle Ages) it does nothing to support purgatory. Indeed, it might be thought to undermine it. The rich man wants help in his torment; none is forthcoming. On the surface, it is simply a heaven/hell story. But as a parable—which I think it is—it seems to be a way of warning Jesus's hearers that those who don't listen to Moses and the prophets will not be convinced even if someone were to be raised from the dead.[21]

Perhaps the most important New Testament passage for the question of the immediate postmortem fate is 1 Corinthians 3:10–15. This is the passage on which Joseph Ratzinger relies for his reinterpretation of purgatory as (only!) a single moment of final fiery judgment, where the fire is actually the Lord himself.[22] There is something to be said for this, though I would locate the moment in question at death, rather than at the final judgment. But a double caution must be sounded. First, the passage is about God's judgment of ministers, *church-builders*, not about all Christians. It might indeed have wider application, but that's not what the passage is about. Second, the salvation, which might come "only through fire" (1 Corinthians 3:15) does not refer to the going-to-heaven story. As becomes clear elsewhere in Paul, it is bodily resurrection. Thus the doctrine of purgatory, which loomed very large 1,400 years later than Paul, is really beside the point. I suspect that some at least of today's purgatory apologists may really be sounding the alarm against an easygoing religion that would shrug its shoulders and say, with Voltaire, *Dieu pardonnera, c'est son métier*: God will forgive; that's his job! No, reply the purgatory people: holiness matters; you need to be purified! The Bible as a whole would emphatically agree. But the impetus for a genuine call to take up the cross, to a spirit-led holiness, is rooted elsewhere than in unwarranted speculations about postmortem processes.

Those who advocate the medieval doctrine of Purgatory have sometimes appealed to Tertullian. He speaks of a *refrigerium*, a cool, refreshing abode for the soul between death and resurrection. But this simply doesn't work. Those resting and being refreshed in Tertullian's imagined temporary abode were happy. They were being neither punished nor purified. Their future bodily resurrection (as opposed to the arrival of their souls at the vision of God) was assured. Those still alive did not need to pray for them, and they were not summoned to do so. At no point, then, does Tertullian's proposal provide a long-range foretaste of the medieval doctrine.

The problem of interpretation here arises, then, only because some much later writers have seen *any* mention of a "waiting period" as the same thing as purgatory. There are some, it seems, for whom a doctrine developed a thousand years later is assumed to be present in embryo in any earlier statement that in any way resembles it. But here the *only* resemblance is that, in both cases, there is an interval between bodily death and bodily resurrection. That is inevitable, as ancient Judaeans and early Christians alike knew well, whenever one takes resurrection seriously. But the way in which writers like Tertullian envisaged such an interval is radically different, both in framework and in detail, from western medieval thought. Insofar as they reflected on the question at all, the early Christians and their Judaean contemporaries never imagined that the interval between death and resurrection was to be a time of purification.

In the absence of other biblical evidence, any argument for anything like the traditional purgatory, even the apparently restrained Tridentine version, will have to rely on distant and shaky inference. Two such lines of thought have regularly been advanced. First, people have suggested that most Christians—except the most devout saints and perhaps the martyrs—are still in need of some punishment for their sins, not least postbaptismal sins. Second, most Christians, with similar exceptions, are not yet in that state of holiness required for seeing the Lord (as in Hebrews) or sufficiently pure in heart to see God (as in the Beatitudes). What was needed, then, was either punishment or purification. Purgatory supplied both.

This idea was perhaps latent from at least the time of Augustine. Once you think in terms of the soul as the vital part of the person, and of heaven as the ultimate destination, the possibility of various stages of postmortem development and/or purification might be contemplated. But when Gregory the Great (540–604) picked up the same theme, then, as the historian Justo González puts it,

> *What for Augustine was conjecture, in Gregory became certainty. Thus, for instance, the theologian of Hippo [i.e., Augustine] had* suggested the possibility *that*

> *there was a place of purification for those who died in sin, where they would spend some time before going to heaven. On the basis of these speculations of Augustine, Gregory* affirmed the existence *of such a place, and thus gave impetus to the development of the doctrine of purgatory.*[23]

The protestant reformers replied to these two points with sharp, and largely Pauline, arguments. First, punishment for sin has been taken by Jesus on the cross. To suppose we need punishing again undermines Jesus's achievement. Second, Paul taught that *bodily death itself finishes sin.* Paul even says this of baptism (Romans 6:7, *ho gar apothanōn dedikaiōtai apo tēs hamartias,* "the one who has died is quit of sin"); how much more, of the bodily death that completes the baptismal identification with Jesus's crucifixion? There is therefore, he concludes, no condemnation for someone in the Messiah.[24] Similarly, when Paul says that he has been crucified with the Messiah, and that the subsequent life he now lives is not his own but that of the Messiah who lives within him (Galatians 2:19–20), it is hard to imagine that he would then say that this new, inner life—the life of the Messiah!—still needs purifying, let alone punishing. "You died," he writes in Colossians 3:3, to which we shall return, "and your life has been with the Messiah, in God." All that remains is for the Messiah to be revealed, and for "you" to be revealed with him in glory. He makes no attempt to warn his readers that some of them at least might need further postmortem purification.

The early Christians agree, of course, that sanctification is vital. It is not an optional extra for a few special saints. But they see this as being supplied through suffering and mortification in the present time, as in 2 Corinthians 4 or Romans 8, and through bodily death. These, as some of the Reformers explained, are the real "purgatory." (I have sometimes wondered if that is why Dante's *Purgatorio* is more popular than either his Heaven or his Hell. It is more like real life.)

But this is what today's purgatory apologists have not taken sufficiently seriously.[25] I think this comes from a residual attachment to some kind of platonic soul. If you start with a dualist anthropology, body plus soul, you may well see bodily death as less important theologically. The soul, as the song has it, "goes marching on," and will still need purifying. But the New Testament's unitary anthropology (to which Paul's language of the "outer person" and the "inner person" in 2 Corinthians 4 is not an exception) tells strongly against this. That's why those who take a nondualist view have experimented with theories either of a "gappy" future—in which the person at death simply goes into a state of nothingness, to be brought back again at the resurrection—or of a fast-forward movement, where the person is taken ahead in time to the moment of cosmic renewal and the general resurrection.[26]

I shall suggest a quite different possibility in the last chapter of this book. But the persistence of purgatory, even among some protestants (including C. S. Lewis here and there), seems to hinge on the idea that most Christians at death are still short of full sanctification, which therefore needs some kind of postmortem work, however much its apologists draw a veil over lurid medieval speculations. Such theologians then reject Paul's teaching that bodily death really does finish sin. I have heard it suggested that this would be a bit of "magic" on God's part, or that it would mean God "zapping" people into a sudden sanctity.[27] That kind of rhetoric is a smoke screen, disguising the absence of argument. The bodily death of a human being is a moment of massive and serious significance, not simply a transition for the soul from one state to another, which would then need a further act of divine manipulation for the person—the soul?—to be free from sin.

In fact, the more we know about psychosomatic human life,[28] the more it makes sense to suppose that Paul meant what he said, and that bodily death brings to a shuddering halt not only our physical desires and actions, both natural and sinful, but the neurological and intentional interconnections, the "heart" and "will," with which the human being is intricately composed. Jerry Walls is right that what matters is the heart, not just the body.[29] But he is wrong thus to assimilate the heart to a platonic soul, and to detach that heart, with its will, thoughts, and attitudes, from its intricate organic link with the body that dies. What then is left to sanctify or purify? Who *are* we then, after that psychosomatic death?

The answer, I suggest, is latent within the New Testament. As a way in, we remind ourselves of what we have seen throughout the present book: that the Bible offers a different metaphysical structure from that of Plato. Heaven and earth are made for one another; the temple is where they come together; in the New Testament that task of coming together is accomplished through the coming of God in Jesus and the spirit; and God's future world, achieved and revealed in and through Jesus, is now overlapping with "the present age." What later theologians would refer to in abstract terms like "transcendence" and "immanence" is here expressed as *the story of creation and new creation*. From a New Testament perspective, you can't create a metaphysic somewhere else—in Athens, say—and then fit God, Jesus, or the spirit into it. John and Paul insist that we must put Jesus himself in the middle of the picture and allow the metaphysic to form around him, drawing on scripture's creation-and-temple theme and pointing to the promise that God will be "all in all."[30]

Within that model, everything looks different. Instead of the faithful straining upward like the ancient and platonically minded pagans, longing to leave this world and return to their true home, we are called to be custodians of the home that God the Creator has made for himself—the earth, made to overlap and integrate with heaven!—and which he will one day come to inhabit fully with his rescuing and transformative power. And we as humans—the royal priesthood—are not simply to be *doing* this work of stewardship as agents. We are supposed to be *modeling* it as image bearers. The New Testament's retrieval of Psalm 8 becomes vital here, especially in the central passage Romans 8:18–39, where the true purgatory is the groaning of all creation, with the church caught up in agonized but spirit-resonating intercession and lament.[31]

The purgatory tradition presents at best a caricature of all this. It offers an overpersonalized and underrealized form of the genuine cosmic anguish, the agony of God's new world struggling to be born. In the Bible, those who have the first fruits of the spirit share in this anguish, not just for their own sake (as though God's drama with the world was solely about *us* and our "destination"!) but because humans have a vital, image-bearing role to play in God's larger plan of new creation. In short, once we tell the story the right way up—with heaven coming to earth, with the homecoming of God, rather than with the citizens of earth finding their way to heaven—many familiar elements will reappear, but they will all look different. Yes, the redeemed will see the face of God. Yes, they will be pure in heart, with the holiness required for seeing the Lord. But this will not be because they have made it to the top of the spiritual ladder. It will be because God has come to them in the grace and word of the gospel, thereby making them clean indeed, as Jesus said in John 15. Or, as John the Baptist said, they will be baptized in the holy spirit and in fire.[32] They will be cleansed through suffering and death and made alive in a new way for the age to come.

How Can the Bible Be Authoritative?

All these debates raise quite sharply the question of biblical authority. Have we, perhaps, allowed the traditions of theological speculation to nudge us further and further away from what Jesus, and the whole of scripture from Genesis to Revelation, seem to have been saying?

I believe the answer is yes. But, as with many gradual developments, there is seldom if ever a clean break. Many teachers have clung to some aspect of God's kingdom coming "on earth as in heaven," resisting the platonic urge to turn everything into "supernatural" categories with the individual soul making its way up to God. Some of the great reforming movements within the church have come about when, for whatever reason, people suddenly realized that an overconcentration on a postmortem future could stifle the urgent (and biblical) call to justice and mercy in the present.

Such debates lie behind many issues in today's church, not least the perennial standoff between those who see a great gulf between "God" and "Caesar" and those who believe that in some sense at least the "powers that be" are ordained by God.

Among the latter, there is just as sharp a divide between those who insist that if the powers are ordained by God we must simply obey them and those who say, as Jesus did to Pilate, that God will therefore hold them to account.[33] At a popular level the same issues show up when certain churches teach their people that any concern about the present world, whether it be the plight of refugees or the homeless, the challenge of ecology and of sustainable living on our vulnerable planet, and so on, are worldly concerns, to be left to the politicians and social workers, and that the only Christian obligation is to show people the way by which, after their death, their souls can arrive safely in heaven.[34] This is then polarized against those who see only too clearly the church's vocation—and long track record—in terms of care for the poor, and indeed of medicine and education. It is important to realize the historical and hermeneutical roots of such controversial questions. That is part of the urgent reason for the present book.

So if we say—as all Christian churches do in their official statements—that the Bible is our authority, what do we mean, and what effect might that have? This is not of course the place for a detailed analysis; I have tried to provide that elsewhere.[35] But if the Bible *as a whole*, not just the Old Testament but also emphatically the New, does indeed tell a coherent overall story about the creator God coming to dwell on earth amid his people, then a choice has to be made between that biblical witness and the much later going-to-heaven master narrative.

One particular irony emerges at this point. The phrase "authority of scripture" has regularly been invoked in the last four hundred years in support of a protestant and/or evangelical understanding of theology, particularly salvation. But this has regularly involved the quest for supposedly authoritative answers *to questions the biblical writers were not addressing.* This is a recipe for muddle and misunderstanding. I am urging that we consider as our primary task the questions the Bible itself is raising, to which it offers striking answers that have not even been noticed.

Equally, of course, some have rejected the idea of scriptural authority as the ultimate norm, arguing that, since the Bible emerged from the life of the church, the church must have the prior claim on ultimate authority. I have heard this argument used ("the church came first!") to privilege the tradition of the church, from whatever century, over any possible correction from scripture. I have also heard it used to privilege today's current thinking, even when not supported either by scripture or by tradition: "the church wrote the Bible," one liberal prelate was quoted as saying, "so the church can rewrite the Bible." This is simply shallow. The New Testament was indeed written from within the church. But it routinely claims authority *over* the church, sometimes sharply, as in Paul's writings to Galatia or Corinth. The writers of the four gospels were not simply reflecting the views of their churches. They believed they were called to *shape* and *direct* those views. To look no further, anyone in that world who starts a book with "In the beginning" is making a striking claim to authority. And what John strongly implied, Paul stated clearly, insisting over and over that his apostolic ministry, including particularly his letters, carried a God-delegated authority.

My case in the present book, however, is not lined up in these terms. I am arguing that the Bible as a whole, including the teaching of Jesus and his first followers, tells a story not about souls going to heaven but about the Creator coming to dwell with his people. In this story, earth and heaven are to be joined together forever, and humans are to be given responsibilities within that new world. This is not, then, about a few verses here and there being ignored or twisted. It is about the entire narrative of scripture as against the dominant narrative of popular western Christianity. This has immediate and urgent implications in church life and practice.

To see the whole Bible as authoritative does not, then, underwrite any particular branch of contemporary church life or teaching. What it does is encourage us to appropriate the Christian tradition with a wise and generous but critical eye. Putting the Bible first means that we can then recognize and celebrate much later church teaching, not least the great fourth- and fifth-century statements of doctrine, for what they were and are. Harnack was wrong: classic trinitarian theology, though by no means always associated with "God's homecoming," does in fact ground that theme. Once we get to know the tune, we can appreciate the key signature. Once we get the biblical starting point right we will be able to recognize which later formularies were appropriate guidelines for their time, and which may be appropriate signposts on the way to ours.

God's Homecoming and the Human Vocation

I have argued that the Bible as a whole presents first the promise, and then the fulfillment, of God's homecoming to his world. Jesus embodies the promised return of YHWH to Zion; the holy spirit indwells the church, anticipating the filling of all creation. This way of telling the story allows one theme to emerge that has not always been given its proper place, namely, *the human vocation*.

The Creator always intended humans to be his means of bringing his wise stewardship to bear on his vibrant new world, and also to join with the rest of creation in articulating the praise of its maker.[36] This human vocation points directly to the two ways in which, in Christian tradition, the Creator has chosen to come into his world: in Jesus himself, and in his own spirit, dwelling in the hearts of human beings to enable them to exercise this glorious human vocation. Christology and pneumatology effectively flesh out the theme of "God's homecoming."

These reflections on Jesus and on his outpoured spirit have often run into difficulty when it comes to thinking about how (what we have sometimes called) "divinity" and "humanity" come together into one. This applies both to the person of Jesus and to the human persons who are indwelt by the spirit. Describing that mysterious but powerful confluence of identity has proved challenging. But once we allow the biblical narrative and metaphysic its full scope, the problem largely disappears. God made humans so that he could become a human—one in particular. He did this so that he could indwell, and work through, more and more humans, equipping them for their vocation as the royal priesthood. In both cases the "humanity" in question is enhanced, not diminished. We should beware of the tendency, in opposing "naturalistic" or reductionist accounts, so to emphasize the divinity of Jesus, and the sovereignty of the holy spirit, that the human vocation, vital in both cases, is reduced or overlooked. This is not simply about appealing for an "Antiochene" position over against an "Alexandrian" one. It is about the Bible's own categories—and challenges.

The work of Jesus and the spirit thus generates what a colleague once called "collaborative eschatology." Humans indwelt by the spirit are charged with the responsibility of being part of the solution to creation's malaise, here and now, in advance of the ultimate redemption. This contextualizes such controversial issues as "divinization" on the one hand and the problem of justification (are we "contributing to our own salvation"?) on the other. Once we realize that the fundamental movement in Christian theology is the coming of God to us, rather than any attempt on our part to get to him, everything that follows is set firmly within the framework of sheer grace.

I see this present book, therefore, as part of another, larger agenda. Systematic theologians have often built up a metaphysic—a way of seeing all of reality—drawn from various philosophical traditions, only bringing the Bible into play for particular passages and proof texts.[37] But the Bible offers its own metaphysic, a vision of all reality in which heaven and earth, though distinct, are designed for a symbiotic relationship within an ongoing purpose. Paul writes in Ephesians 1:10 that God's plan always was "to sum up the whole cosmos in the Messiah—yes, everything in heaven and on earth, in him."[38] The biblical cosmology, so often forgotten by those intent on their souls finding the way to heaven, needs to be retrieved and given its proper place. And in that work the role of human beings can be explored in fresh ways, which will now emerge in the final section of this book.

Section II

SO WHAT? LIVING WITHIN THE REAL BIBLICAL STORY

11

WORSHIP, EVANGELISM, AND PRAYER

Celebrating God's Homecoming: Worship

To focus on God's homecoming is to insist that the whole Christian story is about what theologians have called "grace." That big theological word has meant different things to different people in different contexts.[1] But at its heart it refers to the central Christian belief, rooted in one of ancient Israel's central beliefs, that the God who made the world is a God of love, mercy, faithfulness, kindness, and goodness. "Surely goodness and mercy shall follow me all the days of my life," sang the Psalmist in one of the best known of those wonderful poems.[2] Grace is a sigh-of-relief concept; an it's-all-going-to-be-all-right idea; a truth about God, and hence about the world he made and his purposes for it, on which we can rest secure despite everything. And once you allow the truth of the Word becoming flesh to live among us (John 1:14) really to sink in, you realize that this wasn't a strange, out-of-character thing for God the Creator to do, but the moment above all when at last he came home to do and be what he'd wanted to do and be all along. This realization changes everything, in what we do as renewed humans as much as in how we think about God and ourselves.

We are called to recognize, and celebrate in worship and prayer, the reality of God's homecoming. God, in the person of the spirit, is intending to speak the good news in every language under heaven (Acts 2); God, breathing into and then through Jesus's followers, is sending them out into the world as Jesus himself had been sent (John 20). This must work its way into all aspects of Christian living. The church is meant to be neither more nor less than the community that displays God's homecoming to the world. That community life has always startled outsiders, provoking some to fierce opposition but convincing many (including former persecutors) of the truth of the gospel.[3]

We begin at the center: with worship. Starting there may perhaps allay the fears of some readers. Some may have suspected that I am capitulating to the secularist vision of a purely this-worldly reality, with the glorious gospel reduced to a message of social reform and supposed "improvement." If, after all, we resist the platonic vision that captured the imagination of the medieval church, and with it the countless Victorian hymns that speak movingly about "going home" to heaven, does that mean that we have abandoned the vision of a present spiritual life, and of a hope beyond the grave, that have energized and encouraged so many?

The answer is a resounding No. These final four chapters are designed to fill out that answer.

Doing away with the platonic going-to-heaven story, in fact, allows the genuine biblical vision, including the message of Jesus himself, to stand out. Heaven's rule *has* arrived, and *is arriving*, on earth. It will be completed in the promised "new heavens and new earth." It cannot be reduced to terms of "earth," but it is precisely about the earth *being filled with God's glory*, as scripture always promised. When worship, especially the church's sacramental life, is understood within this true biblical narrative, it will reflect exactly this. The life of the church is supposed to be a forward pointer to the long-promised cosmic reality.

Worship is central to Christian living. Actually, it's central to all human life: "without worship you shrink," wrote the playwright. "It's as brutal as that."[4] This is a general truth: human flourishing depends on looking up, looking beyond, looking deeper, and responding with gratitude, admiration, and aspiration to the vision one has glimpsed. By itself, however, this wide meaning of "worship" can lead in many different directions, some of them dangerous or even destructive. Humans are designed, after all, to reflect the true creator God into the world. But if humans worship idols, the god-reflecting vocation is not canceled. It is distorted, so that we reflect into the world some aspect of, or some force within, the created order. The classic ones are money, sex, and power. We become like what we worship. Instead of shrinking, we are shaped by it: into monsters, if we are worshipping idols, or into truly human beings, if we are worshipping the true creator God. We grow into the likeness of who or what we worship, and we display that likeness to the world.

Yet Jesus didn't say, "If you want to grow instead of shrinking, follow me"; he said, "If you want to follow me, take up your cross." And he promised that, in this quest, those who would lose their lives for his sake would find them, find them richly, find an abundance of life that could be had in no other way. The revolution implied by Jesus's kingdom vision is worked out in the revolutionary worship of his followers. Saying the Lord's Prayer, many have noticed, is among the most revolutionary actions we can ever undertake.

Christian worship, the heart of Christian living, is thus best understood within the framework of biblical thought we have been exploring throughout this book. It is about the response of love and gratitude to the one true God who has come to make his home in our midst. It is about the transformative work of the holy spirit, by whom the church, and every individual disciple, grows into the genuine, heaven-soaked, increasingly human life that was God's will from the beginning. God's homecoming by the spirit initiates and sustains us in the worship of the heaven-plus-earth human being, Jesus of Nazareth, Israel's Messiah and the world's true Lord. God the Creator has come home to his world, and now comes home to his people to lead them in his ongoing mission.

Among the many facets of the worshipping life of the community, we look first at evangelism and prayer.

Announcing God's Homecoming: Evangelism

First, the task of evangelism. Evangelism is both worship in itself (in that it proclaims the mighty acts of God) and the invitation to worship. It invites hearers to discern, and to adore, the God revealed in the gospel. Evangelism, we might say on the basis of the New Testament, is the spirit-powered announcement that the crucified and risen Jesus is the world's true Lord, summoning all people to faith, hope, and the discovery of a new life based on and characterized by love. In other words, it is the declaration (made in a thousand different ways, from large-scale addresses and sermons to local and intimate examples and friendship) that in Jesus the creator God *has come* home to rescue the world, that in the spirit the creator God *is coming* home to dwell among humans. By taking up residence in the hearts of the faithful, the spirit will transform them to be part of God's new creation. This, as Paul says, is the "down payment" for that which is to come. Through the spirit's work, and ultimately in the return of Jesus, his ultimate homecoming, all things will one day be gloriously complete.

The task of evangelism, though in one sense beginning with John the Baptist and then with Jesus, looks back to the prophecy of Isaiah. That is where, in the Greek version, we find the word *evangelizomai*. In Isaiah 40:9, and then in 52:7, the prophet speaks of someone bringing "good tidings" to Jerusalem.[5] In Isaiah 52:8 the messenger announces the news, and then the watchmen on the city walls are to shout the "good news" to their fellow citizens.

The good news in both cases is the same: *YHWH is coming back at last*. And he is coming back to be king. He has won the victory over the dark forces that had destroyed the temple and carried God's people away captive. Now he is coming back to reveal his glory to the whole world (Isaiah 40:5): powerful as a sovereign, gentle as a shepherd (40:10–11). The gospels refer back to this passage and relate it to John the Baptist and Jesus.[6] The natural interpretation is that Jesus's "gospel" message was the news that God the Creator *had* come back to rescue the world; he *was* coming back to call people to be part of his new project; he *would* come back to complete the task in the ultimate new creation (Isaiah 55). In shorthand, we might say: incarnation, spirit, second coming. The gospel is all about the coming of God.

Over and over throughout his public career, Jesus was saying, *This is what it looks like when those promises of God's return and rescue come true.* As with Isaiah moving steadily through the great poem from chapter 40 to chapter 53, the gospel writers lead the eye up from the initial claim of God's return, displayed in Jesus's powerful deeds and explained in his many-sided teaching, to the shocking but vital events of his death and resurrection. *This*, they are saying, *is how it was all accomplished.* John in particular stresses that this was and is the ultimate display of divine glory, upon which, he says, "we gazed." As Jesus said (John 14:9), "anyone who has seen me has seen the father." This is how the prophecy of Isaiah 52:8 was being fulfilled: in plain sight, the people of Jerusalem witnessed the return of YHWH to Zion—even if many of them didn't recognize it.[7]

This *evangelion* is continued through Acts, and is summed up routinely by Paul. The good news is that Israel's God has done what he promised, returning to his people in the person of the Davidic Messiah whose death and resurrection have displayed the divine glory by dealing with the dark power of evil and launching the new creation for all the world.[8] This good news about what *has* happened gives birth to the good news about what *can now* happen: any person, man, woman, child, from any social class (slave or free, wealthy or poor), from any ethnic background (Judaean or Gentile, Greek or barbarian)—anyone at all *can become part of this new creation right now*, by renouncing whatever idols they had been worshipping and by invoking Jesus as Lord. This combined good news then points ahead to what *will* happen. Jesus will return in the end, to complete the job of new creation, to put all things right, and to bring heaven and earth together into one as God the Creator always intended. This is the Christian good news. It's all about the homecoming of the one true God, Creator and rescuer.

Sadly, this isn't what many people think of when they hear the word "evangelism." It isn't what they hear in "gospel sermons." In particular, it isn't what you get if you follow the high road of Platonism, telling people how their souls can get into heaven, let alone how they might avoid ending up in hell. The main trouble with telling the story in those terms is that it doesn't match the Bible's account of Jesus and the gospel. In addition, that way of telling the story easily leads people to suppose that the whole thrust of the story is about the question of whether we've kept God's law, and what happens if we haven't ("we are sinners; we might be going to hell, but God has dealt with that problem if only we will accept his solution"). And that is not the story the Bible is telling.[9]

Don't misunderstand me. Biblical morality was, and remains, hugely important. But the whole story is *not* a moralistic one, focused on how our sinful souls might or might not find their way to heaven. Too often, in the moralized version of the gospel, the whole emphasis is on sin and punishment, not idolatry and victory. This means that the vital message about the overthrow of idols is usually omitted, resulting in many embracing a kind of faith with no understanding of what, for the first Christians, was a kind of "discipleship 101": "you turned to God from idols, to serve a living and true God, and to wait for his son from heaven, whom he raised from the dead—Jesus, who delivers us from the coming fury."[10] Forgetting that larger picture is the high road to unhelpful theologies of atonement.

There is of course a downside to this. Some people—most likely many, as in Jesus's day—persist in idolatry, in lifestyles of mind and body that reject and oppose the possibility of new creation. They are saying, in effect, "I don't want to be part of God's new world; I will continue to worship and serve Mammon, Mars, Venus, or whichever fake divinity is offering what I think I want just now." There are no promises of rescue and fresh vocation for those who insist on going that route. But making this point is not preaching the gospel. It is, at best, a reflex from the true message.[11]

In particular, the message of the cross, so often and rightly a key element in gospel preaching, stands out all the more clearly once the biblical narrative leads the way. On the cross, as in the prophecy of Isaiah 53, the servant bore the sins of the many, taking the weight of the world's wickedness upon himself in order to defeat the usurping power of evil. This accomplished, once and for all, what God did when he overthrew the idols of Egypt at the original Exodus, or the idols of Babylon in the new exodus after exile. The *victory* of God over the idols, accomplished through the death of Jesus in the place of sinful humans, is the sharp focal point of the *coming* of God in the incarnation. God "came home" to die for sinners and so to win the victory, and then to celebrate it and put it into effect.

Telling the story like this draws the resurrection into the center of the message. This is how God's project of new creation has begun. Now that "this world's ruler" has been dealt a fatal blow, Jesus will draw all people to himself.[12] This inclusiveness is the appeal of the gospel: that, in Jesus, the one true God has begun his long-awaited project of new creation, and that by the spirit this is extending out into all the world. That is how God is recruiting people of all sorts to become new-creation people in their turn: new creation in themselves, and the agents of new creation wherever their lives and particular vocations will take them.[13]

My proposal throughout this book is that getting the story the right way up will thus generate whole new ways of telling the truly *good* news of the gospel. These new ways won't "water it down" (people are always suspicious of that). Nor will they parse it out into a more generalized or wishy-washy version of its real self. Where we have often spoken of "heaven and hell" and encouraged people to seek the former and avoid the latter, we ought to speak instead of God's new creation, of the time when the *earth* shall be full of God's glory as the waters cover the sea—and how that *has already begun*, and how people can *already be part of it* here and now by abandoning their idols (harder than it sounds) and worshipping this creator God. Having launched his project of new creation, God is in the business of recruiting volunteers to become part of it: new creation in themselves and agents of new creation in the world. God will put the whole world right in the end. In the present time, he puts human beings right so that they can become, here and now, part of his ongoing putting-right project for the world.

This is not a kind of bonus feature to the promise of salvation. This *is* what salvation (that is, rescue) looks like.

Grasping this point liberates both preachers and hearers from the strange and unfruitful peculiarity of supposing that what's required is for someone to "pray a prayer," to repeat a statement of allegiance to Jesus—and then to wait for however long it takes before they are allowed to "go to heaven at last." In between that sort of conversion and that sort of hope people experience an uneasy balance, knowing one is supposed to behave in a certain way but also being warned not to imagine that one's behavior could be a "work" on which one might rely, compromising one's initial faith. This sounds like a caricature, and indeed it is. But it is, alas, what a great many people have been taught to believe. If we can get the story the right way up, recognizing that it is all about grace from start to finish, we can be liberated from the nervous teaching that holds people back from realizing that the whole point is for God to come home to his world. He comes, here and now, in and through those who are indwelt by the spirit, anticipating the day when Jesus will come again at last and make his home in our midst completely and forever.

This is the context, in particular, where a favorite evangelistic text might come into its own. It is one of the best known homecoming passages in the New Testament. Jesus addresses the lukewarm Christians in Laodicea, and promises:

> *Look! I'm standing here, knocking at the door. If anyone hears my voice and opens the door, I will come in to them and eat with them, and they with me.*[14]

Despite a tradition of this being used to address unbelievers, it is clearly written to Christians. It is addressed, though, to a church that has become arrogant and lukewarm. At the same time, the idea of Jesus coming into the house and eating with friends reminds us strongly of Luke's story of the two disciples on the road to Emmaus, where Jesus, not yet recognized, comes in to eat. There he quietly takes over the role of host, breaking the bread, and that is when they suddenly recognize him. The image of Jesus wanting to come into the house, in other words, opens up, embracing both the puzzled and downcast (as in Luke), and the lukewarm (as in Revelation), and then, quite appropriately, those who are perhaps on the fringe of faith, or just beginning to wonder about Jesus. The Jesus who *has* "come to make his home with us" promises that he *will* do so, again and again: to individuals, to groups, to churches. And the promise, like many biblical promises, includes the sure sign of home: sharing food together. That's what people do at home. The text is truly evangelistic, an archetypal moment in God's promised homecoming—so long as we construe the gospel the right way up.

I have heard many sermons on Revelation 3:20 where the food was not mentioned. This is a shame, because actually it is an ideal text for a sermon at the Eucharist. And I have heard sermons or talks on Revelation 3:20, which interpreted the story in terms of Jesus "coming in" to someone's life *so that they could then go to heaven with him*, which is precisely not the point. The vast and world-changing biblical promise is here beautifully focused on the intimate invitation to invite Jesus in, whether for the first or the ninety-first time, into a life, a home, a fellowship gathering, wherever. As one old hymn puts it:

> *Come, risen Lord, and deign to be our guest;*
> *Nay, let us be thy guests; the feast is thine.*
> *Thyself at thine own board make manifest*
> *In thine own sacrament of bread and wine.*[15]

Above all, Revelation 3:20 breathes the right atmosphere, which is of the *gracious love* of God. This, in Hebrew, is God's *hesed*: his "loving kindness." That, after all, was central to the appeal of the original gospel in the wider world of Greek and Roman society. The Judaeans—at least those who prayed the Psalms, those who read Isaiah 40–55, and so on!—knew very well that their God was a God of astonishing grace and kindness. His forgiveness, after so many terrible times when his people had rebelled, had become legendary, as in Psalms like 106, where the people sin again and again—and God forgives them and restores them each time. The first followers of Jesus saw this gracious forgiveness acted out before their eyes: "[he] loved me," wrote Paul, "and gave himself for me."[16] But the idea of a God who *loved* humans was a strange new idea in the wider world. Zeus and his squabbling children may have taken a fancy to this or that human now and then. But they remained fickle, moody, unpredictable, and often malevolent. Thus nobody, not Homer, not Plato, not Socrates, supposed that a real god would actually *love human beings with an unbreakable love*. The closest I can think of an ancient pagan getting anywhere near this is the Stoic Epictetus, but even he would never have said what the New Testament says on page after page about the true God, and about Jesus: "He had always loved his own people in the world; now he loved them right through to the end."[17] However we explain the gospel, whatever illustrations we use, whatever passages we employ or stories we tell, this astonishing message must always come through.

The idea of a God who loves like that, the center of any true evangelistic message, is hard for many to grasp, particularly if they have not experienced unconditional love and forgiving grace in their own lives. So the message comes loudest and clearest from a community that is embodying the same love in reaching out to their neighbors in every way possible. That is why I argued in *Surprised by Hope* that "evangelism" belongs together with "justice" and "beauty." The good news of new creation makes the sense it's supposed to make when the community that is announcing it is known to care about *putting the world right* at every level and about *celebrating the beauty of the world* in art, music, and every other way.

My main concern here is to alleviate any anxieties that the

way I have outlined the biblical story might cause problems for evangelism. Well, it certainly will be a challenge for some types of evangelism. But once we see that the message is not about us going to be with God (will we get there? Do we have to earn it? How does it happen?) but about God coming to be with us, this doesn't detract either from the evangelistic imperative or the power of the gospel. On the contrary. The announcement of God's coming in Jesus and the spirit—which is in itself an act of worship—holds out the invitation to be part of God's new creation, through the victory of Jesus in his death and resurrection and the present power of the spirit.

Exploring God's Homecoming: Prayer

The second dimension, again worthy of a whole book, is the life of prayer. I have touched on this subject in another recent book so can be brief at this point.[18] Christian prayer is shaped by the twin truths of God's homecoming—in Jesus on the one hand and in the spirit on the other.

Christian prayer is, in other words, essentially *trinitarian* prayer. As in Paul's memorable exposition in Romans 8, it is about the spirit dwelling within us, being fused with our own spirits, so that we find ourselves being shaped according to the likeness of Jesus the Messiah. And that shaping occurs as we share the longings, and even the wordless lament, that the spirit is offering to the father from the depths of the world's horrors and heartaches. This is at the center of worship, as we get to know the true God better and so see more clearly the depth of his ongoing sorrow over his world. We may often find ourselves driven to prayer by urgent need or sudden distress. As in the

Lord's Prayer, the context of the requests for bread, forgiveness, and deliverance are given in the adoration and worship of the earlier clauses, especially "hallowed be thy name."

Saying that Christian prayer is "trinitarian" provides the clue to the shape and pattern of a genuine Christian spirituality. At one level, since classic trinitarian thought has stressed the full divinity of all three members of the Trinity, it is appropriate to direct prayers to any and all of them. The New Testament offers models of prayer to Jesus: Peter shouts "Lord, rescue me!" when sinking into the sea; the early Christians prayed "Come, Lord, come!"[19] We glimpse the prayer to the spirit in the Acts of the Apostles when the apostles lay hands on newly baptized believers and pray for the spirit to come upon them. Prayer to both the son and the spirit has been highlighted in various subsequent Christian traditions. But one well-recognized pattern, from which those are variants, has been to pray *to* the father, *through*, or *in the name of*, the son, *in the power of* the spirit. In other words, such prayer always has at its heart the belief that the one true God *has* come home to this world in the anointed son, Jesus, and that this same God *is constantly* coming home to this world in the presence and power of the spirit. All the prayers that we might find ourselves led to pray—prayers of joy or sorrow, lament or laughter, urgent intercession or patient waiting—all can be framed within God's past and future homecoming.

If we bear all this in mind, we will never suppose that Christian prayer is about calling to a distant God who lives somewhere else. Nor will we suppose that Christian prayer means merely attuning our hearts and imaginations into the ongoing inner life of the present world.[20] God's trinitarian homecoming stands over against the escapist dualism of a distant God and the quasi-pantheism of the world's supposed inner life. The God who remains utterly other has nevertheless come to dwell with us, as Solomon grasped in his famous prayer in 1 Kings 8. The God who made the universe is calling us to be part of the new creation in which his original purposes are being, and will be, gloriously fulfilled.

None of this makes prayer easy. There is a reason why Jesus and his first followers insist that we must persevere in prayer. You only say that sort of thing when the task might seem too daunting, or persisting in it too exhausting. Whatever the form prayer takes, we stand at the threshold, the overlapping place, of heaven and earth. Here there will be glimpses of glory as well as groanings of lament. If we can remember that prayer is a gift of grace, the result of God's homecoming, we might appreciate it more as a central gift and expression of worship.

12

THE SACRAMENTS

God's Homecoming in the Sacramental Universe

Beyond evangelism and prayer, Christian worship centers on the sacraments. And here the whole theme of "God's homecoming" provides a way to clarify a good deal that has been muddled.

God's homecoming may help us understand what people mean when they suggest that the whole world is in some sense sacramental. Perhaps the best-known exposition of this theme is *The World as Sacrament*, by the Orthodox theologian Alexander Schmemann (1921–1983).[1] This way of seeing the world can be glimpsed in the song of the seraphim in Isaiah 6: the whole earth is full of his glory. Taken out of context, that declaration might simply suggest an easygoing pantheism or panentheism—until, of course, we are confronted with a devastating earthquake, a child dying of cancer, or yet another instance of human brutality. Schmemann's thinking never fell into that trap. For him, and I suggest in biblical thought as a whole, what we have come to call "the sacraments" are simply the vivid and dramatic focal points of something that is true of God's presence in the whole world all the time, that, in Hopkins's words, "The world is charged with the grandeur of God." (Hopkins, too, was clear that this was no pantheism, but needed to be seen in terms of God's overall purpose for redemptive new creation.)[2]

There is, of course, a paradox in writing about the sacraments. This is similar to the paradox of writing about music: the music is the reality, and the writing is at best a second-rate signpost to help the reader become a better listener. In the same way, the sacraments are their own language. To translate them into words, as though the words were the "real thing" and the actions were simply vague pointers toward that reality, would be to miss the point.

In fact, any words we use about the sacraments may turn out to be a translation at several removes from the original. If the first level of meaning is contained within the event (Jesus's actions and words), the second level would be the church's response to Jesus, leading to a third level, the church's missional life of outgoing love. Theological explanation would then come in as at least a fourth level, though still quite important. Having said that, for our present purposes it may be helpful to trace explicitly the ways in which the idea of "God's homecoming," in Jesus and the spirit, makes excellent sense of the church's central symbolic actions. Thus, though as I say the whole creation is in one sense already full of God's glory, and though this comes to expression in many events and actions, I focus here on the two events regarded by most of the Christian tradition as sacramental: baptism and the eucharist.[3]

The case I want to present is, in terms of recent scholarship, a robustly new-creational version of what has been argued by various theologians in terms of the present anticipation of God's promised eventual future.[4] Once we see the sacraments of baptism and eucharist through the framework of God's homecoming and new creation's rescue from death, new possibilities emerge.

God's Homecoming in Water: Baptism

Christian baptism looks back to two moments in Israel's scriptures, which display together the twin themes of the present book. In Genesis 1:2, the divine spirit is hovering, brooding like a dove, over the waters, to bring about the extraordinary creation that will shortly appear. At the Exodus, God comes in person to liberate his people from slavery and then to dwell in their midst to lead them through the Red Sea (seen by Paul and others as a baptismal image[5]) to their promised land. As the early Christians saw, creation and redemption point on to the new creation and the second Exodus. The former is accomplished through the homecoming of the spirit, the latter through the homecoming of the incarnate son. The multiple layers of meaning in baptism are almost overwhelming.

Various Judaean groups had used types of ritual washing, but the specifically Christian use and interpretation of baptism begins with Jesus's cousin John. He will have been well aware of biblical resonances. Like some other sign-prophets in both ancient Israel and in his own Judaean world, he knew the symbolism of Exodus and new creation. He did not simply decide randomly to stand by the Jordan and plunge people into the water. He was announcing that it was time for God to become king, for Israel's God, the Creator, to come in person to do what the scriptures had said. And he was promising that when this strange, long-awaited figure arrived he would plunge people not just into water but into the divine spirit. Baptism was thus from the beginning about the double homecoming of God, the arrival of Israel's God and the promise of the spirit. It was issuing a summons, calling people to become part of God's renewed people, celebrating his personal arrival and discovering his personal empowerment.

Matthew, Mark, and Luke tell the story of Jesus's baptism as the direct fulfillment of two key prophecies: Isaiah 40 and Malachi 3. John omits Malachi but highlights Isaiah. The voice crying in the wilderness is preparing the way for YHWH in person. The promised messenger is preparing the way for the Lord to come to his temple. All four gospels then speak of the descent of the dove, interpreting it as indicating Jesus's anointing with God's spirit for his messianic tasks, echoing obvious passages like Isaiah 11 and 42.

The focus on both Jesus and the spirit then points ahead, freighted with the echoes of creation and new creation, of Exodus and new Exodus, into the public career of Jesus and its extraordinary climax. Jesus refers to his forthcoming death as a "baptism." He challenges his all-too-eager followers to be ready for the same fate.[6] The gospel tradition, interestingly, has very little to say for the most part about the work of the spirit. But when suddenly we are presented with a flurry of spirit-promises, as in the "farewell discourses" in John's gospel (chapters 13–17), we should recognize what is going on. The Word *incarnate*, having come home to dwell "in our midst," is promising his own spirit, through whose presence and work the father and the son together will "come home" to his people (John 14:23). The ending of John's gospel, in this respect as in some others, remains tantalizingly brief. But we are clearly informed that Jesus has now bestowed his own spirit on his followers, so that they can carry forward his mission: "As the father has sent me, so I'm sending you."[7]

All this creates the framework within which, for the early church, baptism means what it means. This is worked out in the book of Acts, and by Paul in particular in passages like 1 Corinthians 10, Colossians 2, and Romans 6.

In Acts, the coming of the spirit at Pentecost is the new equivalent of God's coming to dwell in the tabernacle and then the temple. The early church was thereby plunged not only into the life of God's spirit but into several clashes and controversies, many of them focusing on temples. The picture of the early church, engaging with rulers and authorities in Judaea and in the wider Greco-Roman world, is a picture of a new kind of community, cutting across the normal dividing lines in society, and living—to the consternation of onlookers and officials alike—as a new version of the human race, a small working model of new creation. Baptism, in other words, immerses the followers of Jesus into the Jesus-shaped life, living and announcing that in and through him God has become king in a whole new way. They are energized by the spirit to live appropriately, and to speak authoritatively, in a world that was ready for neither.

The story that has baptism as one of its focal points is all about the renewal of humans, not the creation of puppets. That's why baptism bestows fresh responsibility on Jesus's followers. In 1 Corinthians 10, Paul uses the apposite example of the Exodus to remind his hearers that, though many were "baptized into Moses" in the crossing of the Red Sea, many failed to believe and behave appropriately, with predictable results. Protestants have often been worried about anything that, to them, might look like "magic," as though perhaps baptism were thought to produce fully-fledged Christians by some automatic process. That would deny the whole point of recreating people to be genuine humans at last.

However, the long years of medieval western tradition did indeed create a popular impression that baptism would in and of itself confer salvation—albeit with the likelihood of a long time in purgatory to clean up those whose baptism had somehow failed to generate a life of faithful obedience. A different solution to the same problem was offered by those free churches, those designated "Baptist" and many others, who have reserved baptism for adults, or at least teenagers. It is an open question, though, how effective this has been in preventing the problem of a merely nominal commitment and faith.

If, however, we see baptism as the characteristic gift of the God who comes—who *has* come in Jesus, who *is* coming, and who *will* come in the spirit—we are able to see it, neither as the automatic mechanism of salvation nor as a human work in response to the gospel, but as precisely the gift of grace, of God's own loving self. Grace is real; it is concrete; but because it is grace and not magic it does not squash the recipient into passivity, or "do all the work" of salvation. Rather, it creates the necessary context within which faith, hope, and love can grow and flourish, demanding conscious choice and moral effort on the part of the believer. The mystery of grace, and hence the mystery of baptism, is that this choice, and this effort, are recognized as the work of God's spirit, as Paul insists on various occasions.[8] This is the sense in which baptism does indeed work. It is not about God doing some of the work and us doing the rest.

Baptism means *following the embodied God in the way of the cross*. Yes, the cross of course leads to resurrection. That too is given in advance in baptism, as Paul affirms in Romans 6:1–11 and Colossians 2:11–3:11. But we cannot skip quickly over the call to take up the cross. In Romans in particular, Paul actually appeals for this on the basis of baptism; *now* that you've been baptized, *recognize* what it means and put it into practice! Some have supposed, when lamenting the failure of a baptized person to show any signs of faith, that the baptism "failed." But that carries us back into the false either/or. Once we see sacramental grace at the intersection of the homecoming of God in Jesus and the homecoming of God in the spirit, it isn't the baptism that might have failed. What may be lacking is the theological understanding, fellowship, and encouragement. I suspect that our cultural and philosophical climates have made it more difficult to see that grace *confers responsibility*, a responsibility that includes the challenge to seek the further infilling and enabling of the spirit.

There is much more that could be said about baptism. But this is a start. For many, baptism has been seen as an early moment in the journey of the soul to God; I have suggested that it is more biblical, and more fruitful, to see it as a vital moment in God's coming into the world, and into human lives. And this leads us to the sacrament that many traditions have seen as the heart of our common life: the meal that Jesus gave us.

God's Homecoming in Bread and Wine

Everything about this is controversial, including what to call it. I grew up in a church that spoke of "Holy Communion"—until a new rector arrived, who wanted us to call it "The Eucharist," and who did some things a bit differently from his predecessor (though I was too young to figure out what those differences might mean). I was aware of other churches that referred to "The Lord's Supper." I knew that my Roman Catholic friends referred to "The Mass," but that seemed strange, and the explanations offered even stranger.[9] In the earliest church they spoke of "the breaking of bread." By the time Paul is writing to Corinth he refers to "the Lord's meal."[10] Thus the very names we use for the event indicate simultaneously both that it is very special and that it's hard to say exactly how. I now hope that the theme of the present book, the homecoming of God, may provide some help.

It took me years—including my early years in ordained ministry—to figure out why the whole subject, both "what to call it" and "how to do it," was so sensitive. I was aware, for instance, that in some churches you were expected to do things like genuflecting and/or crossing yourself, and in other churches you were clearly expected not to. What was driving all this?

It wasn't just the bad historical memories, though there are plenty of them. Down the street from where I am writing these words, there is a stone cross set in the roadway marking the spot where Bishops Nicholas Ridley and Hugh Latimer, and then Archbishop Thomas Cranmer, were burned at the stake, with the life-or-death question focusing on the meaning of the church's central meal.[11] There were many converging reasons for Cranmer's execution, but at the center was his refusal to accept the Roman doctrine of "transubstantiation."[12] This was a vital element of church teaching at the time, which had been attacked by various reformers in Germany and Switzerland as well as in England and elsewhere.

A great deal depended on this, especially in relation to the power of the church and the clergy, and to the implication of that power in terms of salvation. If the bread and the wine somehow "became" the body and blood of Jesus, and if only the priest could make this happen, the priest wielded (so many supposed) enormous spiritual power over the congregation. But the reformers challenged the theory on which the whole system rested. Likewise, if this event was the "sacrifice" through which sins were forgiven, sins of the dead in purgatory as well as sins of the living here and now, then without this meal people would die unforgiven and risk going to hell. Thus if people started to question the theological basis of "eucharistic sacrifice" as well as "transubstantiation" the system was under threat. But the system was, for the authorities in many countries, part of the bedrock of society. The Reformers' challenge seemed to be undermining the safety and stability of the social fabric as a whole, as well as long-established structures of power. Hence the violent reaction.

Events like the public burning of bishops or archbishops—and, of course, the subsequent martyrdom of many Roman Catholic priests, as the political and religious winds changed direction—have remained in the folk memory of an entire people, even when the details of controversy have faded to a blur. When the predominantly low church Anglicans of the nineteenth century felt under threat by the Oxford movement, with its deliberate revival of elements of "Catholic" tradition, the sixteenth-century *Foxe's Book of Martyrs* enjoyed a considerable revival in popularity.

But the real reason behind the confusion, and the violent controversy, is far deeper than folk memories of martyred heroes. The real reason, as we see as early as Paul's first letter to the Corinthians, is that the meal shared by church members has always been linked directly to the death of Jesus. "Whenever you eat this bread and drink the cup," Paul wrote, "you are announcing the Lord's death until he comes."[13] And "announcing the Lord's death," of course, was central to his gospel, his vocation, and his ministry: "I decided to know nothing in my dealings with you," he said, "except Jesus the Messiah, especially his crucifixion."[14] Touch the bread-breaking, and you touch the nerve center of the gospel. Don't be surprised if this causes a reaction, whether of shock or of delight.

The meal was central to Jesus's intention, to his gospel message. We can't stress enough that *when Jesus wanted to explain to his followers what his forthcoming death would mean, and how they could be folded within that meaning, he didn't give them a theory; he gave them a meal.* You can't translate the meal into a theory, or into a nonphysical spirituality, without serious loss. When Jesus spoke of the broken bread as his body, given for the disciples, he was speaking about his own vocation, to be in himself the inner life of the ongoing community of his followers. "Where two or three come together in my name," he had said earlier, "I'll be there amongst them."[15]

The Last Supper, then, was Jesus's "grid of interpretation," as we might clumsily put it, for what was to happen the next day. It was designed to enable the first disciples, when they recovered from the horror of his death and the shock of his resurrection, to celebrate both his achievement on the cross and his continuing presence with his people. The meal enabled the early church to hold together, in worship and prayer, the theme we have seen to be central to the biblical message: the scripturally promised homecoming of God in the person of Jesus and the power of the spirit, and the future ultimate homecoming of God, filling the earth with his glory.

The meal Jesus bequeathed to his followers carries the multilayered meaning of his whole work. That includes his powerful announcement and embodiment of God's kingdom on earth as in heaven and the ongoing fulfillment and implementation of this work through the spirit. That is why we should not be surprised that controversy has swirled around every aspect of the bread-breaking. If the meal itself proclaims Jesus's victory over evil, it was always likely (as Paul warned in Ephesians 6) that the principalities and powers would try to deflect this challenge to their rule, to distract attention, to stop people becoming gospel-people, Jesus-people.

If you want to distract people's attention, after all, there's nothing like a good controversy. People always find it easier to focus on personalities, cultural assumptions, local traditions, stylistic preferences, and political overtones rather than the actual presence and rescuing power of Jesus and his spirit. Throw into this mix a few brave martyrs and a few garbled historical memories, and, even when people have forgotten the precise details of trials, testimonies, and theological arguments, a sense of tribal loyalty will remain. That will ensure that, when people think of the bread-breaking, they will think, not of Jesus and his kingdom-bringing death and resurrection, but of "them and us," and of "how *they* do it" as against "how *we* do it." This shift of focus has continued for centuries.

The irony is that the bread-breaking symbolizes and puts into effect the Bible's main story, as expounded in this book so far: *the homecoming of God.* Jesus chose Passover as the moment to bring the challenge of his kingdom-of-God message home to Jerusalem and the temple, knowing very well where this would lead. But the original Passover was part of the coming of God to judge Egypt and rescue his people, to lead them in the pillar of cloud and fire, to give them the Torah, to dwell in their midst in the tabernacle—and then to go with them to their promised homeland. By reenacting Passover but with striking innovations, drawing its meaning on to himself and his upcoming death, Jesus was saying *both* that this was the fulfillment of the Passover story, the true Second Exodus for which the prophets had longed and the people had prayed, *and* that it was the start of something new that had been promised long ago by the same prophets. It was the homecoming meal, celebrating what was being achieved then and there and looking ahead to the new world that was thereby opening up.

The meal Jesus inaugurated, and the events it symbolized, had to do with God's project to come in person and free the world, not just from slavery (as in Egypt), not just from exile (as in Babylon), but from a darker reality that characterized both. The real problem was the corruption and horror of death, the ultimate anticreation force, and the idolatry and sin that courted or invoked that death by denying or ignoring the God of creation and covenant. As in Isaiah 54 and 55, consequent upon the saving work of the Servant in Isaiah 53, the renewal of the covenant meant the renewal of creation, a double theme picked up in the New Testament.[16] In Jesus and the spirit, God "comes home" to his world, and to dwell with his people, in fulfillment of the promises and hopes, and especially the promise of forgiveness of sins, meaning (for the Judaeans) the real "return from exile," and (for the Gentiles) rescue from the dark world of idolatry. The bread-breaking, whatever we call it and however we do it, symbolizes and effects this long-promised reality.

To stress God's homecoming, after all, is once again to stress *grace*. All that we do is done within the outpouring of God's loving presence. Tragically, some of the key debates in the sixteenth century, particularly on justification, were oversensitive to the possibility that proud humans might seek to contribute to their own salvation by the performance of "works." As a result, "ritual" became a dirty word, especially in England in the nineteenth century amid the protestant reaction to the high church Oxford movement. Then as now, some traditions became suspicious of anything special that people were doing in conducting the service, whether intoning a liturgy, serving the bread and wine in a particular way, or burning incense. Perhaps, some people thought, these were intended to be "good works" that would please God, and perhaps even earn salvation. Some to this day therefore go to great lengths to keep everything as informal or casual as possible, as though to make it clear that nobody is being ritualistic.

Of course, however "low" the church, there will still be *some* ritual, even if this consists simply of singing worship songs or reading from scripture. Ironic situations arise, such as in some modern charismatic churches where one is expected to raise one's arms in worship but certainly not to make the sign of the cross. "Their" manual acts are idolatrous; "ours" are genuine expressions of worship. This is of course naive, but it can easily creep in. There are many such muddles in churches today.

Now no doubt there have been many muddled Christians, down the years, including clergy and theologians, and in the friendly grace of God the gospel still works powerfully. The biblical view of the human vocation—that we humans are designed to do things that reflect God's glory into the world and the praises of creation back to God—does of course leave it open for some to wonder whether what they "do" in the course of worship might, as it were, force God's hand. But that descent into forms of paganism, or even magic, was not the point—not the point of what most people did, and not the point of the Pauline distinction of faith and works. We should not be surprised or alarmed at the thought that human beings—flawed and failing as we all are, but in principle faithful and obedient—should have a role to play in the event that, again and again, draws together all God's promises and enables God's people to participate personally in them.

Thus practices such as the bringing of bread and wine (God's gift in creation but also the work of human hands) from the congregation to the front of the church ought not to be taken, as I have heard it taken, as a telltale sign of Pelagianism, as though we were trying to contribute to our own salvation. Processions with choirs and music can be and often are God-given ways of lifting hearts and minds into worship. Kneeling down (a practice many churches have long abandoned) is a standard biblical posture for humble prayer. Taking solemn care in distributing the bread and wine gives worshippers the chance to reflect on the enormous and powerful significance of it all. None of these things need be in any way a matter of "ritual" in the sense of "things humans do to impress God." All the human actions involved are designed to take place—to take the *truly human* place—within *the context of grace*, of God's *coming* in love and power to be with his people.

This leads to the two main focal points of controversy: the notion of "sacrifice" and the question of Jesus's "presence" in the bread-breaking service. Whole books have been written about both of these. All I can do here is to point to some ways in which reframing the question in terms of God's homecoming may help to find new ways forward.

First, sacrifice. The great controversies in earlier centuries focused on the question of whether Jesus Christ was or was not being recrucified in every Mass. Traditional Catholic teaching assumed the biblical viewpoint that at certain moments past events could become present afresh, as when Judaeans celebrating Passover declared that God was bringing *them* out of Egypt then and there. Thus, with time and history looping backward or forward on themselves, the breaking of consecrated bread became part of the single, one-off event of Jesus's crucifixion.

That was not, though, how the early Protestants heard it. What they heard, and what many ordinary folk believed, was that the priest was sacrificing Christ afresh—not only a shocking idea in itself, but suggesting that Jesus's death was not after all a finished achievement, and needed continual supplementation. So when Protestants spoke of "sacrifice" in their liturgies (that of Archbishop Cranmer providing a famous example), they did so, not in terms of the bread-breaking, but in terms, borrowed from Romans 12:2, of offering to God "ourselves, our souls and bodies, to be a living sacrifice." That in turn horrified devout Roman Catholics, who concluded that it was the Protestants who were adding an extra sacrifice to Jesus's one, unique self-offering. All this produced, and still produces, multilayered confusion.

But the real confusion here is that the sacrificial system in the Old Testament was in any case never about humans doing things to impress God. Nor was it—despite much misunderstanding—about animals being punished in the place of guilty humans. The one animal in Leviticus that has the people's sins confessed over its head is the scapegoat, which is precisely the one that is not killed.[17] Many have supposed that the point of sacrifice was to enable sinners to come into the presence of the holy God. But the biblical theme of God's homecoming stands this on its head. The point of the Levitical sacrifices, placed in the canon of scripture right after the coming of God to the tabernacle in Exodus 40, was to cleanse both the place and the people *to enable the holy God to come and be at home there*. Sacrifice was primarily about *God's* homecoming, getting the house clean and tidy for his presence. The important thing then is to set the event in the biblical context where it began, namely, that of the coming of God to his people in Jesus the Messiah and then his coming to dwell within them through the holy spirit. The bread-breaking thus looks forward, as Paul said, to the final coming of Jesus.[18] The present "homecoming" anticipates that final moment.

This, finally, brings us to the central puzzle of traditional eucharistic theology: the question of the presence of Jesus the Messiah in the bread-breaking service, and in relation to the bread and the wine in particular. The great Eucharistic controversies of the Reformation period in particular were predicated on the western narrative of salvation as going to heaven. But when we tell the salvation story in the way the Bible tells it, then a new way of looking at the bread and the wine will open up in front of us.

Think of it all in terms of space, time, and matter. First, space or place: what Jesus did at the Last Supper was related directly to his solemn prediction of the fall of the temple, the place where heaven and earth met. In the bread and wine, he brought together past promises with present and future fulfillment. His followers were now to form a heaven-and-earth community, not just in Jerusalem, but wherever they went in their new worldwide mission.[19] Putting together the themes we studied in the first part of this book, we are promised that in the "new heavens and new earth" the whole creation will be filled to overflowing with the divine glory. The heaven-and-earth space of the temple is the model for the heaven-and-earth space of the church's life.

So too with time: God's promised future comes back to meet us in the present, just as ancient events come forward into fresh fulfillment. The prophetic books are full of this. In Isaiah 40–66, the covenants with Abraham or with David are renewed, and the "new heavens and new earth" are anticipated. In Isaiah 55:1–3, anyone who is thirsty is invited to the waters, and God will make with them all "an everlasting covenant, my steadfast, sure love for David." The covenant with David, made centuries earlier, would be fulfilled in a new way. The prophet's hearers are invited to stand between that past and that future, to share in the blessings of new creation here and now, bringing heavenly reality to birth in creation's renewed fruitfulness.

If this is true of space and time, what about matter? What can we say, what *must* we say, about the bread we break and the wine we share?

Here, in the story of the Last Supper, we see Jesus, who—as the four evangelists have been telling us in their different ways—is the embodiment, the "incarnation," of Israel's God. He denounces the Jerusalem temple (the place where sins could be forgiven, and their effects wiped away); he prophesies its fall. Then he celebrates a (significantly modified) Passover meal with his closest disciples, foretelling the ultimate new Passover to come. He speaks to them of his forthcoming death as the means of covenant renewal and forgiveness. He gives them bread and wine, not only as signposts to that death but as the way in which they can share in its innermost meaning. This is how his very life, and with it his forgiveness and healing, can become theirs.

So far, we might think, so good. But at this point interpretations have traditionally divided. The traditional Roman view of what "happens" to the bread and the wine was based on the theology of Thomas Aquinas, who drew on the distinction made by Aristotle between "substance" and "accidents." The "substance" was the real thing, the vital interior reality, not detectable by the senses. The "accidents" were the outward appearance and composition, the things that were deemed to be "accidentally true" of an unseen substance. This allowed for the fact that the bread and wine still looked, smelled, felt, and tasted like bread and wine. According to the theory, it was their "substance" that changed into the true body and blood of Jesus, not their "accidents."

The protestant reformers were only too aware of how the subtle Aristotelian theory had, for many generations, been lost on ordinary worshippers. At the popular level, many believed that the priest was simply performing a bit of theological magic, through which the bread and wine would be miraculously transformed into the actual physical stuff of Jesus's body and blood. The Reformers by and large took the view that this popular belief was generating superstition and idolatry, giving the priest supernatural properties and some kind of divine authority. Most were agreed that Jesus was present in the Lord's Supper, but the question was what exactly that meant and how it worked. Some spoke of the bread-breaking as "visible words," as though the words one might "hear" through the action of breaking the bread were the deeper reality, with the meal being merely a signpost in that direction. Other theories were tried, and have been much discussed.

But the biblical hinterland within which Jesus's action and words at the Last Supper make the sense they make is that of ancient Israel's sense of space, time, and matter. What happens when we put the traditional questions, and more specifically the meal itself, into the context of the story of God's homecoming, of creation and new creation?

My proposal is that we should understand all this, and with it an entire theology of eucharistic presence, in terms of the present anticipation of the promised filling of all creation with God's glory. Here at the original Supper we have the spirit-anointed king, prophesied by the scriptures, speaking of how his own death was to put the world right, and speaking of the bread and the wine as his own body and blood. The evangelists see Jesus's public career in terms of the long-promised return of YHWH to Zion. Jesus brought his work into sharp and climactic focus in his action in the temple and his Last Supper. This was what it looked like when YHWH returned to Zion: God in Christ holding out the bread and wine to humankind. Paul, John, and others see the gift of the spirit as the advance sign, the *arrabōn*, pointing forward to the long-promised filling of all creation.[20]

The picture then comes together in Jesus's Passover-echoing words, his actions with the bread and the wine, and (in John) his promise of the spirit. The early Christian writers are showing how, at last, heaven and earth were being joined. The bread and the wine can be seen as true gifts coming forward to us from God's future, like the grapes from the promised land that the Israelites were able to sample while still in the wilderness.[21] The bread and wine, thus filled with the glory of God, sustain those who feed on them as "glory-people." One could even say that Paul's famous line in Romans 8 is true of those who receive the bread and wine: those he justified, them he also glorified.[22] We are presented, close up and personally, with new creation that we can eat and drink. The church is thus refreshed, again and again, as the small working model of new creation, nourished by the spirit who feeds Jesus's people with his own life and love. Jesus is the embodiment of the God who had promised to come home to his people. Jesus's spirit is the homecoming God who fills his people and energizes them as the living anticipation of the long-awaited filling of all creation. Both of these long strands of biblical hope come rushing together in the rich multilayered sacramental event, which we might receive as Jesus's gift of himself as we look forward to the final coming and feast.

Seen from this point of view, all the old anxieties about the danger of idolatry surrounding the Eucharist can be avoided. The Eucharist is to the material world what the Sabbath is to the prominent Judaean view of time: it is the advance reality of what we are promised in the end. This is where the Bride meets the Bridegroom in a mystery-laden engagement party, anticipating the eventual marriage. New creation bears the imprint of the incarnate son; it is saturated, in advance, with the holy spirit. The Eucharist is the moment within present time when the triune God comes home to be with his people, anticipating the final coming and the renewal of all creation. Once we learn to think in the full sweep of scripture, instead of merely drawing on bits and pieces to fit in with preconceived unbiblical philosophies, there is every reason to encourage devotional practices that reflect this new-creational reality.

We are therefore fully justified, I believe, in giving appropriate reverence to what we are learning to see as advance fruits of new creation. Of course, the question remains as to what counts as "appropriate." But my hope here is simply to alert nervous protestants to the possibility that there might indeed *be* appropriate forms of reverence, and that making everything as informal as possible might actually be inappropriate and irreverent. Anxiety about idolatry must not block the glad recognition of God's new creation. And, though the bread-breaking does indeed focus first and foremost on Jesus's forthcoming death, its meaning is fully displayed in the new covenant he establishes, and in the new creation that results from his defeat of evil on the cross.

Thus the crucifixion—Jesus's loving offering of himself to death for the sins of the world—remains central and vital, as it has been in some of the great protestant liturgies, not least that of Thomas Cranmer. But what is changed, in the proposals I am putting forward, is the result that flows from it. I am here following through on the narrative that stands behind the paean of praise in Revelation 5:

You are worthy to take the scroll;
you are worthy to open its seals;
for you were slaughtered and with your own blood
you purchased a people for God,
from every tribe and tongue,
from every people and nation
and made them a kingdom and priests to our God
and they will reign on the earth.[23]

The death of the lamb—who is simultaneously the Lion of Judah—results in the new creation, with the redeemed humans at last taking up their original vocation as the image-bearers, the royal priesthood, reflecting God's wise sovereignty into the rest of creation and reflecting the praises of creation back to the Creator. The Eucharist brings both the cross and new creation into focus, particularly once we understand the presence of Jesus in terms of the anticipation of the ultimate new creation.

If this is so, we understand better how the Eucharist gives energy to the church's mission. Once we have tasted new creation, we are commissioned to *be* new-creation people, in both senses: human beings newly created, and human beings now able to bring about new creation in the world. We are commissioned for the church's age-old tasks of healing, educating, caring for the poor, speaking the truth to power, and in every possible way bringing advance signs of God's redemption and healing to the creation that groans in travail.[24] These and a thousand other vocations all flow from the death of Jesus, winning the victory over the powers of darkness and death. They all flow from the inauguration of new creation at his resurrection, glimpsed already in the bread and wine of the supper. The Eucharist, as many theologians have seen, *defines* the church: "There is one loaf; well, then, there may be several of us, but we are one body, because we all share the one loaf."[25]

All this leads naturally to the second major area where the idea of God's homecoming makes fresh and challenging sense. We turn to the question of the unity-in-diversity of the multi-ethnic, spirit-filled people of God.

13

THE POLYCHROME CHURCH AS THE SIGN TO THE POWERS

The Problem of Divided Churches

One of the greatest tragedies in the Christian world over the last several centuries is that the church has divided, again and again, along ethnic lines. And there is a further tragedy attached to this. Though many have felt excluded by these ethnic divisions, many others have scarcely even noticed.

The biblical picture of God's homecoming—fulfilled in Jesus and the spirit—stands over against any such ethnic division. In the present chapter I want to look in some detail at two passages in Paul that make the point so strikingly that it is hard to credit that people missed it. You might have thought that, with the fresh excitement of Bible translation as part of the sixteenth-century Reformation, people reading scripture in their own tongue for the first time would have heard, loud and clear, the message that the people of God (as defined by their allegiance to Messiah Jesus and indwelt by his spirit) were, by those very definitions, a *single* family composed of *many nations*. You might particularly assume this when you consider that two of the vitally relevant biblical passages are from two of Paul's great letters, Romans and Ephesians, which in other ways were central to the Reformers and their successors.

My purpose in the present chapter is to show how the theme of God's homecoming, promised in Israel's scriptures and celebrated as a fresh reality in the early Christian writings, produced almost immediately a vision of the polychrome church, the world's first great experiment in multiculturalism.

But it's worth taking a moment to consider how far the church has strayed from this biblical vision, seemingly ignoring scripture's central imperative all the while insisting loudly on the inspiration and authority of scripture. I think there are two reasons to be pondered.

First, if the main aim of Christianity is for people's souls to find their way up to heaven to be with God, then the question of how they organize themselves here on earth is of far less importance, except insofar as it might affect their chances of making it through purgatory and up to heaven in the end. The reformers challenged the prevailing view of how you might get to heaven, not the "going-to-heaven" narrative itself.

Second, we should note an unintended effect of the welcome and necessary effort, a few hundred years ago, to give people access to scripture and liturgy in their own language. The Western church of the medieval period was more or less ruled by Rome, with scripture and liturgy in the same Latin whether you were in Scotland or Sicily. Most societies were fairly stable in terms of ethnic background and makeup. Travelers and migrants could be incorporated into local communities and local churches without any perceived necessity to split off into different nationalities. But when scripture and liturgy were translated into German, French, English, Spanish, and so on—not to mention languages from farther afield—then it would become natural for people to meet in language groups, which would inevitably mean gatherings defined by ethnicity. By the time a century or so had gone by, a large European city might well find itself playing host to a German church, a Portuguese church, and many others besides.

Meanwhile, the Bible, to which the eager protestant groups were supposedly giving allegiance over and above previous church tradition and authority, was saying things like:

> *After this I looked, and lo and behold a huge gathering which nobody could possibly count, from every nation and tribe and people and language . . . They were shouting out at the tops of their voices, "Salvation belongs to our God, to the one who sits on the throne, and to the lamb!"*[1]

And again, in Paul's famous speech in Athens:

> *The God who made the world and everything in it . . . made from one stock every race of humans to live on the whole face of the earth, allotting them their properly ordained times and the boundaries for their dwellings. The aim was that they would search for God, and perhaps reach out for him and find him. Indeed, he is actually not far from each one of us, for in him we live and move and exist.*[2]

There is no word for "stock" in the Greek of the first sentence in that quotation. It simply reads "from one," *ex henos*. Some early manuscripts inserted *haimatos*, "blood," to clarify the unitary nature of the human race. Part of Paul's point was that the creator God stands above, and relates equally to, all humans everywhere. He made them all and cares for them all. Indeed, this passage became an important passage in the abolitionist movements of the nineteenth century, especially since the King James version, to which reference was regularly made, followed the manuscripts that had "blood." Different pigmentation, indeed—the Mediterranean world was well used to humans of many different ethnicities and skin tones—but the same blood. And the puzzle remains: Why then did the Western churches of the last few centuries not insist on cross-cultural, multiethnic communities of Jesus followers—as their first-century predecessors in melting-pot cities like Antioch or Corinth had done so clearly? And why have some political leaders, appealing not least to would-be "Christian" populations, bewitched their followers into thinking in terms of the "pure blood" of "people like us" being "poisoned" by other strands?

I suspect that to answer that question would require an expertise in sociology and other fields, which I do not possess.[3] But what we can do is look at the two New Testament passages that show clearly the theological basis of the early Christians' practice of the polychrome community.

Paul's Vision of the Church: Ephesians 2–3

One could make the case for the multiethnic people of God on the basis of almost any of Paul's letters. Galatians, which I think was the first to be written, is emphatic: all baptized Jesus believers belong in one and the same family, whether Judaean or Greek, slave or free, male or female.[4] Paul was pushing back hard at the suggestion that Gentile converts had to become formally and officially Judaean in order to belong to the true people of God. When he expands that horizon in a passage like Colossians 3 it's clear that he has more in mind than simply overcoming the Judaean/Gentile boundary:

> *In this new humanity there is no question of "Greek and Jew," or "circumcised and uncircumcised," of "barbarian, Scythian," or "slave and free." The Messiah is everything and in everything!*[5]

But it is in Ephesians that we get one of the fullest expositions of the same point. What was in Colossians almost a throwaway line, though an important one, here becomes a major topic in itself.[6]

Ephesians is all about the church, and especially about its unity. God the Creator always intended to bring together in the Messiah all things in heaven and on earth (Ephesians 1:10), and the coming together of Judaean and Gentile in the Messiah's family is the remarkable and powerful sign of that in the present. I suspect that the Reformation tradition, eager to demonstrate the doctrine of justification by grace through faith from Romans and Galatians, may often have been happy to note the emphatic statement of this great truth in Ephesians 2:1–10, and may have then passed over somewhat more lightly the "Therefore"—or, in my translation, "So then"—with which Paul opens the vital argument of Ephesians 2:11–22.

Paul's overall theme is precisely the coming of God. First, the coming of God in the person of the Messiah, to make peace between the different ethnic groups. Then, the coming of God in the person of the spirit, to make the resulting multiethnic community into the new temple where God now lives. God's homecoming results directly in the community in which the different ethnic groups discover themselves to be the single family that the Creator always intended and has now brought about. As we learn to read Ephesians 2 as a whole, we discover that the two halves of the chapter—verses 1–10 and 11–22—belong tightly together. *The reason the Gentiles can be welcomed into the single family of God is because the Messiah has dealt with their sin.* They used to be excluded from God's people because they were "idolaters" or "sinners." Now, because of Jesus's death, appropriated by faith, they are idolatrous sinners no longer. The coming of God to save people "by grace through faith" (Ephesians 2:8) is thus the necessary preparation for the unifying of the human race in Messiah and spirit. In terms of modern Pauline scholarship, the "old perspective" is the vital precondition for the "new perspective," and without the "new perspective" the point of the "old" would be lost.[7] That unifying across traditional boundaries is the sure sign, every bit as sure as Jesus's resurrection, that sin and idolatry has indeed been dealt with on the cross.

So Paul begins by sketching the previous plight of the non-Judaean peoples:

> *So then, remember this! In human terms, that is, in your "flesh," you are "Gentiles." You are the people who the so-called "circumcision" refer to as the so-called "uncircumcision"—circumcision, of course, being something done by human hands to human flesh.* (Ephesians 2:11)

In other words, the ethnic distinction and its markers are not ultimate realities. They did, however, have a powerful effect:

Well, once upon a time you were separated from the Messiah. You were detached from the community of Israel. You were foreigners to the covenants which contained the promise. There you were, in the world with no hope and no god! (Ephesians 2:12)

Paul is clearly emphasizing the vast chasm that separated God's ancient people from all surrounding nations. But he does so in order to insist on the remarkable nature of the gospel through which the barriers have come down:

But now, in Messiah Jesus, you have been brought near in the Messiah's blood—yes, you, who used to be a long way away! He is our peace, you see. He has made the two to be one. He has pulled down the barrier, the dividing wall, that turns us into enemies of each other. He has done this in his flesh, by abolishing the law with its commands and instructions. (Ephesians 2:13–15a)

This last comment, about "abolishing commands and instructions," has nothing to do with *moral* commands. It has everything to do with the commands that separated ancient Israel from the nations: circumcision, the food laws, the sabbath, and not least access to the inner shrine of the temple. In all this, Paul's vision of the long-term divine purpose picks up the theme already stated in Ephesians 1:10 and applies it to the joining together, in the present time, of the different categories of humans:

The point of doing all this was to create, in him, one new human being out of the two, so making peace. God was reconciling both of us to himself in a single body, through the cross, by killing the enmity in him. (Ephesians 2:15b–16)

Killing, of course, is what enemies have traditionally done to one another. But now, enmity itself is killed—rather as captivity is led away captive (Ephesians 4:8). And all this results from *the coming of God in the person of the Messiah*. Paul here echoes one of the classic "coming of God" passages from Isaiah 52:7, where the messenger announces the "good news" of peace and salvation, declaring to Zion, "Your God reigns." This leads the eye up, first, to the coming of YHWH to Zion (Isaiah 52:8), and then—though this turns out to be a different way of saying the same thing—the coming of the "servant" who, against all the odds, turns out to be "the arm of YHWH" in person, suffering vicariously for the people (Isaiah 52:13–53:12).

So the Messiah came and gave the good news. Peace had come! Peace, that is, for those of you who were a long way away, and peace, too, for those who were close at hand. Through him, you see, we both have access to the father in the one spirit. (Ephesians 2:17–18)

This language of "access," following closely from the mention of the "dividing wall" in verse 14, tells us already that Paul is thinking in terms of the Jerusalem temple, where the wall separating the "court of the Gentiles" from the innermost courts carried a sign, warning non-Judaeans that to come further would be punishable by death. No, says Paul: you now have "access." As often in Paul's writing, these earlier hints are then brought out into explicit statements as he draws the chapter together:

> *This is the result. You are no longer foreigners or strangers. No: you are fellow citizens with God's holy people. You are members of God's household. You are built on the foundation of the apostles and prophets, with Messiah Jesus himself as the cornerstone. In him the whole building is fitted together, and grows into a holy temple in the Lord. You, too, are being built up together, in him, into a place where God will live by the spirit.* (Ephesians 2:19–22)

The last phrase ("where God will live") is not referring to some future time. The Greek is simply "into a dwelling-place of God," *eis katoikētērion tou theou*. That word *katoikētērion* is the same word used in the prayer of Solomon in 1 Kings 8, at the dedication of the temple as the place where God would dwell.[8] *The coming of God in the person and work of the Messiah, accomplishing peace and salvation, is matched by the coming of God in the person and work of the spirit, indwelling the single multiethnic family that constitutes the new temple.*

This fact about the church, not least in its first-century context, should take one's breath away. It certainly proved a challenge to the civic authorities as well as the casual onlookers in the various places where the Pauline mission took root. Ancient society was carefully segregated. You knew where you were—and where everyone else was. But the gospel of Messiah Jesus sliced straight through all those divisions. The vision for a multiethnic family of God was not an add-on to the primary message of one's sins being forgiven so one could go to heaven;

the multiethnic family of God, accomplished through the sin-forgiving work of Jesus and the renewal of the spirit, simply *was and is* the primary message. It was the sign that in Jesus the living God had come "home" to the territory of humans; that he had dealt with the problem of idolatry and sin that had kept the peoples apart; and that in the spirit he had come to *be* at home there.

In recent times some scholars have pushed back at the idea that the shared fellowship of Judaeans and Gentiles was as important to Paul as the forgiveness of sins. Might it not, some have suggested, just be a matter of "table manners"?[9] Ephesians 3 insists that it is far more than that. It is the active and effective sign of the sin-forgiving gospel:

> *The secret plan is, the purpose that's been hidden from the very beginning of the world in God who created all things . . . that God's wisdom, in all its rich variety, was to be made known to the rulers and authorities in the heavenly places—through the church!* (Ephesians 3:9–10)

In other words, the church is designed, intended—and equipped by the spirit!—to display the multicolored reality of God's original creation, as the signpost to the principalities and powers that think they run the world. A new creation, a new way of being human, has arrived in their midst. In that spirit, Paul offers his great prayer for God to "come home" to the church, ending with the idea of the divine "fullness" that we have seen to be central to the biblical hope:

> *My prayer is this: that he will lay out all the riches of his glory to give you strength and power, through his spirit, in your*

> *inner being; that the Messiah may make his home in your hearts, through faith; that love may be your root, your firm foundation; and that you may be strong enough . . . to grasp the breadth and length and height and depth, and to know the Messiah's love—though actually it's so deep that nobody can really know it! So may God fill you with all his fullness.* (Ephesians 3:16–19)

The same theme continues into the second half of the letter, when Paul writes of the multiple ministries within the church. "The one who came down is the one who also 'went up'—yes, above all the heavens!—*so that he might fill all things.*"[10] The different manifestations of the spirit's gifts in the multiple vocations within the church are to be understood as the present effects of the same divine work that will in the end fill the whole creation. Once more Paul is picking up the biblical theme of the Creator's intention to "be at home within," and so to fill, the whole creation, and of the church as the present anticipation of that eventual result.

This theme points on to the other passage that is vital for our present theme: Romans 15:7–13.

Unity as the Sign of Hope: Romans 15

Those of us who have often lectured on Romans know the danger: we spend so long on the magisterial chapters 1–8 that we don't leave long enough to do justice to the vital section of chapters 9–11 . . . and then, even more, we run out of time to deal properly with chapters 12–16. But Romans 15:7–13 is not just an added extra, a few tips for church life once the serious business of "how to get saved" has been dealt with. Romans 15 is a carefully planned and performed peroration. It leads the eye back to where the epistle began, with Jesus as the Davidic Messiah, raised from the dead, and the nations of the world hailing him as their Lord and finding him as their hope.[11]

Comparing the two passages makes the point. Here is the opening of the letter:

> *Paul, a slave of the Messiah, King Jesus, called to be an apostle, set apart for God's good news, which he promised beforehand through his prophets in the sacred writings—the good news about his son, who was descended from David's seed in terms of flesh, and who was marked out powerfully as God's son in terms of the spirit of holiness by the resurrection of the dead: Jesus, the royal Messiah, our Lord! Through him we have received grace and apostleship to bring about believing obedience among all the nations for the sake of his name . . .* (Romans 1:1–5)

And here—with only Paul's plans and closing greetings still to come—is the triumphant matching conclusion:

> *Welcome one another, therefore, as the Messiah has welcomed you, to God's glory. Let me tell you why: the Messiah became a servant of the circumcised people in order to demonstrate the truthfulness of God—that is, to confirm the promises to the patriarchs, and to bring*

the nations to praise God for his mercy . . . [as] Isaiah says once more,

There shall be the root of Jesse,
The one who rises up to rule the nations;
The nations shall hope in him.

May the God of hope fill you with all joy and peace in believing, so that you may overflow with hope by the power of the holy spirit. (Romans 15:7–9, 12–13)

As I have remarked before, scholarly and popular readings of Romans alike have tended to marginalize the theme of Davidic Messiahship. But it was central and vital for Paul. In Jesus, God's purposes for Israel had been fulfilled. Now—as prophets and psalms had foretold—the doors stood open for people from every ethnic background, not of course to replace "the circumcised people," but, exactly as in Ephesians 2 and 3, to supplement and enlarge them. In this remarkable conclusion, the nations will come to praise the God of Israel precisely for his *mercy* in rescuing idolatrous outsiders.

As many scholars now agree, when Paul quotes a biblical passage he regularly has the whole paragraph or chapter in mind, even though he may only quote a single line.[12] (If Paul had spelled out all that he really meant at every point then a letter like Romans might have been as long as a treatise by Aristotle . . . which would have been quite impractical.) Here the line in question is from a passage we have already seen to be a key scriptural promise: Isaiah 11:10. The opening of Isaiah 11 is of course *messianic*, picking up from the predictions of the coming king in Isaiah 9:2–7; it is also *new-creational*, picking up from the vision of a world at peace in Isaiah 2:2–4. Here in chapter 11 the messianic theme is explicit and laid out at length. The "shoot" that will "come forth from the stock of Jesse" will be anointed with the spirit of YHWH so that, under his just judgment, the world will be put right. "With righteousness he shall judge the poor, and decide with equity for the meek of the earth," dealing decisively with the wicked who have ruined his beautiful creation (Isaiah 11:4).

The result will be the coming together of the nations. Paul here sees the joining of Judaean and Gentile in the church, overcoming their ancient separation, as the vital and hopeful sign that this promise is coming true. Isaiah 11 speaks of a reconciliation in the animal kingdom, with the wolf and the lamb lying down together. I agree with those commentators who suggest that the passage should be read both literally (as a prophecy of a new creation in which all species will live in peace) and metaphorically (as a prophecy of the reconciliation of previously warring nations; wild animals can serve that literary purpose elsewhere, as with the "lion" of Assyria[13]). Certainly Paul's vision of new creation in Romans 8 incorporates the literal meaning, and the metaphorical, too, as his theme of reconciliation of previously hostile ethnic groups, specifically Judaeans and Gentiles, is brought here to a climax. The monsters of Daniel 7 are nightmarish beasts, symbolizing the various violent empires. Now, Isaiah declares, the lion will eat straw like the ox, while the cow and the bear will feed side by side. Paul, picking up this perspective, sees the multiethnic church as the sign to the world of this coming new creation, the new world in which everything will be put right and all peoples will live in peace.

Paul has here, in other words, woven tightly together the

double strands of biblical promise, the double theme of God's homecoming. The Messiah, anointed by the spirit of YHWH, will put into effect YHWH's coming in judgment and salvation. The result will be that "the earth will be full of the knowledge of YHWH as the waters cover the sea" (Isaiah 11:9). The verse Paul quotes comes immediately after this, bringing us back to David (the shoot coming out of Jesse's roots) and thus tying together Isaiah 11:1–10 as a rounded whole. The rule of the Messiah over the nations will result in the whole creation being filled with the knowledge of YHWH, and thus with a rich harmony and peace.

That is the context in which Paul's concluding blessing has its particular resonance:

> *May the God of hope* fill you *with all joy and peace in believing, so that* you may overflow *with hope by the power of the holy spirit.* (Romans 15:13)

In other words, the *present* "filling" of the united transethnic church is the sure sign of the promised "filling" of all creation. The echoes of Ephesians are not far away. And that is why, as in Ephesians, the very existence of this church, worshipping together as a single family across traditional and ethnic lines, is the sign, both to believers and to the wider world, of the Isaianic hope, the Romans 8 hope, the hope for the new creation in which all things are put right.

That is why the mutual "welcome," as Paul begins it in Romans chapter 14, is so vital: "Welcome someone who is weak in faith, but not in order to have disputes on difficult points," 14:1. This is also where he ends in 15:7: "Welcome one another, therefore, as the Messiah has welcomed you, to God's glory." He is addressing the potentially fraught situation in Rome, in which a few small house churches, perhaps scattered across different parts of the huge, teeming city, might hear of one another's existence, but might also have suspicions about divergences from Judaean customs of food and sabbath.[14] But Paul is careful to lay out his foundational argument for mutual welcome, in chapter 14, without being specific about the ethnic connotations ("some of us like doing things this way, some prefer to do them that way, so don't judge one another—leave that to the Messiah!"). This is not, we should note, a first-century version of a laissez-faire Enlightenment doctrine of "tolerance." It is the direct result of Paul's insistence, rooted in the death and resurrection of Jesus and in the gift of the spirit, that "there is no distinction between Judaean and Greek" (Romans 3:22; 10:12), which is itself based, not on a who-cares easygoing relativism, but precisely on Paul's belief that, in Messiah Jesus, God's long plan to give Abraham a family of "many nations" had been fulfilled.[15] The western Enlightenment has tried to achieve by tolerance what in scripture is God's gift of love.[16]

Paul finally makes things explicit in chapter 15. His language about the strong and the weak was all along a way of cooling down overheated scruples, switching attention from ethnic labels to personal likes and dislikes. His aim is visible and celebratory unity:

> *May the God of patience and encouragement grant you to come to a common mind among yourselves, in accordance with the Messiah, Jesus, so that, with one mind and one mouth, you may glorify the God and father of our Lord Jesus the Messiah.* (Romans 15:5–6)

One mind and one mouth; that is Paul's intention. Unity in worship is not an optional extra for people who might hear of other worshipping groups elsewhere in town but would harbor suspicions about them. No: for Paul, the mutual cross-cultural welcome is of the very essence of the gospel: "Welcome one another, therefore, as the Messiah has welcomed you, to God's glory" (Romans 15:7). That is the sign of hope: the hope that the God who brings the wolf and the lamb to lie down together will one day fill all creation with his glory, as he is presently filling the worshipping church to overflowing. The God whose messianic homecoming in Jesus has resulted in the new gospel regime, in which all nations, peoples, tribes, and languages are equally welcome, is the God whose homecoming in the power of the holy spirit causes the church to overflow with hope. In the multicultural, multiethnic church, joined together as a single family, we glimpse the truth of the gospel, the hope of all creation being liberated from corruption, the hope of the whole world being filled with God's glory as the waters cover the sea.

What the Monochrome Church Misses

Three things are clear to me as I reflect on all this. First, I cannot escape the sense that the decline of the biblical hope in western Christianity, and the preponderance of same-color churches, are closely related.

By "the decline of the biblical hope" I mean not only the liberal denial of bodily resurrection, though that has been devastating enough. I refer to the fact the western fixation with the going-to-heaven story has all but obliterated the new-creational hope of which the Bible actually speaks. Even those who insist on the bodily resurrection of Jesus often conclude from that, not that new creation has been launched on earth as in heaven, but that there is indeed a life after death and that by believing in Jesus we can obtain it.

By "the preponderance of same-color churches" I do not just mean "Black churches" or "white churches" or any single ethnic church community. I mean, equally, the ways in which denominations, and individual churches within denominations, reflect distinctions of class and wealth as well as color and culture. If, after all, we have given up the hope that the earth shall be full of God's glory, that the wolf and the lamb will lie down together, in favor of the nebulous platonic heaven of popular imagination, why should it matter that the worshipping church reflect the many strands of ethnicity and culture represented in any particular locality? Some might think: As long as folk are being trained in heavenly-mindedness, why should it matter if people who look and sound different from ourselves (and who perhaps "do things a bit differently") are worshipping in a different building, half a mile down the road, rather than "with one heart and voice" together with ourselves? But if we hold to the biblical hope, rooted in God's homecoming in Messiah and spirit, and issuing in the combined new heavens and new earth, then it matters enormously.

I know how hard it is to make even small steps in the right direction. Few of us take kindly to having the style and content of our regular worship disrupted. But if the church is called to be the small working model of new creation, and if in that new creation there is "neither Jew nor Greek, slave nor free, no 'male and female,'" then we have no choice. The huge multicultural gathering of Revelation 7 is not meant as a vision simply for the ultimate future. It is to be reflected in actual worshipping communities here and now. To think otherwise would be like someone saying "In the resurrection I will be sinless; so there's no point trying to battle with sin here and now." No: *because* in the future life we will be sinless, and united across all ethnic and other differences, it is all the more important that we anticipate this as far as possible in the present. God's homecoming in Messiah and spirit has already become a reality. It is not something for which we are still waiting.

The second thing that has become clear to me is that the churches of the west, particularly in the many protestant traditions, have drifted so far away from the Bible (despite often insisting loudly on its supreme authority!) that my argument in this chapter may well appear strange, dangerous, and utterly foreign. Some will react to what I say not just with the personal animosity that doesn't want its normal life to be disrupted, but with a political suspicion: perhaps the call for multicolored unity is simply a "politically correct" attempt to introduce a multiculturalism that arises, not from Christianity, but from Marxism or some equivalent. After all, it is not that long ago that strict racial segregation was not only enforced by law among the supposedly God-fearing people of southern Africa as well as the southern states of America. Many have assumed that this was "what the Bible teaches," referring of course to passages in Israel's scriptures about the people of God not mixing with idolatrous foreigners, without noticing that this was one of those points where the gospel of Jesus effected a huge (and always intended) change in exactly that area.

This, again, may be partly because Romans 15 fell off the back of many popular readings of the great epistle. All this may have something to do with the rejection in certain quarters of fresh readings of Paul in which the coming together of Judaean and Gentile are seen as the direct correlation of justification by faith. But a true multiculturalism was all along a Christian innovation. It results directly from the gospel of grace, from the message of the God who has come home in Jesus, who comes home in the presence and power of the spirit, and who will come again to complete the work of cosmic renewal toward which the church is called to act as a signpost, a beacon of hope.

It is of course bizarre that some contemporary political movements try to impose or foster a kind of multiculturalism on supposedly secular grounds, giving the impression that the idea arises from a philosophical or political source quite other than Christian faith. It can't be done; this is another classic example of the post-Enlightenment world trying to get the fruit of the gospel while cutting off the root.[17]

The truth is that if the church forgets part of its core message—and for Paul the multiethnic church was the living embodiment of that core message—then we shouldn't be surprised if people try to get to the same result by other means. Jesus had to face a similar problem: the kingdom was breaking in, and the men of violence were trying to get in on the act.[18] Within Enlightenment modernity, right-wing Hegelians developed the idea of progress while left-wing Hegelians embraced the hope of revolution. Both were parasitic on Jewish and Christian eschatology, but in both cases they were filling in the gaps left by an increasingly platonic church that had forgotten its own inaugurated eschatology and had its eyes solely on heaven. We need, as a matter of urgency, to reclaim the multicultural vision (as well as the visions of social improvement and/or radical change) from within a specifically Christian, gospel-shaped agenda. It isn't enough to have the church simply joining in with this or that current movement, which in any case usually happens half a generation too late. We need to be creative, front-foot theologians, pastors, and teachers, leading the way into, and celebrating, the reality of which the various secular movements of the last few centuries have been, at best, parodies.

The third thing that has come home to me strongly in recent years is the difficulty that awaits someone like me, an elderly white male, saying this kind of thing. Some years ago I was speaking on these topics in a seminar in Los Angeles when an African American woman theologian said, graciously but firmly, that, when she hears someone like me talking about a multicultural church, she and others like her will inevitably hear me saying "You all now get to become honorary white males." Perhaps that is a danger I cannot avoid, even though of course it is the last thing I intend. I do not blame the questioner. Her natural reaction was perhaps inevitable, granted the back history of church life in America and elsewhere, and granted the efforts that are still made in some quarters to maintain not only ethnic segregation but male-only church leadership. There is food for thought, and room for improvement, for us all.

The community of which Paul speaks is precisely polychrome. As in Ephesians 3:10, the multicolored splendor of the creator God is to be revealed through the church. The principalities and powers always tend toward a monochrome, drab uniformity, squashing everything into the same shape and dealing violently with the bits that refuse to conform. But God's creation isn't like that, and his new creation isn't supposed to be like that either. So when Paul insists on "neither Judaean nor Greek," he doesn't mean (as today's jargon has it) that people's "identities" are thereby "erased." Paul can and does address Judaeans as Judaeans and Gentiles as Gentiles. He can speak of himself still as a Judaean, and he can make a theological point out of his identity, even while at the same time making it clear that this does not give him a higher status in the Messiah's family than his Gentile siblings.[19]

Perhaps the early twenty-first century, in which the question of identity has been blown up beyond all previous imaginings, is not the most helpful time to keep a clear head on what the New Testament is saying. Equally, perhaps it is precisely these questions, raised by our contemporaries, that rightly compel us to be more precise and nuanced in our reading and exposition. Let's be clear: equality does not mean uniformity. The ground is even at the foot of the cross. But those who stand on that even ground—and together sing their hearts out in joy and gratitude—are, and remain, a community drawn from every nation, people, tribe, and tongue.

14

LIFE BEYOND DEATH AND THE CALLING OF THE CHURCH

What Are We Waiting For?

The normal story that almost all modern Christianity tells comes into sharp focus at funerals. We assume, along with most of western culture, that the point of Christianity is "to go to heaven when you die." But that, as we have seen, brings its own problems, not least because this is not after all the story that the Bible, both Old and New Testaments, is actually telling.

Funerals are therefore hard, in at least two senses. They are hard for those who have loved and lost a friend or family member, even when they have a strong faith and a clear hope of a future time in which all shall be well once more. But they are also hard for the people who organize the service, and who preach or teach at it. People come to funerals expecting the "going-to-heaven" narrative in hymns, prayers, and homilies. It has saturated western culture, whether or not people actually believe it. Almost whatever a preacher says, many hearers will think that he or she "must really" be talking about the recently deceased person going to heaven. They will mentally decode any other statement or hint into an oblique way of saying the same thing. They will ask, for reassurance, "Where is he now?" or "Where is she now?" Many preachers know perfectly well that the biblical hope is focused on new creation, on the new heavens and new earth into which God's people will be raised in new and immortal physical bodies. But they still find it deceptively easy to add extra remarks about how Jesus, having died, was "raised to glory," or how those who have died have now "gone home."

Well-known hymns reinforce this:

When Christ shall come, with shout of acclamation,
and take me home, *what joy shall fill my heart.*[1]

I pointed out in *Surprised by Hope* that this was a translation of a Swedish original that said things rather differently. I have sometimes managed to alter the words on a service sheet so that they read "and heal his world" instead of "and take me home." But, as students have sometimes said after a lecture, you can understand what the teacher is saying for a short while, but after a couple of minutes your mind will flick back into default mode.

How then do we approach the question of death? How can we combine wise teaching about the recently departed with the biblical emphasis on new creation, and on the bodily resurrection that will enable God's people to take an active share in that new creation? How can the theme of God's homecoming, which we have been exploring throughout this book, bring fresh clarity, not only to what we say about death and beyond, but to the life and vocation of God's people here and now? That is the subject of this final chapter.

An introductory note: the right time to explore and teach the still-surprising and often-unknown biblical truth about death, and God's ultimate purposes beyond it, is not at the funeral. Funeral sermons should in general be quite brief, clear to the point of simplicity, and full of gentle consolation and hope. But congregations need to be taught throughout the year to think biblically, in a way that sadly has not happened even in those churches that pride themselves on their "biblical" beliefs. And thinking biblically, to say it again, means being grasped by the story of the God who comes to us and who will come again when Jesus returns and the spirit transforms all creation. It is this double "coming" (Jesus and the spirit) in this double time (present and future) that we must now explore.

One final introductory comment, repeating something I have often said before: *all our talk about God's future is a set of signposts pointing into a fog*—or, if you like, into the bright mist of God's still-hidden purposes. The signposts should of course be pointing in the right direction. The theologian, the exegete, and the preacher must make sure that they are. But the signposts do not provide an advance photographic guide to what we shall see when God's future arrives to make its home with us.

The Double "Coming"

From one point of view, thinking about Christian eschatology under the heading of "God's homecoming" ought to be easy. "He will come again in glory to judge the living and the dead," we say in the Creed, "and his kingdom will have no end." Well and good. I have expounded the "second coming" in some detail in *Surprised by Hope*, and I'm not going to repeat what I said there.[2] I would simply stress two things.

First, the early Christians seem to have been quite reticent when it came to precise predictions about God's ultimate future. Many early Christian references to the second coming of Jesus use the language of scripture to speak of "that day." As in the Hebrew Bible, such phrases are flexible. "The day of YHWH" might refer, for some prophets, to the coming fall of Jerusalem, or the Northern Kingdom, or indeed Babylon, but other prophets could use it with other referents.[3] Likewise, the early Christians were far more cautious about what precisely Jesus's second coming would involve, and when it might happen, than some of their modern expositors would wish. Jesus stressed that only the father knew about future timings. That has not stopped many theological castles being built in thin air.[4]

Second, in line with our earlier expositions in the present book, the purpose of Jesus's second coming will not be to scoop his people up and take them back with him to heaven, *away from* this world. His aim will be to complete the work accomplished in his death and resurrection; that is, to bring his healing and restorative rule *to* this world, in the creation of the new heavens and new earth. The incarnate second person of the trinity, the human being who is the ultimate image of God, will come to do both what God wants to do and what God created humans to do, namely, to bring his wise order to the world.

But there is a further, less obvious fulfillment of the same theme, which emerges when we consider the eschatological work of the spirit. I have suggested throughout this book that the personal coming of God—the return of YHWH to Zion—takes place within, and brings into sharp focus, the larger theme of God's intention to fill all creation with his personal presence and glory. God made a world that is other than himself. He made it out of love, and with that love he will fill it with himself. But because it is love, God's coming to the whole creation will enable it to be even more gloriously itself, in all its odd, quirky, pluriform originality. Creation, when transformed into the promised new creation, will be more truly itself, more truly unusual and unique in its million parts, and at the same time will be gloriously filled with God's loving presence. And I have suggested that this filling may best be understood in terms of the work of the holy spirit.

That is why the spirit's filling of the church in the present time, enabling it, as we have seen, to be gloriously varied as well as united, is the true anticipation of the ultimate divine purpose for the whole creation. The holy spirit has already been poured out on the church, and through the church into the world, from Pentecost onward.[5] But at last the spirit will come afresh on the whole creation, filling it with divine glory as the waters cover the sea, and raising God's people from the dead to share in the running of this new world.[6] When we put the picture together (adding texts like Genesis 1 and Romans 8 into the mix!) we may cautiously suggest that Jesus's second coming will be the moment when the spirit, having groaned in labor pains, will finally give birth to the new heavens and new earth. This will be God's homecoming indeed, in all senses.

This narrative thus provides a rich and multilayered framework for thinking about God's future for the world and for humans, not least in the puzzling interval between bodily death and bodily resurrection. God's promise to come in person to save and judge *has been* fulfilled in Jesus and *will be* fulfilled at his future coming. God's promise to fill the earth with his glorious presence *has been and is being* fulfilled in the life of the church and *will be* fulfilled in the final new creation. All our specific reflection on the detail of the future hope, and of intermediate states, must be understood within this framework.

Between Death and Resurrection

The obvious though revolutionary answer to the question of personal continuity between bodily death and bodily resurrection is hiding in plain sight. The early Christians seem not to have been particularly interested in the question that so exercises modern people, especially at funerals ("where are they now?"). But they supply us with the material from which a good answer can be given. Jesus's first followers, I suggest, would have answered in terms of the holy spirit: the spirit who dwells within us in the present will continue to sustain us between death and resurrection. Failing to see this, the tradition has replaced the spirit with a platonic soul. Hence the problems we have seen, and many others.

So how does this work out? As we have seen, the biblical theme of God's homecoming focuses on two types of "coming": the filling of all creation with the knowledge and glory of God, and the personal return of YHWH to Zion. The New Testament sees the latter fulfilled in Jesus. It sees the former fulfilled both in the spirit's present work in the church and the believer, and in the promised future renewal of all creation. Once God's spirit has come to dwell in a person, and to be (so to speak) fused with their own spirit, *God himself provides the continuity between the previous bodily life and the future one.* The New Testament then speaks of God's people after bodily death in terms of their being "with the Messiah," and the best way to understand that "being with" is, I suggest, in terms of the spirit. The double homecoming of God, which will be complete at Jesus's final return when the spirit breathes glorious and renewing life throughout creation, is anticipated even in the unmapped interval between bodily death and bodily resurrection.

Perhaps the best way to begin this exposition is with the last words of Jesus in Luke's gospel. Quoting Psalm 31:5, he prays "Here's my spirit, Father! You can take care of it now!"—or, in the better-known New Revised Standard Version, "Father, into your hands I commend my spirit."[7] I suspect that many modern Christians, reading this, make no distinction between "spirit" and the more familiar "soul" and understand the passage in terms of the latter. However, as we have seen, the New Testament nowhere uses "soul" in that sense. Jesus's words are then echoed by Stephen, the first martyr, in his dying prayer, "Lord Jesus, receive my spirit."[8] This, indeed, is in line with the comment in Ecclesiastes: bodily death means that "the dust returns to the earth as it was, and the breath [Hebrew *haruach*, Septuagint *to pneuma*] returns to God who gave it."[9] Paul, in a strange but significant passage dealing with a sharp disciplinary problem in Corinth, speaks of the spirit being rescued after the death of the body.[10]

The backstory for all this is Genesis 2:7, where God breathes into the new-made human nostrils the "breath of life." The other obvious reference point is Ezekiel 37, where God promises that he will cause "breath" (*ruach/pneuma*; that is, wind or spirit) to come into the dry bones that have been reassembled into corpses, and make them live (37:5). YHWH says to the prophet:

> *Prophesy to the breath, prophesy mortal, and say to the breath: Thus says the Lord YHWH: Come from the four winds [*mēarbach ruchoth; ek tōn tessarōn pneumatōn*], O breath, and breathe upon these slain, that they may live.*[11]

Ezekiel does so, and the previously dead bodies are filled with "breath" (wind or spirit would be equally good renderings), and they stand up, a huge multitude. The interpretation follows naturally: God will do the unthinkable, opening the graves of exile and bringing his people back to their own land:

> *I will put my spirit within you, and you shall live, and I will place you on your own soil; then you shall know that I, YHWH, have spoken and will act, says YHWH.*[12]

We today hear the words "spirit," "breath," and "wind" as three different things, separable at least in thought. But the regular use of *ruach* in Hebrew, and *pneuma* in Greek, to summon up all three as a single complex entity is apparent here, when the "four winds" come to "breathe" on the slain, meaning that God's "spirit" will come and animate them. This close connection is difficult to grasp for those of us accustomed to a hard dividing line between "natural" phenomena such as human breath and a "supernatural" phenomenon like God's spirit. But from Genesis onward this distinction was never so hard and fast. And behind Genesis 2:7 there stands Genesis 1:2, where the "wind of God," the powerful *ruach elohim* or *pneuma theou*, "swept over the face of the waters" (NRSV). My sense is that if we could interview the people who wrote, edited, and prayed all these texts we would discover that they saw the whole mysterious phenomenon, which we separate out into different entities, as closely interrelated. Breath, in humans and animals alike, and indeed the wind that brings fresh air to all, are the vehicles and means of God's life, given to God's living creatures and then given back at the end of present bodily life.

This last point is dramatically illustrated in one of the great Psalms of creation. The Psalmist celebrates the wonderfully rich variety of God's creation—earth and sky, plants and animals, and humans taking their place in the midst of it all. God has made it all "in wisdom," as Proverbs said, and as John and Colossians imply.[13] And it is all animated by God's powerful breath, his *ruach*. This remains God's possession. He can take it away again—and then restore it:

> *When you take away their breath, they die, and return to their dust. When you send forth your spirit, they are created, and you renew the face of the ground.*[14]

Despite the apparent difference ("breath" and "spirit") within that translation, the Hebrew for both words is *ruach*, and the Septuagint renders them both as *pneuma*. From there we might discern a straight line to Paul's language about the spirit of God as both the present possession and the agent of resurrection. And, I suggest, the vehicle (if that is the right word) for the life in between the two.

To understand how this might work, helping us to address our question about where, and indeed "what," human beings are between bodily death and bodily resurrection, we might turn to Paul's language about the close interrelation between God's spirit and the human spirit:

Who knows what is really going on inside a person, except the spirit of the person which is inside them? Well, it's like that with God. Nobody knows what is going on inside God except God's spirit. And we haven't received the spirit of the world, but the spirit that comes from God, so that we can know the things that have been given to us by God.[15]

And then, even more remarkably:

Don't you know that anyone who joins himself to a prostitute is one body with her? "The two shall become one flesh"—that's what it says. But the one who joins himself to the Lord becomes one spirit with him . . . Don't you know that your body is a temple of the holy spirit within you, the spirit God gave you, so that you don't belong to yourselves? You were quite an expensive purchase! So glorify God in your body.[16]

Paul is thus visualizing our individual human spirit as being fused together with the divine spirit, so that they form a unity. I do not think most Christians, including most theologians, have reflected sufficiently on this. If we did, we should discover a vital clue to our question about continuing life between death and resurrection. God's spirit, and our spirit joined together with God's spirit, provide the postmortem reality that most Christians have tried to describe in terms of the "soul."

We should also add, from Romans:

You didn't receive a spirit of slavery, did you, to go back again into a state of fear? But you received the spirit of

> *sonship, in whom we call out "Abba, Father!" When that happens, it is the spirit itself giving supporting witness to what our own spirit is saying, that we are God's children. And if we're children, we are also heirs . . .*
>
> *In the same way, the spirit comes alongside and helps us in our weakness. We don't know what to pray for as we ought to; but that same spirit pleads on our behalf, with groanings too deep for words. And the Searcher of Hearts knows what the spirit is thinking, because the spirit pleads for God's people according to God's will.*[17]

This close correlation of the divine spirit with the spirit of a believer stands under the overall rubric of verses 8–11, the passage to which Psalm 104:29–30 points clearly enough:

> *But you're not people of flesh; you're people of the spirit (if indeed God's spirit lives within you; note that anyone who doesn't have the spirit of the Messiah doesn't belong to him). But if the Messiah is in you, the body is indeed dead because of sin, but the spirit is life because of covenant justice. So then, if the spirit of the one who raised Jesus from the dead lives within you, the one who raised the Messiah from the dead will give life to your mortal bodies, too, through his spirit who lives within you.*[18]

Taken together, all this suggests that Paul sees an intimate correlation of the divine spirit, defined here in terms of being the agent of new life, and the human spirit of the believer. When we place this in the context of our argument, concerning the gift of the spirit as part of the homecoming whereby

God has "come home" to be with, and within, human beings, we see how far-fetched it would be to suppose that God's spirit might come and dwell within a person on a merely temporary basis, as a transient, passing phenomenon between their baptism (and coming to faith) and their bodily death. Rather, I suggest, what Paul says of the postbaptismal Christian applies equally to the postmortem Christian:

> *Don't you see: you died, and your life has been hidden with the Messiah, in God! When the Messiah is revealed (and he is your life, remember), then you too will be revealed with him in glory.*[19]

This statement holds together the passage just quoted from Romans 8 with the hope Paul articulates in Philippians 1:

> *I'm pulled both ways at once: I would really love to leave all this and be with the Messiah, because that would be far better. But staying on here in the flesh is more vital for your sake.*[20]

This idea of being "with the Messiah" after death can also be spoken of in terms of being "at home with the Lord":

> *We know that while we are at home in the body we are away from the Lord. We live our lives by faith, you see, not by sight. We are confident, and we would much prefer to be away from the body and at home with the Lord.*[21]

This passage does not mean that Paul envisions a disembodied postmortem existence as the final state. What he says in this passage comes within the larger picture, sketched immediately before, of the promise of eventual resurrection:

> *Yes: in the present "tent," we groan under a great weight. But we don't want to put it off; we want to put on something else on top, so that what is doomed to die may be swallowed up with life. It is God who has been at work in us to do this,* the God who has given us the spirit as the first installment and guarantee.[22]

Would Paul then say that this "first installment and guarantee," the present possession of the spirit, would be withdrawn after death, to return later on in order to raise the believer to new bodily life? That seems highly unlikely. Far more natural, I suggest, to suppose that when God the father gives the spirit to dwell within an individual (or indeed a church, as in 1 Corinthians 3) this is not intended as a short-term injection of spiritual power, sufficient to drive faith, hope, and love until the time of bodily death but to be discontinued thereafter. *When the spirit has come home to a person, the spirit, fused together with the human spirit and holding it in continuing life, will stay "at home," holding that person in life, through and after bodily death, and on to the point where the same spirit will raise that person from the dead.* Though Paul never says this in so many exact words (he was not troubled by our question), when he speaks of being "with the Messiah," and "with the Messiah in God," he could equally well have said that the spirit, having come to dwell in a believer so that the believer has become "one spirit" with Jesus, will then sustain them after bodily death within the mystery of the holy trinity. The coming of God in the Messiah and the coming of God in the spirit have always belonged closely together. "Hidden with the Messiah in God" would be one way of saying just that. The continuing life of believers after death, which Paul assumes in various passages, such as, for instance, 1 Thessalonians 4:14–18, can be understood in exactly this way.

In other words, insofar as the spirit has shaped, guided, led, energized, and animated the believer in this life, the spirit will not abandon such a person after their bodily death. We might even say, with a cautious boldness, that in shaping and directing the believer, not least in enabling him or her to "put to death the deeds of the body" (Romans 8:13), the spirit's own self, having come "home" to that person, has been shaped afresh. (This is not unlike something I would also want to say, that the incarnate son was shaped by his friendships with Peter, Mary, and the rest.) We have so often spoken of the effects of the spirit's work on the believer that we have not usually stopped to think of the effects of that work *on the spirit's own self.* With all due allowance for divine foreknowledge, and for the fact that God has "prepared good works ahead of time" as the road his people must travel (Ephesians 1:10), we may still speak of the effects *on the spirit* of the filling of this or that person. That is why the eventual promise of God's presence filling the whole creation, with the present filling of the church as its anticipation, enables the spirit-filled church to "abound in hope" (Romans 15:13).

The mode of existence that may be predicated for believers between bodily death and bodily resurrection may then, I suggest, be seen in terms of sharing the inner life of the triune God—specifically, the life of the spirit. This, I think, is a better and more biblical and theological way of saying what John Polkinghorne memorably said, that at death God will download our software onto his hardware until he gives us new hardware to run the software again for ourselves. Delightful though that illustration may be, it is simply a pointer to what I take to be the reality: that the spirit who has shaped believers has also been shaped by that same process. The spirit who inspired and enabled this or that work of grace, generosity, costly witness, creative endeavor, martyrdom, wisdom, learning, and outgoing love is now forever afterward shaped by that work, as an artist is known as the one who painted this picture or composed that symphony. In biblical terms, this is how God "has kept us among the living" (Psalm 66:9), which, literally translated, might be "who places our breathing selves in life," with "breathing selves" as a rendering of *naphshēnu.* The Coverdale translation "who holds our souls in life" shows how easily the Hebraic concept of the breathing self could morph, in later readings, into the platonic idea of the soul. But if we hold our biblical nerve we can see a straight line from the Psalmist's celebration of YHWH's keeping of the faithful person in life to Paul's insistence that, after death, the believer's life is "hidden with the Messiah, in God." And I am suggesting that the best way of understanding this—the way that is then pulled out of shape by the introduction of the platonic soul—is to see the spirit's own self as the place where, and the means by which, the person remains "with the Messiah, which is far better."

This way of approaching our question has one particular obvious benefit. It cuts in a single stroke through all the tortured speculation about postmortem existence that so troubled the late medieval period. The protestant reformers were correct in their arguments, rooted in Paul's theology, against the then dominant doctrine of purgatory. But we can now go further. The reformers continued to think in terms of the progress, and state, of the immortal soul. But once we think instead in terms of the spirit, and of the spirit of believers becoming one with the holy spirit, it makes no sense to imagine anything in the immediate postmortem state of existence other than the experience of being "with the Messiah in God," held and sustained by the spirit that has called, guided, and sanctified the believer during the present life.

One might be tempted to say that we could still refer to this state of being as "heaven." But that could be seriously misleading. The early Christians did not use that word to denote or describe this reality. Nor is this "state of being" the ultimate destination, which the going-to-heaven story would inevitably imply for a modern Christian. The eventual goal is bodily resurrection, within the full new creation. Talking of "heaven" all too easily allows people to go back into the "normal" mode, the "getting-into-heaven" narrative so familiar in the western Christian tradition.

What's more, the philosophically inspired dream of a progress toward the vision of God, the "beatific vision" of widespread speculation, misses the point that Jesus so clearly articulated: "Anyone who has seen me has seen the father" (John 14:9). We do not need to look elsewhere than at the incarnate Jesus. Indeed, we must not. If we do, we will inevitably construct a Jesus of our own imagining. The theologian may imagine a Jesus more like whatever philosophical idea of the father he or she already holds. The skeptical historian may imagine a Jesus who never thought of himself as other than a prophet. No: *he*, Jesus, is "the image of God, the invisible one, the firstborn of all creation" (Colossians 1:15). He is the true reflection of the father—at the same time as he is the true embodiment of what humans were made to be.

You cannot then start off (though many still try) with a picture of God drawn from speculative theology or philosophy, or simply from intuition, and then try to imagine the incarnate son as the embodiment of that God. Nor can you begin with a reductionist would-be historical imagination of "what was possible in the first century" and hence "what Jesus must have been like" despite what the gospels say. "Nobody has ever seen God," says John at the climax of his Prologue. "The only-begotten God, who is intimately close to the father—he has brought him to light" (John 1:18). Literally, he has *exegeted* him, has explained and unfolded and displayed before the astonished world who its Creator really is. As we have seen, this includes, and indeed highlights, not only the signs of new creation such as the turning of water into wine, but also the signs of the love through which that new creation comes about: God incarnate weeping at the tomb of his friend (John 11:35), washing the feet of his followers (13:2–20), dying in the place of sinners (18:40). When we read this, we are close to what John says in the famous fourteenth verse of the Prologue: "The Word became flesh, and lived among us. We gazed upon his glory." And when we are reminded one last time of what the risen Jesus says to his followers, we discover that the mission of the son becomes the mission he passes on to his followers:

"Peace be with you," Jesus said to them again. "As the father has sent me, so I'm sending you."
With that, he breathed on them.
"Receive the holy spirit," he said.[23]

The basic point I am making—that the holy spirit is the mode and means of our continuing life beyond the grave and in anticipation of the resurrection—can be seen in Paul's language about the spirit as the *arrabōn*, the "down payment" of the future inheritance. The indwelling spirit is the first fruits of what is to come. The spirit, having shaped and sanctified the life of the believer, carries the believer's personal continuity through bodily death, which completes purification, and on toward resurrection. To return once more to Colossians 3:3: the believer, having died, is "hidden with the Messiah in God." As Paul continues in that passage: "When the Messiah is revealed (and he is your life, remember), then you too will be revealed with him in glory." When we put this together with Romans 8:9–11 the point is clear. All the Messiah's people are indwelt by his spirit; therefore, though the body is dead because of sin, the spirit is life *dia dikaiosynēn*, through "righteousness," God's covenant justice embodied and enacted in Jesus. Death finally deals with sin; the life-giving spirit provides ongoing continuity and eventual resurrection. Paul sees the believer as a little temple, and the family of Jesus believers as the new, worldwide temple, sanctified and purified as required.[24]

Perhaps we could put it like this. Bodily death finishes off the old psychosomatic "you." To cling to it, or to imagine a soul that is a personal possession, something other than the indwelling spirit, is to sidestep the co-crucifixion of which Paul speaks in Galatians 2:19–21. Perhaps it is even to cherish a little pride after all. However—to paraphrase 2 Corinthians 5:1–5: "When the spirit has indwelt someone, they become more truly the person God always intended them to be. That new humanity, that 'real me' or 'real you,' is already there in God's heavenly purposes, waiting to become a heaven-and-earth reality at the resurrection. Their present groaning is the longing for what is mortal to be swallowed up by life. God himself has prepared you and me for this very thing, giving us the spirit as the down payment." Once the spirit has indwelt and shaped a person, the spirit—precisely as the "down payment" of what is to come—doesn't stop being their true life.

Thus, in Paul's mind at least, when (through the grace of the gospel) the spirit comes to indwell a person, the spirit "clothes himself" with that person, as in the well-known passages about Gideon and others.[25] The spirit is then the true inner reality of that person, not overriding what we think of as their unique and specific personality, but fused together with their spirit, celebrating, refining, cleansing, and enhancing its God-given reality. If that's what one might mean by *theōsis*, so be it: filled with the fullness of God.[26] Then, after psychosomatic death has brought to an end all personal sin, from heart to will to action, the already indwelling spirit lives on, within the mystery of the creative outflowing love of the Trinity. We are thereby not simply "remembered" by God, as some have suggested. We are sustained in living being "with the Messiah" in—dare we say—the ever-expanding mystery of the Trinity.

This, I think, is what Paul refers to as being "absent from the body and present with the Lord," or "departing and being with the Messiah, which is far better"—in both cases, still awaiting resurrection. This will be a genuine time of conscious delight, a *refrigerium* in the sense that a third-century north African like Tertullian might hope for, neither punitive nor purgative, but the refreshing and awesome gladness of being "hidden with the Messiah in God."[27] Call this paradise if you like, though the early Christians hardly ever do. I have already warned about the dangers of calling it "heaven": the New Testament never does, and such language will at once be misunderstood, in a dualist or escapist direction, as a reference to the normal going-to-heaven story. Call it the mystery of the Trinity. The great biblical narrative, as we have insisted throughout this book, is not about humans making their way from earth to heaven, being purified on their upward journey. It is about God, Creator, Lord, spirit, coming to dwell with, among, and within humans. This, I think, is the best biblical account we can give of what it means for a Jesus follower to have died in the body and to be awaiting resurrection.

I believe it is appropriate for those still alive to pray for those in that postmortem state. We do not know whether they pray for us, but I see no reason why not. Protestant nervousness about praying for the departed stemmed entirely from the proper anxiety about colluding with the false doctrine of purgatory and the multiple abuses it generated. But once we consider the faithful dead as spirit-grounded humans, being with the Messiah and beholding the face of God, with no purgatory to worry about, we can pray with them and for them, for their continuing life of refreshment while awaiting resurrection at the coming great renewal. They will already have been shaped by the spirit into their own particular variation on the general human vocation, the calling to be the royal priesthood, which encompasses tasks from the political to the sacramental, joining heaven and earth in advance. Once we give personal eschatology its full Trinitarian shape, that many-sided genuine-human vocation comes back at last into view. There will then be no need for those caricatured and parodic speculations that have stolen time, energy, and indeed joy from western Christianity these many years.

Thus the homecoming of the one true God, in its two promised forms (Jesus and the spirit) and its two historical foci (present and future), provides the biblical framework from within which these tricky and historically contentious questions can be addressed.

We can sum up the argument of this book, and its forward movement, by stating briefly the double biblical promise of God's homecoming in Jesus and in the spirit, and the present fulfillment of that double promise.

I have argued earlier that the first Christians understood the gift of God's spirit as the present fulfillment of God's ancient promise to come home to his creation, filling it with his glory and knowledge. This promise will ultimately be fulfilled in the new creation when God is "all in all," when creation is set free from its present slavery to corruption. The present gift of the spirit to Jesus's followers, the divine homecoming that was launched at Pentecost, thus constitutes them already as the first fruits of that new creation. They are already given an active role in mission, ministry, and not least the prayer of lament so vividly described in Romans 8.[28]

Second, God's promise to return to Zion to judge and to save will be finally fulfilled at Jesus's second coming, the "appearing" spoken of in Colossians 3:4 and 1 John 3:2, the time when the heavenly reality at present hidden from earthly sight will be unveiled, and Jesus will be seen as Lord of all. His first coming, with the Word becoming flesh, tabernacling in our midst, and displaying his astonishing and loving glory to human gaze, was and is the decisive anticipation of that final event, the present homecoming that guarantees the final one.

In between the present and the future "comings," both of the spirit and of the son, the gospel—the message of the son in the power of the spirit—catches us up into God's purposes. The gospel draws us into faith and obedience; it sends us out in mission and ministry; after our bodily death, it sustains us "with the Messiah in God," against the day when we share his spirit-given resurrection and his royal and priestly vocation in his new heavens and new earth. Paul encapsulates this, at the climax of his greatest letter, in a trinitarian conclusion and blessing that embodies the biblical message in which all life is suffused with God's Messiah-shaped and spirit-given glory:

Isaiah says once more:

There shall be the root of Jesse;
the one who rises up to rule the nations;
the nations shall hope in him.
May the God of hope fill you with all joy and peace in believing, so that you may overflow with hope by the power of the holy spirit.[29]

Comfort, Comfort My People

All this comes together, then, not simply in terms of an answer to the question, "Where are they now?" but in the practical life and work of the spirit-filled church in the present. To expound this briefly in conclusion I turn back to one of the classic biblical passages about God's homecoming: Isaiah 40:1–11.

We have already seen that the passage promises the return of YHWH to Zion:

In the wilderness prepare the way of YHWH, make straight in the desert a highway for our God . . . the glory of YHWH shall be revealed, and all people shall see it together, for the mouth of YHWH has spoken.[30]

Within the larger context of the whole Bible, one is bound to notice a bifocal reality. First, the prophet is promising to the exiles in Babylon—and to the downcast remnant in desolate Jerusalem—that YHWH will return in glory. This promise was reiterated in Ezekiel. When, after many of the exiles had returned, the people were, to put it mildly, less than fully satisfied, the prophets Zechariah and Malachi reiterated the point. He would indeed be returning soon, so the careless priests and faithless people had better watch out. But then, second, the gospel writers insist that John the Baptist was fulfilling the role of the "voice in the wilderness," and that the "coming one" for whom he was preparing the road was none other than Jesus.

But Isaiah 40:1–11 is more complicated than simply a prophetic prediction. As with Isaiah 6, or 1 Kings 22, we are presented with a scene in the heavenly court, where God is consulting with his heavenly host and (in this case, unlike those others) calling them to bring comfort to his people. The words "comfort, comfort" in the famous opening line of the chapter are in the plural: God is commanding the angels and archangels to console and reassure his people.[31] It is in response to that command that a voice calls out the instruction to prepare YHWH's homecoming path (verse 3). It is in further response that another voice summons the prophet to "cry out" (verse 6), and assures him that, even if the people to whom he is to shout out the news are as frail as flowers, blown away by the wind, God's word will stand forever (verse 8).

The whole paragraph, which functions as an overture to the great poem we know as Isaiah 40–55, then reaches its climax with what seems to be a further heavenly command to the earthly heralds who are to bring the message of comfort.[32] The heralds must lift up their voices and shout to Jerusalem that

God is indeed coming back, coming with his powerful "arm" ready to put things right (verse 10), coming as a gentle shepherd to look after the lambs and the mother sheep (verse 11). These themes are then worked out in the larger poem through the work of the "Servant of YHWH" who turns out to be the embodiment of YHWH's "arm" (Isaiah 53:1), and who is called to bring the message of rescue and hope not just to Zion, not just to the exiles, but to the whole world (Isaiah 49:6). *And in the New Testament that summons is freshly applied not just to Jesus but to the apostles, in the power of the spirit*—specifically of course Paul, for whom Isaiah 49 seems to have been a vital part of his personal vocation.[33]

I am suggesting, in other words, that we should read Isaiah 40:1–11 not just bifocally ([a] the God of creation and covenant returning to Jerusalem; [b] Jesus as the embodiment of this God, coming to bring justice and salvation) but trifocally, or, perhaps better, trinitarianly. The message of comfort is not only for the Judaean exiles, or desolate Jerusalem, but for the whole world. Any ancient reader of Genesis 1–11 would know that the Judaean exile in Babylon, as predicted in Deuteronomy 27–29, was simply the dramatic outworking of the primal "exile" from the garden. The early narrative led to Babel in Genesis 11; the prophetic warnings had pointed to the sinful people of God being exiled and ending up in Babylon. It's the same story, writ large. The promise of return from exile, and of God returning after his sin-caused absence, then applies not only to Judaeans but to the whole world. As the Psalms and Isaiah say again and again, when the creator God does for Israel what he has promised to do, then the whole world will be brought into the resulting redemption. The promise of YHWH's return, and the fulfillment of that promise in Jesus, are then completed by the work of the spirit, the comforter, YHWH "coming home" afresh to dwell with, and to work redemption through, the faithful followers of Jesus. And with that insight we are invited to read Isaiah 40 in terms of the church's spirit-given vocation.

In other words, just as the prophet was standing in the divine council, listening to the original command of God in verses 1–2 and then to the voices crying out in verses 3 and 6, so the faithful followers of Jesus are called *to stand humbly in the divine council in order then to stand boldly in human councils.* In the power of the spirit we are to lift up our voices to declare the homecoming of God, the God who comes to put everything right at last, the God whose personal touch is to be known through his gentle care of those in special need.

We need, then, to pray and plan, to prophesy and put into practice, what it would look like if verses 9 to 11 were to come true in the power of the spirit. The close-up focus of Isaiah in the sixth-century BC is basic. The gospel picture of the life and redeeming work of Jesus is built on it. Now, as those indwelt by God's spirit stand in the divine council, celebrating the homecoming of the triune God, we are commissioned and equipped to display and announce to the world the comfort of God. We celebrate the homecoming of the father and the son by invoking the homecoming of the spirit.

We are to be people of prayerful power, as in verse 10: YHWH comes with might and his arm rules for him. Come, holy spirit, we pray, move afresh in your world; raise up among your people the prophetic vision and the organizational skill to launch strategies of powerful justice in which God's reward and recompense will be lived out in the world. And we are to be people of gentle grace, as in verse 11: he will feed his flock like a shepherd. Come, holy spirit, we pray, move afresh among your people, and pour out the pastoral vision and the organizational skill to launch strategies of healing and hope in wounded and fearful communities—communities that can easily turn to bitterness, anger, and violence but that, by the spirit's grace, may find the way to reconciliation and hope. Come, holy spirit, so that in our worship we may stand humbly in the divine council in order that in our witness we may stand boldly in human councils, from the neighborhoods and cities where we live, all the way up to the great councils of state and international relations. Come, holy spirit, come as the God of all comfort.

If all this feels impossible, a nice dream we have to forget in the messy and dangerous reality of our world, we need to read and pray Isaiah 40 again, this time right through to the end of the chapter. For God, the nations are like a drop from a bucket; he brings princes to naught and rulers to nothing. The chapter closes with the great promise that we should take for ourselves as we look out at our traumatic world and seek the fresh vocation through which God will return once more in the power of the spirit: "Why do you say, My way is hidden from YHWH? . . . Have you not known? . . . YHWH is the everlasting God . . . he does not faint or grow weary . . . He gives power to the faint, and strengthens the powerless."[34] We need that reminder every time we are rightly overwhelmed by the tragedy and agony of our world. The church's vocation is never triumphalistic, but always, as Paul knew, worked out through our own weakness, apparent powerlessness, and even failures. Yes: "Even youths will faint and grow weary, and the young will fall exhausted" (verse 30)—we know that, we feel that, but, as in verse 8 (and then again at 55:11) the word of God remains the solid rock: "those who wait for YHWH shall renew their strength; they shall mount up with wings like eagles, they shall run and not be weary, they shall walk and not faint."[35]

That should be our prayer for ourselves and our communities: the prayer of the homecoming of the triune God. God promised Israel he would return. God fulfilled that promise in Jesus. God now longs to fulfill it again, and again, through the holy spirit, the comforter. The doctrine of the trinity is not, after all, a strange philosophical fantasy of thinkers who have lost their biblical roots. When we recover those roots, and learn to understand the whole narrative of the faith in these terms, we find that we don't need complex medieval interpretative strategies. The coming of the triune God is all the hermeneutical framework we require. As we read the Bible prayerfully we are confronted, again and again, with the triple reality of the God of all comfort.

This gives us the complex lens (I am thinking of varifocal spectacles) through which to read the whole scripture. We move from the close-up lens of ancient Israel, of creation and covenant, to the midrange lens of the incarnate son, in whom all God's promises find their "yes" and through whom all things are made new. Then, lifting up our eyes to the long-range lens, we see before us the hope, and the church's task, of spirit-given comfort, reconciliation, and healing.

The gospel message has all too often been shrunk. It has been turned into a self-help message of how we might find our way up to heaven, and then sometimes (particularly in the modern Western churches) of how to have a happy life while we wait for that eventuality. But the promise of God's powerful and comforting homecoming works in the opposite direction. It is gloriously fulfilled in the son, and powerfully implemented through the spirit—which means, through those in whom the spirit dwells, those who confess Jesus as Lord and savior in the full Isaianic and gospel sense. Let us pray afresh in our own day for the power of the spirit, that through new vision and vocation, through the work of churches and individuals, there may be signs of hope, glimpses of glory, justice, and mercy lived out so that all flesh may see and know the God who is father, son, and spirit, the God who comes home with the message of comfort, the gentle shepherd who will put all things right at last, the powerful wind that fills us now and will one day fill all creation.

NOTES

PREFACE

1. UK ed., 2007; US ed., 2008.
2. Steve Bouma-Prediger and Brian Walsh, *Beyond Homelessness: Christian Faith in a Culture of Displacement*, 16th anniversary edition (Eerdmans, 2023).
3. Miroslav Volf and Ryan McAnnaly-Linz, *The Home of God: A Brief Story of Everything* (Brazos Press, 2022).
4. J. Richard Middleton, *A New Heaven and a New Earth: Reclaiming Biblical Eschatology* (Baker Academic, 2014).
5. J. Moltmann, *The Coming of God: Christian Eschatology* (Fortress, 2004).
6. See, e.g., the preface to Tom Holland, *Pax: War and Peace in Rome's Golden Age* (Abacus, 2024).

CHAPTER 1: THE STORY OF SCRIPTURE

1. See, e.g., Francesca A. Murphy, *God Is Not a Story: Realism Revisited* (Oxford University Press, 2007). I am agreeing with her overall reaffirmation of "realism" while insisting that the narrative dimension remains vital.
2. See, e.g., Alexander Schmemann, *For the Life of the World* (St. Vladimir's Seminary Press, 2010 [1974]). Original title *World as Sacrament.*
3. Out of many, I have in mind, e.g., Hans Boersma, whose many elegant and learned works consistently advocate a thoroughgoing platonic understanding of the Bible as well as Christian thought. On the platonic tradition and its gradual entry into Christian thought and practice from the third century onward, see the clear and helpful introduction in Andrew Louth, *The Origins of the Christian Mystical Tradition: From Plato to Denys* (Oxford University Press, 2007 [1980]). And see chaps. 7–10 herein.
4. Plutarch, "On Exile," 607A–F (in Plutarch, *Moralia*, vol. VII, Loeb Classical Library [Harvard University Press, 1959], 564–71).

5. John Betjeman, *Uncollected Poems* (John Murray, 1982 [1955]), 69.
6. See N. T. Wright, *For All the Saints: Remembering the Christian Departed* (SPCK and Morehouse, 2003). The quotation is from Philippians 1:23.
7. E.g., Isaiah 11:9; 1 Corinthians 15:28.
8. 2 Kings 6:17; Revelation 4:1–2.
9. E.g., Isaiah 55:10–11; Acts 14:17.
10. John 14:23.
11. 1 Corinthians 8:1–3.
12. The first reference to "heaven" (Romans 1:18) is about God's wrath being revealed "from heaven" against ungodliness and injustice; the second (10:6), quoting scripture, asks rhetorically, "who has gone up to heaven?" in order to stress that now God's word has come *from* heaven to be "near you."
13. See N. T. Wright, *Into the Heart of Romans* (SPCK and Zondervan, 2023).
14. I am grateful here to Haley Goranson Jacob, *Conformed to the Image of His Son* (InterVarsity Press, 2018).
15. The one occurrence outside Matthew is John 3:5. On Jesus's "kingdom"language, see N. T. Wright, *Jesus and the Victory of God* (SPCK and Fortress, 1996), part 2.
16. See chap. 6 herein. On the long plan of God see especially, e.g., Ephesians 1:10.
17. "O God of Bethel, by whose hand," by Philip Doddridge (1736).
18. Plutarch, "On Exile," 607A–F (in Plutarch, *Moralia*, vol. VII, Loeb Classical Library [Harvard University Press, 1959]), 564–71. For Plato, "the soul is naturally divine and seeks to return to the divine realm" (Louth, *Origins of the Christian Mystical Tradition*, 3).
19. Revelation 6:9; 20:4; see the discussion further on. Other uses of *psychē* in the New Testament, e.g., James 1:21, 5:20 are best understood in terms of the underlying Hebrew *nephesh*, which means "life" or "living being."
20. Matthew 16:26.
21. Romans 8:16; the whole passage is important. See too 1 Corinthians 2:11–16.
22. Psalm 42:5–6, 11, 43:5 (New Revised Standard Version). John Goldingay, in his striking recent translation, renders the key phrase, "Why do you bow low, my entire being, and why are you in turmoil within me?" That phrase "my entire being" indicates well enough that "soul"—as commonly understood today—is inadequate and misleading. See John Goldingay and Tom Wright, *The Bible for Everyone* (SPCK, 2018), 548.
23. See N. T. Wright, *The Resurrection of the Son of God* (SPCK and Fortress, 2003), 87–89. Those in Sheol are *rephaim*, "shades."
24. On the passage, see the important discussion in Wright, *The Resurrection of the Son of God*, 162–75.
25. Prayer of Azariah 64.
26. 1 Corinthians 15:20–28.
27. See, e.g., Romans 9–11 and chap. 14 herein.
28. For this view of Genesis 1 and 2, see my fuller treatment in N. T. Wright, *History and Eschatology: Jesus and the Promise of Natural Theology* (Baylor University Press and SPCK, 2019), chap. 5, drawing on several contemporary scholars such as John Walton, J. Richard Middleton, Greg Beale, and others.
29. See J. Richard Middleton, *The Liberating Image* (Brazos Press, 2005).

30. New Living Translation "living person"; English Standard Version "living creature"; Revised New Jerusalem Bible "living being."
31. I refer to the patriarch as Abraham for simplicity's sake, even though until chapter 17 he has the shorter name of Abram.
32. See this emphatically stated in Revelation 5:10, 20:6.
33. 2 Peter 3:10 is regularly cited here as a problem, since in some readings it seems to suggest that the whole original creation will be destroyed, leaving God to make the new one ex nihilo. The underlying Greek text is problematic because of somewhat wild variations in the manuscript tradition. But the meaning seems to be that when all that has infected God's perfect world with corruption and decay has been swept away, then "the earth and all the works on it will be disclosed." This is then similar to Paul's envisaged scenario in 1 Corinthians 3:12–15, where the coming fire will burn away all that is not from God, leaving only the true apostolic work to stand out. See my fuller discussion in *Resurrection of the Son of God*, 284–86, 462–63.
34. I speak of the "canonical" gospels to differentiate them from much later collections of supposed Jesus-material, e.g., the so-called *Gospel of Thomas* (on which, see my *Judas and the Gospel of Jesus*). And I am referring, of course, to the heart of the "Christian" Bible. The question of the continuing Judaean understanding of Israel's scriptures, and the implicit dialogue between that and Christian readings, introduces several other large questions, important but not for our present argument.
35. C. S. Lewis, *Studies in Words*, 2nd ed. (Cambridge University Press, 2013), chap. 1.
36. As Paul expounds more fully in 1 Corinthians 15:50–53, the point to which he refers again briefly in 2 Corinthians 5:4, speaking about the desire not to "put off" the physical body, so as to be left with a bare soul, but to "put on something else on top." The new body will be, in our popular language, not *less* physical but *more* so.
37. See too the famous promise in Revelation 3:20, that those who hear Jesus knocking and open the door will find that he comes in to make his home with them; see chap. 11 herein.
38. See the full discussion in Wright, *Surprised by Hope* (HarperOne, 2008), 136–49, and the discussion of the key passage, 1 Thessalonians 4:13–18, in Wright, *Resurrection of the Son of God*, 214–18.

CHAPTER 2: FILLING THE EARTH WITH GLORY

1. The Hebrew text simply has *kabod*, "glory"; the Septuagint adds *meta*, "with." For all this, see Wright, *Resurrection of the Son of God*, chaps. 3 and 4.
2. E.g., Daniel 12:1–3.
3. Cf. Psalm 50:12, 89:11; and cf. Exodus 9:29, 19:5.
4. Psalm 96:10–13, see also 98:7–9.
5. Jeremiah 23:23–24.
6. Wisdom 1:7, 12:1. The decontextualized use of one phrase from 1:7 in modern liturgies ("the Spirit of God fills the whole world") can all too easily be heard as affirming some kind of uncritical pantheism.

7. Wisdom 1:6–8.
8. Deuteronomy 4:39; also Joshua 2:11.
9. Psalm 99:1.
10. Psalm 11:4; see also, e.g., 33:13–15, 103:19.
11. Psalm 103:19.
12. Isaiah 66:1.
13. Psalm 115:16.
14. Deuteronomy 26:15.
15. Ecclesiastes 5:2.
16. Deuteronomy 10:14–15.
17. Isaiah 57:15.
18. Genesis 1:1; see, e.g., Exodus 20:11; 2 Kings 19:15; Nehemiah 9:6; and frequently in the Psalms, e.g., 102:25.
19. 1 Kings 8:10–13, 27–30.
20. See 1 Kings 8:48 with, e.g., Daniel 6:10, 9:20.
21. 1 Kings 8:54–61.
22. The "name": see 1 Kings 8:16, 29; Exodus 20:24; Deuteronomy 12:11; 1 Kings 9:3, 11:36, 14:21; 2 Kings 21:7, 23:27; 2 Chronicles 6:20, 7:16, 12:13, 33:7; Psalm 74:7. On the significance of God's "name" in a place, see, e.g., Carmen Imes, *Bearing God's Name: Why Sinai Still Matters* (IVP Academic, 2019).
23. 1 Kings 8:20–21.
24. Psalm 27:4.
25. Isaiah 2:2–4.
26. Micah 4:4–5.
27. Isaiah 9:6–7.
28. Isaiah 11:9.
29. On Paul's use of Isaiah 11 in Romans 15, see chap. 13 herein.
30. Habakkuk 2:12–14.
31. See Numbers 10:11. The exact chronology is not relevant to our present purposes.
32. Numbers 13:25–14:10.
33. Numbers 14:10–12; cf. Leviticus 9:4, 23–24.
34. Numbers 14:13–14.
35. Numbers 14:17–18, echoing Exodus 34:6–7.
36. Numbers 14:20–23.
37. Psalm 72:20.
38. 72:3–4.
39. 72:8–11, 15–17.
40. 72:12–14.
41. 72:18–19.
42. Ezekiel 10–11. See chap. 4 herein.
43. E.g., Psalm 104:21, 27–30, leading directly to vv. 31–32: "May the glory of YHWH endure forever; may YHWH rejoice in his works—who looks on the earth and it trembles, who touches the mountains and they smoke."
44. Romans 15:13.
45. Luke 19:41–44.
46. John 1:14, 2:21.

CHAPTER 3: CREATION AND TEMPLE: THE GLORY COMES TO DWELL

1. For the whole theme, see Wright, *History and Eschatology*, chap. 5, and the further material there; and see especially Middleton, *Liberating Image*.
2. See exactly this sense, in relation to the Jerusalem temple, at Psalm 132:8, 14.
3. Exodus 19; 1 Peter 2; Revelation 1, 5, and so on. See especially Wright, *History and Eschatology*, chap. 5; N. T. Wright, *Virtue Reborn* [US title *After You Believe*] (SPCK and HarperOne, 2010).
4. N. T. Wright, *Paul and the Faithfulness of God* (SPCK and Fortress Press, 2013), chap. 10.
5. Romans 4:13, 8:12–30.
6. E.g., Psalm 2:7–9.
7. That, at least, is one interpretation of the relevant Hebrew phrase, which could also mean "beside him" or "over him."
8. Genesis 28:13–15.
9. Genesis 28:16.
10. For the idea of stones marking God's homemaking promises, compare Joshua 4:1–24; in Habakkuk 2:9–11 the stones in the wall of the house will themselves cry out against the idolatrous inhabitants, imitating Babel in their selfish lust for security.
11. See, e.g., Exodus 3:18, 5:1, 10:9, 12:12; Numbers 33:4; compare Isaiah 19:1; Jeremiah 43:13.
12. Exodus 19:4–6.
13. See N. T. Wright, *The Day the Revolution Began* (SPCK and HarperOne, 2016).
14. Exodus 24:9–11.
15. Cf., e.g., John 1:18; Colossians 1:15.
16. Exodus 33:20, 23.
17. E.g., Hans Boersma; see chap. 10 herein.
18. Leviticus 10:1–7.
19. Exodus 33:1–3.
20. Exodus 33:12–16.
21. Exodus 40:34–35.
22. See particularly Volf and McAnnaly-Linz, *Home of God*.
23. Jacob Milgrom, *Leviticus: A Book of Ritual and Ethics* (Fortress Press, 2004); and Milgrom's multivolume commentary on Leviticus in the Anchor Bible series. There is indeed a biblical doctrine of "penal substitution," but it is not based on the idea of Jesus replacing sacrificed animals. See my discussions in *The Day the Revolution Began* (HarperOne, 2016) and chap. 2 of my *Into the Heart of Romans* (Zondervan, 2023).
24. Leviticus 17:11. I owe a great deal here to the work of my colleague David Moffitt: see especially his *Rethinking the Atonement* (Baker, 2022).
25. 1 Samuel 4:3.
26. 1 Samuel 4:6–9.
27. 1 Samuel 4:19–22.
28. 1 Samuel 5.
29. 2 Samuel 7:11b–16.
30. 2 Samuel 11.
31. 1 Kings 8:6, 10–11.

32. 1 Kings 8:12–13; see Exodus 19:9 and so on. The "forever" in Solomon's prayer is of course an overreach; as God makes clear, the promise to place the divine name in the temple is conditional on obedience.
33. 1 Kings 8:20–21.
34. 1 Kings 8:27.
35. 1 Kings 8:29–30.
36. 1 Kings 8:43.
37. 1 Kings 8:48.
38. 1 Kings 8:59–60.
39. 1 Kings 9:6–9.
40. 2 Kings 12:28; cf. Exodus 32:8.
41. 2 Kings 17:5–41.
42. Jeremiah 4:23.

CHAPTER 4: THE DEPARTING AND RETURNING GLORY

1. Ezekiel: 43: 1–2, 4–5.
2. Ezekiel 44:1–3.
3. Ezekiel 47:1–12.
4. Ezekiel 48:35.
5. Ezekiel 36:35–36.
6. Ezekiel 34:25–31.
7. Isaiah 35:1–6.
8. Isaiah 40:4–5, 10–11.
9. Isaiah 52:7–10.
10. Isaiah 40:8.
11. Isaiah 55:10–13.
12. Isaiah 59:15–16, 20.
13. Isaiah 60:1–3, 19.
14. Isaiah 61:1–3.
15. Isaiah 63:9.
16. Isaiah 64:1–2.
17. Isaiah 66:1–2.
18. Isaiah 66:15, 22.
19. Zephaniah 3:14–17.
20. Haggai 2:4–9.
21. Zechariah 1:16. This translation is that of Nicholas King, *The Bible: A Study Bible Freshly Translated by Nicholas King* (Kevin Mayhew, 2013). Most standard English versions make this a past tense ("I *have returned*" or near equivalent); other exceptions include New International Version ("I will return"). Goldingay implies an immediate future rather than a past event ("I'm turning back to Yerushalaim in compassion"). The Hebrew is *shabti*, as in 8:3, which is normally rendered as future. The Septuagint *epistrepsō* is unambiguously future, as are the other Greek verbs in the verse.
22. Zechariah 2:10–13 (2:14–17 Masoretic Text/Septuagint).

23. Zechariah 8:2–3.
24. Zechariah 9:9–10, 14.
25. See Wright, *Jesus and the Victory of God*, 615–24; Wright, *Paul and the Faithfulness of God*, 104–7, and frequently (see index, s.v. "YHWH, return of").
26. Malachi 3:1–3.
27. Malachi 4:5–6.
28. Isaiah 35:4, leading at once to the promise of blind eyes being opened—the promise echoed by Jesus in, e.g., Matthew 11. Perhaps part of the point is the need for blind eyes to be opened to see clearly what is going on.
29. Isaiah 40:5.
30. Isaiah 52:8, following the word about the messenger announcing to Zion, "Your God reigns."
31. I assume that this book was written sometime in the late second century BC.
32. 2 Maccabees 2:7–8. "The place" is a reference to the temple.
33. For other second-temple signs of the unfulfilled "glory appearing" promise, see Wright, *Paul and the Faithfulness of God*, 104–7, with notes.
34. Matthew 5:23, 8:4, 23:18.
35. Josephus, *Jewish War*, 6:299–300.
36. bYom 21b: see *Paul and the Faithfulness of God*, 106 n. 134.
37. On messianic movements, see N. T. Wright, *The New Testament and the People of God* (SPCK and Fortress, 1992), 307–20; Wright, *Jesus and the Victory of God*, chap. 11; M. V. Novenson, *Christ among the Messiahs: Christ Language in Paul and Messiah Language in Ancient Judaism* (Oxford University Press, 2015).
38. E.g., Ezekiel 34:23–24.
39. Isaiah 55:3.
40. John 20:19–23.

CHAPTER 5: THE HUMAN FACE OF THE GOD WHO COMES

1. A recent example: S. J. Duby, *Jesus and the God of Classical Theism* (Baker Academic, 2022).
2. See especially N. T. Wright, *History and Eschatology: Jesus and the Promise of Natural Theology* (Baylor University Press, 2019), chap. 3.
3. See the "Interlude," chap. 7 herein.
4. On Bultmann, see especially Wright, *History and Eschatology*.
5. In what follows, I am running in parallel to Richard Hays, *Echoes of Scripture in the Gospels* (Baylor University Press, 2016). I am exploring one particular thread within a much larger tapestry.
6. Mark 1:7–8.
7. Mark 1:11.
8. Mark 9:2–13, ending with the disciples' puzzled question about "Elijah" who was expected to "come first" (Mark 9:11). "First" here clearly refers to a sequence in which Elijah is to be followed by YHWH.
9. On the different parties, groups, and expectations, see, e.g., N. T. Wright, *The New Testament and the People of God* (Fortress Press, 1992), part 3. The Sadducees, so

far as we can tell, were neither wanting nor expecting any great change; they were clinging to their precarious quasi-aristocratic power.

10. Matthew 1:23.
11. Matthew 28:18.
12. See Wright, *The Day the Revolution Began.*
13. See Wright, *The New Testament and the People of God*, 302–7; and see, e.g., J. T. Pennington, *Heaven and Earth in the Gospel of Matthew* (Baker Academic, 2007).
14. See Wright, *History and Eschatology* chaps. 2, 4; and "Hope Deferred: Against the Dogma of Delay," in *Early Christianity* 9, no. 1 (2018): 37–82.
15. See N. T. Wright, *Jesus and the Victory of God* (Fortress Press, 1997), chap. 12.
16. On the problems connected with notions of "miracle," see Wright, *History and Eschatology* chaps. 1–2.
17. Matthew 11:4–6.
18. Matthew 12:31–32.
19. See Wright, *History and Eschatology*, chap. 5.
20. Matthew 11:2–15, quoting Isaiah 5.
21. Matthew 11:7–15, 17:10–13.
22. Matthew 11:28–30.
23. Luke 8:39.
24. I have argued this case more fully in Wright, *Jesus and the Victory of God*, chap. 13.
25. Luke 19:42–44. The idea of God "visiting" for judgment is clear in passages like Jeremiah 31:44, Septuagint (Masoretic Text 48:44).
26. Luke 24:25.
27. Acts 2:1–4; see N. T. Wright, *The Challenge of Acts* (SPCK and Zondervan Academic, 2024), chap. 2.
28. John 14:9.
29. John 2:19; Mark 14:58.
30. John 2:21.
31. John 20:12. This point is made by Rowan Williams, following B. F. Westcott (see Williams, *On Christian Theology* [Oxford: Blackwell, 2000], 186f.; cf. Wright, *Resurrection of the Son of God*, 668).
32. See too 1:33, 3:5–8, 34, 4:23–24, 6:63, and especially 7:37–39. These remain cryptic without the much fuller material in chaps. 14–16, and the denouement in 20:19–23.
33. John 15:26–27, 16:7–15.
34. John 20:21–23.
35. Isaiah 63:11; Haggai 2:5; Nehemiah 9:20. See chap. 7 herein.
36. John 20:15.

CHAPTER 6: THE APPARENT EXCEPTIONS

1. For parallel explorations, cf. J. Richard Middleton, *A New Heaven and A New Earth* (Baker Academic, 2014). Several of the points herein have already been discussed in more detail in Wright, *Resurrection of the Son of God*, and Wright, *Surprised by Hope*.

2. Luke 23:42.
3. Luke 23:43. The "placard" is noted in all four gospels: Matthew 27:37; Mark 15:26; Luke 23:38; John 19:19.
4. Cf. Philippians 1:3; 2 Corinthians 5:8.
5. Elsewhere in 2 Corinthians 12:4; Revelation 2:7.
6. On Tertullian, see chaps. 9, 10 herein.
7. John 14:23.
8. The new *Cambridge Greek Lexicon* gives three regular classical meanings: a place to stay, a pause or waiting time on a journey, a resting place. It adds a fourth, "residence"—but cites only the New Testament for this, presumably with the "normal" reading of the present passage in mind.
9. See too *Orientis Graeci Inscriptiones Selectai*, ed. W. Dittenberger (1903–1905), 527:5, rendered by LSJ (Liddell and Scott's *Greek-English Lexicon*) as "quarters" or "billets" for troops: that is, precisely not their permanent "homes." Also Philo *Moses* 1.316, referring to soldiers who remained in camp. LSJ offers "apartments" for John 14:2, 23.
10. *Strom.* 2.18.96.2.
11. John 14:18–21, 23–26, 28.
12. This becomes particularly important in the discussions in chap. 14 herein.
13. See the full discussion in my *Resurrection of the Son of God,* 364–71.
14. On this passage see my *Resurrection of the Son of God*, 225–36.
15. 1 Corinthians 15:28.
16. Mark 10:21 / Luke 18:23; and see Matthew 6:30 / Luke 12:33; see, e.g., Colossians 1:5; 2 Timothy 4:8; 1 Peter 1:4.
17. Luke 16:19–31; see the full discussion in Wright, *Jesus and the Victory of God,* 255–56.
18. On the phrase in Judaean writings see *Resurrection of the Son of God* 437–38; and H. L. Strack and P. Billerbeck, *Kommentar zum Neuen Testament aus Talmud und Midrasch.* 6 vols. C. H. Beck, 1926–1956. 2:225–27.
19. The verse in question reads, "Changed from glory into glory, / Till in heaven we take our place / Till we cast our crowns before thee, / Lost in wonder, love and praise." The first line is taken from 2 Corinthians 3:18, and the rest from Revelation 4:10, both of which are references to present realities, not simply future ones.

CHAPTER 7: THE HOMECOMING OF GOD: FILLED WITH THE SPIRIT

1. I am here developing the line of thought I began to pursue in Wright, *History and Eschatology*, chap. 8.
2. Isaiah 63:11–14.
3. Haggai 2:4–5.
4. Haggai 2:6–9.
5. Nehemiah 9:19–20.
6. See Wright, *Into the Heart of Romans*, chaps. 4–7, on Romans 8:12–30.
7. Romans 8:22.
8. Romans 8:23.

9. Romans 8:21; see too Galatians 1:1–5, where the gift of the spirit is seen as the beginning of the fulfillment of the "inheritance" promise; see my *Galatians* (Eerdmans, 2021).
10. See the fuller discussion in chap. 9 herein.
11. Isaiah 11:9.
12. 2 Corinthians 4:6.
13. The only other New Testament occurrences are referring to the "fulfilling" of the time for Jesus to be "taken up" (Luke 9:51) and the moment when the disciples' boat is "filling up" with water (Luke 8:23).
14. See, e.g., Acts 4:8, 31; 6:3, 5; 7:55; 9:17; 11:24; 13:9, 52. I have developed this understanding of Acts 2 a bit further in my recent *The Challenge of Acts* (SPCK and Zondervan, 2024).
15. John 14:23–24.
16. John 7:37–39.
17. 1:14, 2:21.
18. Some have read 7:37–38 differently, with Jesus as the one out of whose heart will flow rivers of living water. But this would make little difference to the understanding of 20:19–23 I am proposing.
19. John 12:20–32.
20. Matthew 5:28–41
21. John 20:31. I follow those who, noting the absence of the definite article before "Jesus," conclude that the *subject* of the sentence is "Messiah, son of God" and that "Jesus" is the *complement*—which matches the opening remark in 1:45, which could be rendered roughly "we've found the Messiah, and it's Jesus."
22. See too the "royal" overtones of this vocation in 2 Samuel 14:17; 1 Kings 3:9.
23. Mark 1:15
24. John 16:8–11.
25. John 12:31.
26. See the detailed discussion in N. T. Wright and Michael F. Bird, *Jesus and the Powers* (SPCK and Zondervan, 2024), 62–63, and the larger context. On the relevant Acts passages, see N. T. Wright, *The Challenge of Acts* (SPCK and Zondervan, 2024).

CHAPTER 8: SWITCHING THE SCRIPT? THE BIBLE AND THE CHRISTIAN TRADITION

1. See Wright, *The Resurrection of the Son of God*, chap. 3.
2. A clear and winsome exposition of this point of view is offered by Ephraim Radner, *Time and the Word: Figural Reading of the Christian Scriptures* (Eerdmans, 2021).
3. Apart from a brief period of independence from the 160s BC to 46 BC; see Wright, *The New Testament and the People of God*, part 3; Wright, *Paul and the Faithfulness of God*, chap. 2.
4. E.g., Luke 7:50, 8:48.
5. Ben F. Meyer, *The Aims of Jesus* (Fortress Press and SCM, 1979).
6. On the "intermediate state" and similar questions, see chap. 14 herein.

7. A good example of Paul saying exactly this is in Philippians 3:2–11.
8. For this theme, and a strong refutation of it in relation to the early period, see M. V. Novenson, *The Grammar of Messianism: An Ancient Jewish Political Idiom and Its Users* (Oxford University Press, 2017), chap. 6.
9. See especially Peter Brown, *The Ransom of the Soul: Afterlife and Wealth in Early Christianity* (Harvard University Press, 2015).
10. Luke 24:13–35.
11. See the veiled criticism by C. E. B. Cranfield, *A Critical and Exegetical Commentary on the Epistle to the Romans*, vol. 2 (T & T Clark, 1979), 867. He speaks of Paul's vision of "vast and splendid reaches of the truth of Christ which lie beyond the ken of all Marcionites and semi-, crypto-, and unwitting, Marcionites."
12. A good example from the earlier exegetical period: Eduard Schweizer, *The Letter to Colossians: A Commentary* (Augsburg, 1983 [1976]), 22, interprets "Christ is the end of the law" as "the end of all self-righteous judgments."
13. On Romans 10:4, see e.g., Wright, *Paul and the Faithfulness of God*, 1165–76, esp. 1172.
14. See N. T. Wright, *Paul and His Recent Interpreters* (SPCK and Fortress, 2015), part 1.
15. 2 Corinthians 3:6.
16. 1 Corinthians 1:23.
17. See, e.g., Wright, *Paul and His Recent Interpreters*, part 2; Wright, *History and Eschatology*, chaps. 2, 4. It is unfortunate that E. van Driel, *Rethinking Paul: Protestant Theology and Pauline Exegesis* (Cambridge University Press, 2021), one of the few recent systematic theologians to wrestle with current Pauline scholarship, perpetuates the false either/or of "covenant" and "apocalyptic."
18. Luke 24:25–26.
19. Luke 24:27.
20. E.g., Galatians 4:21–5:1, on which, see Wright, *Galatians*.
21. On Sabbath, see N. T. Wright, *Scripture and the Authority of God*, 2nd ed. (SPCK; HarperOne, 2011), chap. 9; and Wright, *History and Eschatology*, chap. 5.
22. Matthew 8:11. See Genesis 12, 15; Psalm 2, 47; Isaiah 49; and the whole argument of Romans, Galatians, and Ephesians. Also, Revelation 7:9, "a huge gathering which nobody could possibly count, from every nation and tribe and people and language."
23. See, e.g., Galatians 2:11–21, with the discussion in my *Galatians*; and Ephesians 2:11–22, on which, see chap. 13 herein.
24. See, e.g., Romans 14.
25. Mark 7:19.
26. Luke 23:34; Acts 7:60; Romans 12:19–21.
27. Romans 15:7–13; see chap. 13 herein.
28. For that particular view, in the Isaiah Targum, see Wright, *Jesus and the Victory of God*, 590.
29. See, e.g., John 12:31, 14:30, 16:11, 33; Colossians 2:15; Revelation 6:2, 19:1–8, 11–21; and Jesus's cryptic saying at Matthew 10:28; Luke 12:4–5. See Wright, *The Day the Revolution Began*.
30. See, e.g., Peter Carnley, *Resurrection in Retrospect* (Cascade Books, 2019),

pleading explicitly and somewhat plaintively for a platonic view. See my brief comments in *History and Eschatology* chap. 6, and the earlier critique in *The Resurrection of the Son of God*, 643, and elsewhere (see the index). I am reminded of the cartoon in which a Mother Superior is complaining to the bishop about a death-watch beetle in the convent roof, to which he replies, "It may help to think of it as a metaphor."

31. See Louth, *The Origins of the Christian Mystical Tradition*; and Wright, *The Resurrection of the Son of God*, chap. 3; Wright, *History and Eschatology*, e.g., 190.
32. 1 Corinthians 15:20–28.
33. See Wright, *The Resurrection of the Son of God*, chap. 4.
34. Mark 10:35–45. On Bar Kochba, see Wright, *The New Testament and the People of God*,165–66, and, e.g., P. Schäfer, *The History of the Jews in the Greco-Roman World* (Routledge, 2003).
35. See N. T. Wright, *Paul: A Biography* (SPCK and HarperOne, 2018).
36. Romans 10:2.

CHAPTER 9: GOD'S ARRIVAL ON EARTH OR THE SOUL'S ARRIVAL IN HEAVEN?

1. Harnack's magnum opus was originally published in 1894 and has gone through many subsequent editions in German, English, and other languages.
2. On Marcion's view of the Hebrew scriptures, see, e.g., B. Strawn, *The Old Testament Is Dying: A Diagnosis and Recommended Treatment* (Baker Academic, 2017), especially chap. 5.
3. On the problems with "historical criticism," see Wright, *History and Eschatology*, chaps. 2, 3, 4.
4. See Wright, *Jesus and the Victory of God*, throughout; and, more popularly, N. T. Wright, *The Challenge of Jesus* (SPCK and InterVarsity Press, 2001); and N. T. Wright, *Simply Jesus* (SPCK and HarperOne, 2011).
5. 2 Corinthians 10:5.
6. See Wright, *Scripture and the Authority of God.*
7. Galatians 4:1–11, on which see my *Galatians.*
8. See Henry Chadwick, "The Chalcedonian Definition," in *Selected Writings*, ed. William G. Rusch (Eerdmans, 2017 [1983]), 101–14. See the discussion in Wright, *History and Eschatology*, 303.
9. Wright, *Paul and the Faithfulness of God*, chaps. 2–5.
10. See Wright, *The New Testament and the People of God*, 199.
11. See especially Louth, *Origins of the Christian Mystical Tradition*; and see particularly chap. 10 herein.
12. Brown, *Ransom of the Soul*, 9. For a full picture of the relevant material in the period we would want to add Irenaeus of Lyons (AD 130–202), on whom see Wright, *The Resurrection of the Son of God*, 513–17. I am grateful to the historian Tom Holland for alerting me to Brown's book when it came out.
13. Brown, *Ransom of the Soul*, 12.
14. Brown, *Ransom of the Soul*, 13. Origen did indeed believe in the resurrection but

interpreted it significantly differently: see Wright, *The Resurrection of the Son of God*, 518–27.

15. See, e.g., Plutarch "On Exile."
16. See, e.g., J. Le Goff, *The Birth of Purgatory* (University of Chicago Press, 1984 [1981]); Stephen Greenblatt, *Hamlet in Purgatory* (Princeton University Press, 2001).
17. See now Wright and Bird, *Jesus and the Powers*, especially chaps. 2, 5.
18. See chap. 10 herein.
19. The earlier frescoes I have in mind include the remarkable paintings (1499–1502) of Luca Signorelli in the Chapel of San Brizio within the cathedral of Orvieto.
20. See Wright, *Paul and His Recent Interpreters*, chap. 3; n.b. especially the statement of Barth in Church Dogmatics 4.1.622–23, quoted in Wright, *Paul and His Recent Interpreters*, 86.
21. See Wright, *Into the Heart of Romans*, chaps. 5, 6.
22. See Wright, *History and Eschatology*, chap. 1.
23. C. S. Lewis, *Miracles: A Preliminary Study*. Fontana 1960 [1947].

CHAPTER 10: THE IMAGINED GOAL AND THE UNNECESSARY JOURNEY

1. Hans Boersma, *Five Things Theologians Wish Biblical Scholars Knew* (Eerdmans, 2022); and Boersma, *Seeing God: The Beatific Vision in Christian Tradition* (Eerdmans, 2022). I also have in mind J. Saward, *O Sweet and Blessed Country: The Christian Hope for Heaven* (Oxford University Press, 2005).
2. See my fuller critique: "The Vision of God and the Kingdom of God: Theological and Ecumenical Reflections," in *Rhetoric, History, and Theology: Interpreting the New Testament*, ed. T. D. Still and J. A. Myers (Fortress Academic, 2002), 257–73.
3. Isaiah 6; Exodus 33:17–23 (but see Exodus 24:9–11). Jesus declares that the angels who look after vulnerable children always behold God's face (Matthew 18:10).
4. See P. Gooder, *Only the Third Heaven? 2 Corinthians 12:1–10 and Heavenly Ascent* (T & T Clark, 2006).
5. So M. Bockmuehl, *Revelation and Mystery in Ancient Judaism and Pauline Christianity* (Eerdmans, 1990), 175–77.
6. The privileging of "sight" has its own problems, as those of us who have written about world*views* have discovered.
7. Revelation 5:10; see 1:6, 20:6; and see Romans 5:17; 1 Peter 2:9; and see my exposition of this in *After You Believe* (HarperOne, 2010; UK title: *Virtue Reborn*).
8. Saward, *Sweet and Blessed Country*, 52–55.
9. See Wright, *History and Eschatology*, chap. 8; and Wright, *Surprised by Hope*, part 3.
10. This builds on the previous discussion in my *Surprised by Hope*, chap. 11.
11. See especially Greenblatt, *Hamlet in Purgatory*.
12. See, e.g., J. Ratzinger, "Eschatology: Death and Eternal Life," in *Dogmatic Theology* (Catholic University of America Press, 1988 [1977]), chap. 9.

13. E.g., Paul J. Griffiths, "Purgatory," in *The Oxford Handbook of Eschatology*, ed. J. L. Walls (Oxford University Press, 2008), 427–45.
14. See Wright, *Surprised by Hope*, chap. 11, part 2.
15. 1 Thessalonians 4:15, 17; 1 Corinthians 15:51; see Daniel 12:2.
16. Gergely M. Juhász, *Translating Resurrection: The Debate between William Tyndale and George Joye in Its Historical and Theological Context* (Brill, 2014).
17. See particularly Wright, *History and Eschatology*, throughout.
18. See again Boersma, *Five Things*.
19. This supplements the argument in my *Surprised by Hope*, chap. 11, part 2.
20. 1 Corinthians 15:29. See the discussion in Wright, *The Resurrection of the Son of God*, 338–40.
21. See the discussion in Wright, *Jesus and the Victory of God*, 255–56.
22. Ratzinger, "Eschatology: Death and Eternal Life," 228–33.
23. J. L. González, *The Story of Christianity*, vol. 1, *The Early Church to the Dawn of the Reformation*, 2nd ed. (Bravo, 2010), 288 (my italics). I owe this reference to Amy Hollingsworth.
24. Romans 8:1; see Wright, *Into the Heart of Romans*, 28–61.
25. For instance, Jerry Walls in his various writings.
26. I think this is what J. T. Turner is arguing in his proposal of "eschatological presentism," e.g., J. T. Turner, *On the Resurrection of the Dead: A New Metaphysics of Afterlife for Christian Thought* (Routledge, 2019).
27. David Brown, "No Heaven without Purgatory," *Religious Studies* 21 (1985); J. Polkinghorne, *The God of Hope and the End of the World* (Yale University Press, 2002), makes the first point; Jerry L. Walls makes the second, in *Purgatory: The Logic of Total Transformation* (Oxford University Press, 2012).
28. That word itself suggests a bipartite reality, offering an implicit concession to Plato while insisting that he must not have the last word. I use it heuristically.
29. Jerry L. Walls, *Heaven, Hell, and Purgatory: A Protestant View of the Cosmic Drama* (Brazos, 2015), 137.
30. This is one of the central arguments of my Gifford Lectures, *History and Eschatology* (2019).
31. On the use of Psalm 8 in Romans 8, see especially H. G. Jacob, *Conformed to the Image of His Son: Reconsidering Paul's Theology of Glory in Romans* (IVP Academic, 2018); and my *Into the Heart of Romans*, chaps. 5–7.
32. Matthew 3:11.
33. See Romans 13:1–7; and Bird and Wright, *Jesus and the Powers*. For Jesus and Pilate, see John 19:11.
34. See, e.g., Saward, *Sweet and Blessed Country*.
35. See my *Scripture and the Authority of God*.
36. On this whole theme, and its interrelation with other key themes, see Wright, *History and Eschatology*, chap. 5.
37. H. Boersma, already mentioned, is a vigorous advocate for this view: see recently *Five Things* and his many longer works. See too R. R. Reno, *The End of Interpretation: Reclaiming the Priority of Ecclesial Exegesis* (Baker Academic, 2022), which argues specifically that the Bible should *only* be read through the lens of later creedal orthodoxy. We might compare the series of biblical commentaries,

written by systematic theologians, published by Brazos Press in the early years of the century.

38. Ephesians 1:10. This statement becomes thematic for the whole book: see N. T. Wright, *The Vision of Ephesians* (SPCK and Zondervan, 2025).

CHAPTER 11: WORSHIP, EVANGELISM, AND PRAYER

1. See the important survey by John Barclay, *Paul and the Gift* (Eerdmans, 2015), part 1.
2. Psalm 23:6.
3. See Wright, *History and Eschatology*, chap. 8; see R. Stark, *The Rise of Christianity* (HarperOne, 1996).
4. P. Shaffer, *Equus*, Act 2.
5. Some interpreters, and translators, have read 40:9 in terms of Jerusalem being the "herald," but I think the Hebrew text, and the parallel with 52:7, makes this less likely.
6. Matthew 3:3; Mark 1:3; Luke 3:4–6; John 1:23. They describe the message in terms of the same Greek verb: Mark 1:14–15; Luke 3:18.
7. As in Luke 19:41–44.
8. On "gospel" in Paul, see the index to Wright, *Paul and the Faithfulness of God*. For the summaries of Paul's preaching, see, e.g., Acts 12, 14, 17, and his own comments in 1 Corinthians 1–2.
9. On this point, and what follows in terms of atonement theology, see Wright, *The Day the Revolution Began*.
10. 1 Thessalonians 1:9–10.
11. On the negative side of the story, see my *Surprised by Hope*, chap. 11, section 4. (Page numbers vary in the UK and US editions.)
12. John 12:31–32.
13. See, e.g., Ephesians 2:8–10.
14. Revelation 3:20.
15. G. W. Briggs, "Come, Risen Lord" (1931).
16. Galatians 2:20.
17. John 13:1. On Epictetus, see Wright, *Paul and the Faithfulness of God*, 223–27.
18. See Wright, *Into the Heart of Romans*, chap. 6.
19. 1 Corinthians 16:22.
20. See the chapter on prayer in N. T. Wright, *Simply Christian* (SPCK and HarperSanFrancisco, 2006).

CHAPTER 12: THE SACRAMENTS

1. Schmemann, *The World as Sacrament*, (Darton, Longman and Todd, 2010 [1974]); republished as *For the Life of the World*.
2. Hopkins, "God's Grandeur"; see Wright, *History and Eschatology*, chap. 8.
3. I say "most of" because a few groups, such as the Salvation Army, do not use the sacraments.

4. E.g., G. Wainwright, *Eucharist and Eschatology* (Epworth Press, 1971); J. Moltmann *The Church in the Power of the Spirit* (SCM, 1977), chap. 5.
5. 1 Corinthians 10:1–2.
6. Mark 10:35–45.
7. John 20:21.
8. 1 Corinthians 15:11; Colossians 1:29.
9. The word originates from the concluding sentence of the Latin service, "Ite, missa est," meaning roughly "Go—there is a dismissal," i.e., "you are dismissed." But the word "missa" was then taken as a noun, referring to the whole event: "Go, the Mass is complete."
10. Acts 2:42; 1 Corinthians 11:20; in the latter passage I have translated *deipnon* as "Supper" (in my *New Testament for Everyone*, 3rd ed., 2019) but actually the Greek word refers simply to the main meal of the day, particularly a formal or celebratory one.
11. Ridley and Latimer: October 16, 1555. Cranmer: March 21, 1556.
12. On Cranmer and the detail of his developing theology, and the key and subtle issues at his trial, see above all D. MacCulloch, *Thomas Cranmer: A Life* (Yale University Press, 1997).
13. 1 Corinthians 11:26.
14. 1 Corinthians 2:2; he later (15:3–4) puts this in the larger context, including the resurrection.
15. Matthew 18:20. A remarkably similar saying is found in the early rabbis, about two or three coming together to study Torah and finding that the *Shekinah*, the tabernacling presence of God, is there with them: Mishnah *Aboth* 3:2. See Wright, *Jesus and the Victory of God*, 297.
16. E.g., 2 Corinthians 3–5.
17. Leviticus 16.
18. 1 Corinthians 11:26.
19. As we have seen, this is picked up in, e.g., Ephesians 2:11–22; see too, e.g., Colossians 1:27.
20. 2 Corinthians 1:22, 5:5; Ephesians 1:14; and compare the theme of "first fruits" in, e.g., Romans 8:23.
21. Numbers 13:23.
22. Romans 8:30.
23. Revelation 5:9–10.
24. Romans 8:18–30.
25. 1 Corinthians 10:17.

CHAPTER 13: THE POLYCHROME CHURCH AS THE SIGN TO THE POWERS

1. Revelation 7:9–10. It would be absurd to suggest—though I have sometimes heard it said—that this multilingual and multicultural reality *only* relates to the ultimate postmortem future, not to the church in the present time.
2. Acts 17:24, 26–28.

3. One alarming set of answers to the question emerges from the important recent study of D. G. Hummel, *The Rise and Fall of Dispensationalism* (Eerdmans, 2023).
4. For full details, see my *Galatians*.
5. Colossians 3:11.
6. On Ephesians see N. T. Wright, *The Vision of Ephesians* (SPCK and Zondervan, 2025).
7. See Wright, *Paul and His Recent Interpreters*, chaps. 2–5.
8. 1 Kings 8:13, 39, 43, 49.
9. E.g., Stephen Westerholm; see Wright, *Paul and His Recent Interpreters*, 123–28.
10. Ephesians 4:10.
11. I have spelled this out with full annotation in my 2023 essay "The Sign of New Creation: Romans 15:7–13," in *It's About Life: The Formative Power of Scripture; Essays in Honour of Rikk E. Watts*, ed. B. Bell et al. (Regent College Publishing, 2023), 219–37.
12. See particularly R. B. Hays, *Echoes of Scripture in the Letters of Paul* (Yale University Press, 1989); discussed in Wright, *Paul and His Recent Interpreters*, 96–102.
13. Isaiah 5:29.
14. On the whole theme of "welcome" and its biblical resonances for Paul, see Oliver Wright, "A Theological Reading of the 'Welcome' Offered by God and Christ in Romans 14–15 Using the Septuagint," *Heythrop Journal* 65, no. 3 (2024): 292–305.
15. Romans 4:11–12, 16–17; and see the whole theme of Galatians 3:1–4:7.
16. On the many ways in which the Enlightenment produced parodies of Christian truth, see Wright, *History and Eschatology*, chaps. 1, 2.
17. See now e.g. James Davison Hunter, *Democracy and Solidarity: On the Cultural Roots of America's Political Crisis*. Yale University Press, 2024.
18. Matthew 11:12; see Luke 16:16, and note Wright, *Jesus and the Victory of God*, 225, 296, 446, 468.
19. Romans 11:1; Galatians 2:15; Philippians 3:2–11.

CHAPTER 14: LIFE BEYOND DEATH AND THE CALLING OF THE CHURCH

1. Carl Boberg, translated by S. K. Hine, "How Great Thou Art." See the brief discussion in Wright, *Surprised by Hope*, chap. 2, section 3.
2. Wright, *Surprised by Hope*, chaps. 7, 8, 9.
3. Isaiah 2:12, 22:5; Jeremiah 46:10; Amos 5:18; Joel 1:15; Zephaniah 1:14.
4. Matthew 24:36.
5. Acts 2; in John 20 Jesus breathes out his spirit on his followers on the evening of Easter Day.
6. Romans 8:8–11 with, e.g., 5:17; see, e.g., Wright, *History and Eschatology*, chap. 8.
7. Luke 23:46.
8. Acts 7:59.
9. Ecclesiastes 12:7, cf. 3:21; Job 34:14; Psalm 104:29–30; Isaiah 42:5, 57:16; Zechariah 12:1. In Numbers 16:22 God is invoked as "the God of the spirits of all flesh," as also 27:16.

10. 1 Corinthians 5:5.
11. Ezekiel 37:9.
12. Ezekiel 37:14.
13. See Psalm 104:24; cf. John 1:3–5; Colossians 1:15–20.
14. Psalm 104:29–30.
15. 1 Corinthians 2:11–12.
16. 1 Corinthians 6:16–17, 19–20.
17. Romans 8:15–17, 26–27. For details, see Wright, *Into the Heart of Romans*.
18. Romans 8:9–11.
19. Colossians 3:3–4.
20. Philippians 1:23–24.
21. 2 Corinthians 5:6–8.
22. 2 Corinthians 5:4–5. On all this, see Wright, *The Resurrection of the Son of God*, 361–72.
23. John 20:21–23.
24. Ephesians 2:21–22.
25. Judges 6:34; also with Othniel, 3.10.
26. Ephesians 3:19.
27. See chap. 10 herein on Tertullian's view of life beyond death.
28. On the latter point, see Wright, *History and Eschatology*, chap. 8.
29. Romans 15:12–13.
30. Isaiah 40:3–5.
31. The word for "comfort" in the Greek version is *parakaleite*, cognate with John's word for the holy spirit, the *paraklētos*, "comforter" or "advocate" (John 14:15, etc.).
32. With, e.g., J. Goldingay and David Payne, *A Critical and Exegetical Commentary on Isaiah 40–55* (T & T Clark International, 2006), vol. 1: 86; and mindful of the obvious parallel in 52:7, I take verse 9 in the sense of the American Standard Version ("O thou that tellest good tidings to Zion") against, e.g., the New Revised Standard Version ("O Zion, herald of good tidings").
33. See my *Paul: A Biography*, 369–70.
34. Isaiah 40:27–29
35. Isaiah 40:27–31.

INDEX

Aaron, 47, 59, 60, 61–62
Abihu, 59, 60
Abraham
  call of, 19–20, 62
  God's promises to, 19, 54–55, 105
  God's renewed covenant with, 250
  God's work through family of, 52–53
  meetings with God, 55
"accidents" *vs.* "substance," 251
"age to come," 124
allegory, 160–61
All Souls Day, 197
Apocrypha, 201–2
Aquinas, 184, 185, 186, 197, 199, 251
Aristotle, xiv, 5, 251
Ark of the Covenant, 61, 63–64
arrabōn, 252, 295
"at home with the Lord," 121–22, 193, 289
Augustine, 5, 183, 185, 199, 205–6

baptism, 137, 202–3, 206, 210, 236–40
Bar Kochba rebellion, 170, 180
"beatific vision," 60, 184, 186, 189, 190–93, 293
Benedict (pope), 197
Betjeman, John, 6
Boersma, Hans, 190, 307n3
"breath," 19, 141, 284–86
Brown, Peter, 181–83, 199
Bultmann, Rudolf, 94

Caleb, 42
Callirhoe (Chariton), 118
Calvin, John, 187, 198
Catholic teaching, 4, 241–42, 247–48, 251
Chadwick, Henry, 185
Chalcedonian Definition, 174, 179
Christianity
  central doctrines of (*See* doctrines, Christian; *specific doctrines*)
  de-Judaizing of, 94
  development of thought in, 180–89
  God's homecoming central to, 3–4, 10, 17, 20–21
church. *See also* early Christians
  authority of the Bible and, 152–53, 210–13
  decline of biblical hope in, 272–76
  defined by Eucharist, 255
  development of teaching in, 180–89
  God's homecoming displayed and declared through, 220, 221, 302
  God's love embodied in, 230
  going-to-heaven story in (*See* going-to-heaven story)

church (*continued*)
intercession and lament of, 209, 297
Marcionism and, 159–60, 165, 171
mission of, 145–46, 249, 254–55, 322n19
multiethnicity in
filling of all creation anticipated by, 266–72
and homecoming, 257, 260–61, 263, 264–66, 274, 275
Paul's vision for, 258–66
resistance to, 257–58, 272–77
unity and welcome, 259–60, 261, 266–72
as new Temple
and gift of the spirit, 109–10, 112, 136, 138–39
this-worldly nature of, 166
with worldwide scope, 138, 165–66, 264, 295
platonic influence on (*See* Platonism)
power of, 241–42
present filling with holy spirit
equipped for mission by, 37, 110–11, 131, 139–40, 145
filling of all creation anticipated by, 86, 129–31, 134–37, 146, 195, 252, 282, 298
this-worldly to otherworldly "shift" taught by, 23–24, 89–91, 149–50, 153–55, 158, 163–65
unity of, 136, 195, 260, 266–72
vocation of, 4, 194–95, 302, 303
as working model of new creation, 146, 195, 252–53, 273
"citizens of heaven," 123
Clement of Alexandria, 161, 181
comfort, God's message of, 300–302
coming king
linked to promised filling of creation, 40, 43–45, 47, 84, 89
linked to YHWH dwelling forever in the midst of his people, 64, 66
linked to YHWH's return to Zion, 40, 83–84, 88–89, 92, 95–97
rule of, 38–40, 43–44, 83, 167
Council of Trent (1545–63), 196–97
Cranmer, Thomas, 15, 241, 248, 254
creation
baptism and, 236
"destruction" of, 21, 309n33
divine purpose for, 18, 20–21, 47, 282
as fulfillment of God's promises to Abraham, 55
as heaven-plus-earth reality, 18, 50
present filling of, earth, present "filling" with God's spirit
renewal of (*See* creation, promised filling of; new creation)
Tabernacle and, 20, 61, 108
Temple and, 18–19, 20, 37, 45, 50–52
work of spirit in, 141–42, 143, 236
creation, promised filling of. *See also* new creation
Eucharist and, 252
God's homecoming and, 20, 92, 283, 298
heaven and earth united in, 8, 9, 30, 195
Jesus's embodiment of, 120, 130, 131
early Christians' understanding of, 45, 88, 112, 168, 298
as gospels' main theme, 92, 97, 98, 108, 113
gospel writers' understanding of, 112, 130, 131
Jesus's final fulfillment of, 131, 139
judgment and justice in, 20, 30–32, 40, 43–44
with knowledge and glory of God, 8, 38, 40, 41, 46, 124, 130, 135

pointers to
creatures looking to God for food, 46
filling of Tabernacle, 43, 61, 62–63, 85–86, 108, 134, 135
filling of Temple, 38, 45, 47, 86, 90, 108, 109, 135, 136
promise of coming king linked to, 40, 43–45, 47, 84, 89
return to Zion as specific focus of (*See* Zion, YHWH's return to)
salvation and, 11
spirit's present work anticipating
proclaimed by Isaiah, 86
through church, 86, 129–31, 134–37, 146, 195, 252, 282, 298
unthwarted by wickedness, 41–43
as vision of messianic kingdom, 38–41, 43–45, 135
creational monotheism, 4, 46
creeds, 174, 178, 179, 185
Cyprian of Carthage, 16, 158, 181–82, 200

Dante, 184, 186, 197
David, 64, 65–66, 67, 105, 250
death
bodily, 206, 207–8, 295, 296
early Christian view of, 169, 283
funerals and, 278–80
intercession and, 202, 203, 297
of Jesus (*See under* Jesus)
platonic view of, 169, 207, 208
psychosomatic, 208, 295, 296
Deism, 102–3
disciples
cleansing of, 142–43
expectations of Messiah, 163, 168
filling with spirit, 109, 138
Jesus's breathing on, 111–12, 140, 141–43
Last Supper significance for, 243
mission of, 99, 139, 142
new temple and, 112, 117, 138–39
sins forgiven/retained by, 112, 143–45
doctrines, Christian
atonement, 311n23
creeds, 174, 178, 179, 185
fourth- and fifth-century context for, 184
going-to-heaven story and, 176–77
Harnack's thesis and, 173, 174, 175–76
Incarnation, 174, 176
"justification by faith," 186–87, 196
purgatory (*See* purgatory, doctrine of)
vs. story of scripture, 176–77, 178
transubstantiation, 242
Trinity, 213, 304
Dream of Gerontius (Newman), 197
dualism, 5–6, 13. *See also* Platonism

early Christians. *See also* disciples
connections made by
coming king and filling of all creation, 130
coming king and YHWH's dwelling forever in the midst of his people, 64, 66
coming king and YHWH's return to Zion, 83–84, 88–89, 92, 95–97
God's homecoming as central story for, 3, 4, 10, 16–17, 23, 45, 66
Israel's scriptures as context for, 45, 49–50, 57, 90–91, 158, 164, 165
Jesus's fulfillment of OT promises for, 45, 88–89, 298
multiethnic communities of, 259
Platonism foreign to, 191
spirit's equipping of, 37, 110–11, 129–30, 131, 139–40, 145

early Christians (*continued*)
spirit's fulfillment of OT promises for, 45, 88, 131, 298
witness and mission of, 99, 101–2, 112, 169, 294
earth. *See also* world
creational monotheistic view of, 4, 46
dualistic view of, 68
God's rule over, 10, 12
God's transcendence, immanence and, 37
promised filling of (*See* creation, promised filling of)
relationship to heaven (*See* heaven-and-earth metaphysic)
earth, present "filling" with God's spirit
heaven–earth intersection and, 8, 9 (*See also* heaven-and-earth metaphysic)
in Israel's scriptures, 28, 31, 32, 86 (*See also under* Tabernacle; Temple)
through gift of the spirit, 16, 17, 298 (*See also under* spirit of God)
Eli, 63
Elijah, 27, 34–35, 70, 103, 105, 119, 313n8
Elisha, 70, 103
Emmanuel promise, 66
Emmaus, 107, 158, 163, 168, 228
Epicureanism, 29, 102–3, 183, 188
eschatology. *See* creation, promised filling of; second coming
"eternal life," 124
Eucharist, 240–55
church's mission and, 249, 254–55, 322n19
controversies over, 241–44, 247–54
God's homecoming and, 243, 244–45, 252–55
names for, 240–41
evangelion, 224
evangelism, 222–31
Exile
vs. home and worship, 56–57
Israel's sin and, 66, 69, 301
promised return to Zion and, 301
Exodus–Exile narrative, 57–63, 236, 237, 301. *See also* Tabernacle; Temple
Ezekiel, 72, 285

Flavius Josephus, 119, 155–56, 157–58
food, sharing, 228–29
food laws, 166–67
funerals, 278–80

Gentiles, 166, 261, 265, 269, 277
Gledhill, Ruth, 7
Gnosticism, 181
God (YHWH)
comforting message of, 300–302
heavenly domain of, 9–10, 29–30, 32–33
intention to dwell in the world, 10, 12, 18, 20, 37, 52
judgment of
at filling of all creation, 30–32, 107
at return to Zion, 40, 84–85, 86
"visiting" for, 107, 314n25
love of, 140–41, 229–30, 282, 294
presence with Israelites, 57–63, 65–66, 301
departure from, 45, 60–61, 63–64, 71, 72 (*See also* Tabernacle; Temple)
purposes for creation, 18–21, 34, 47, 51, 163–64, 282
purposes for humans, 51–52, 59, 69, 163–64, 301
return of (*See* Zion, YHWH's return to)
sovereign, saving rule of, 10, 12
transcendent and immanent nature of, 37, 68, 208

viewed as "distant," 93, 102–3
work of, through humans, 19–20, 37, 47, 102 (*See also* vocation of humans)
"going to be with God," 34–35, 37, 50–51, 59–60
going-to-heaven story
church and theological developments leading to, 172–77, 180–89, 190
cultural assumptions informing, 12, 92–93
"heaven" misunderstood in, 7–12, 28–29, 68
hermeneutics and, 12, 89–90, 304
impact of
on atonement theories, 225
on biblical interpretation and teaching, 17, 21, 22, 92–93, 94, 99–100, 150, 304
decline of biblical hope, 272–73
divisions within church, 257
Eucharistic controversies, 249
on evangelism, 225–26, 227–28
fragmentation of gospels, 94
on purgatory doctrine, 189, 195–96, 197–99, 205
on view of intermediate state, 293
on view of second coming, xi–xii, 22–23, 119–20
language assumptions informing, 21–22
philosophical assumptions informing, 29, 93, 102–3, 183, 188 (*See also* Platonism)
"soul" misunderstood in, 7, 12–16, 211
widespread belief in, 3, 6, 12, 13, 21–22, 23, 278–79
going-to-heaven story, lack of support for
in broad story of scripture, 20
apparent exceptions, 114–28
in early Christian beliefs (*See* early Christians: God's homecoming as central story for)
in historical documents, 155–56
in Israel's scriptures
creation story, 18, 19
Abraham's family, 34–35, 36, 54, 55–56, 59–60, 62–63
prophets and psalms, 84, 85, 202
in New Testament, 11–12, 22–23, 47–48, 97, 98, 113
Goldingay, John, 308n22, 312n21
González, Justo, 205–6
gospel
ethnic barriers removed by, 262, 264–65, 272, 274
moralized version of, 225–26
platonic interpretation of, 5, 17–18, 94 (*See also* going-to-heaven story)
between present and future "comings," 298–99
gospels, 95–112
canonicity of, 309n34
coming king linked to YHWH's return in, 92, 96–97, 106, 108
fragmentation of, 94
God's homecoming depicted by, 92, 93, 98, 100, 113, 223–24
Israel's scriptures as context for, 95–96, 97–98, 99, 105, 302
misreading of, 92–95, 99–100
grace, 219, 239, 240, 245–46, 247, 302–3
Great Divorce, The (Lewis), 22
Gregory the Great, 205–6

Harnack, Adolf von, 172–73, 174–77, 200, 213
heaven
as God's domain, 9–10, 29–30, 32–33, 34, 125
God's transcendence, immanence and, 37

heaven (*continued*)
medieval view of, 184, 187
misunderstanding of, 7–12, 29, 68, 124, 126–28, 308n12 (*See also* going-to-heaven story)
NT use of term, 11, 191, 293
Reformers' view of, 187
relationship to earth (*See* heaven-and-earth metaphysic)
translation from Hebrew and Greek, 8, 9–10, 28–30, 125
treasure in, 124–25
heaven, kingdom of, 4, 12, 30, 50, 56, 99–100
heaven-and-earth metaphysic. *See also* earth; heaven
as bipartite, 8, 34, 320n28
in broad story of scripture, 8
final heaven–earth union in, 8–9, 125, 128, 195, 215, 252, 260 (*See also* new creation)
God's homecoming and, 18, 30, 51, 112
God's sovereign rule and, 9, 32–34
heaven as God's sphere in, 9–10, 29–30, 32–33
human vocation and, 51–52, 97, 209
intersection of
God's judgment at, 30–34
prayer at, 233
Tabernacle as, 9, 37, 61–62, 109
Temple as, 9, 18–19, 35–37, 68, 109, 117
in Israel's scriptures, 18, 20, 28–29, 51
one-directional movement in, 34–37
overlapping and interlocking nature of, 8–9, 29
"transcendence" and "immanence" expressed in, 37, 208
Hegel, Georg Wilhelm Friedrich, 5, 188
hell, 184
Hellenistic philosophy, 176
Hellenization thesis, 172–73, 174–77, 200
hermeneutics
academic study and, 93–94
creational monotheism and, 4
Epicureanism and, 29
going-to-heaven story and, 12, 304
homecoming framework for, 301–5
language assumptions and, 21–22
morality and, 57–58
OT approaches, 150, 152, 160–62
OT–NT continuity and, 89–91
platonic interpretation and, 17–18
Hillelite School, 181
historical criticism, 93, 175
holy spirit, xv. *See also* spirit of God
homecoming of God, 298
central to Christianity, 3–4, 10, 17, 20–21
church doctrine and (*See* doctrines, Christian)
church practices and, 302–4
baptism, 236–40
church unity, 260, 271–72
death and funerals, 202, 203, 278–80, 297
Eucharist, 243, 244–45, 252–55
evangelism, 222–31
grace, 302–3
hermeneutics, 299–305
in polarized culture, 211
prayer, 220, 231–33, 302, 304
teaching, 4–5, 189, 280
worship, 219–22
church tradition and, 213
creation intended for, 18–19, 20–21, 51, 52
distortions of (*See* going-to-heaven story; Platonism)
early Christians' understanding of, 3, 4, 10, 16–17, 23, 45, 66
grace and, 219, 245–46, 247, 302
heaven–earth union and, 30, 125, 128

human vocation and, 19, 51, 53–54, 194, 213–15
as main point of Christianity, 3–4
miracles as signs of, 104
scriptural authority and, 212–13
stones marking promises of, 56n10, 311
in story of scripture, 10, 17, 18–22, 46, 56, 57, 298 (*See also* gospels; Israel's scriptures; New Testament)
two modes of fulfillment in, 65, 79, 140, 283, 298 (*See also* Jesus; spirit of God)
homecoming of God (*continued*)
two times of fulfillment in, 130–31, 282–83, 298 (*See also* creation, promised filling of; earth, present "filling" with God's spirit)
two types of "coming" in, 283 (*See also* creation, promised filling of; Zion, YHWH's return to)
hope, biblical
decline of, 272–76
of God's homecoming, 91, 303–4
multiethnic church as sign of, 266–72
Hopkins, Gerard Manley, 234–35
"house" and "household," 65–66, 116–21
"How Great Thou Art" (Boberg), 279
humans
baptism and renewal of, 238
God's work through, 19–20, 37, 47, 102
as image at heart of Temple-creation, 18–19, 47, 51–52, 61–62, 97, 250
interior lives of, 14–15 (*See also* soul)
psychosomatic life and death of, 208, 295, 296, 320n28
true self for, 295–96
Hume, David, 102

identity, 276–77, 295–96
idolatry, 53–54, 60, 61, 225, 226, 261
immanence, 37, 68, 208
"in Abraham's bosom," 125–26
Incarnation, 140, 174, 176, 223, 226
indulgences, sale of, 196
intermediate state (between bodily death and bodily resurrection), 283–99
God's homecoming and, 282–83, 284, 288–89, 297–98
going-to-heaven story and, 278–80, 293
vs. "heaven," 293, 296–97
"paradise" and, 115, 296
purgatory and, 198, 202, 204–5, 207
"soul" and, 13, 15, 198, 283, 284, 287, 292
sustained by holy spirit
God's spirit–human spirit connection, 284–88
personal continuity, 295–96
theological implications of, 292–94, 297
"with the Messiah," 121, 283–84, 288–92, 293, 296, 297–98
Irenaeus, 158, 181, 200
Israel
as chosen family, 33, 53, 55, 58–59, 69
God's dwelling in midst of, 57–63, 65–66, 301
departure from, 60–61, 63–64, 72 (*See also* Tabernacle; Temple)
restoration of (*See* Zion, YHWH's return to)
Israel's scriptures. *See also* Old Testament; *specific promises*
as context for early Christians, 45, 49–50, 57, 90–91, 158, 164, 165
as context for gospels, 95–96, 97–98, 99, 105
as context for salvation, 151–52, 155–56
heaven-and-earth metaphysic in, 18, 20, 28–29, 51
homecoming theme in, 54–57, 58–63, 85–86

Israel's scriptures (*continued*)
message of comfort in, 300–302
"soul" in, 15, 308n23
Tabernacle and Temple in (*See* Tabernacle; Temple)
this-worldly message in, 150–52
vision of messianic kingdom in, 38–41, 43–45

Jacob, 53, 54, 55–56
Jeroboam, 70
Jerusalem, 40, 64. *See also* Zion, YHWH's return to
Jesus
ascension of, 138, 168–69
baptism of, 237
breathing spirit on disciples, 111–12, 140, 141–43
as coming king, 40, 64, 66, 88–89, 92, 96–97
as Davidic Messiah, 267–70
death of
atoning and cleansing nature of, 142–43, 295
as baptism, 237
first-century Judaean expectations, 157, 158
linked to Eucharist, 242–43, 254
God's homecoming in, 282–83, 298
declared in evangelism, 222–23
early Christians' understanding of, 4, 10, 16–17, 281
and human vocation, 214–15
and multi-ethnicity, 260–61
"heaven" and "soul" as used by, 13–14, 191
Incarnation of, 140, 174, 176, 223, 226
John the Baptist and, 138, 168–69, 300
Judaean context for, 169–70, 172–73, 175
"kingdom" language and vision of, 12, 30, 94, 170, 175, 221–22, 308n15
miracles of, 94
mission of, 49–50, 57, 139–40, 294
OT promises affirmed and redefined by, 98, 100–102, 106–7, 120, 175
parables of, 4, 98, 125
platonic construct foreign to, 191
presence in Eucharist, 247, 249–53
promised filling of all creation fulfilled by (*See under* creation, promised filling of)
promised return to Zion embodied by (*See* Zion, YHWH's return to)
resurrection of, 46–47, 112, 118, 157, 168–69
sacrifice of, 247–49
second coming of (*See* second coming)
Tabernacle and, 64, 91, 108, 109
Temple confrontation, 47, 97, 106, 165, 249, 250
as Temple replacement, 64, 108–9, 117
as true reflection of the father, 293–94
"Jews" (term usage), xv
John, Gospel of, 108–12, 139–46
John the Baptist, 95, 103, 105, 223, 236–37, 300
Joseph, 52–53
Josephus (*See under* Flavius Josephus)
Joshua, 42
Joye, George, 198
Judaean–Gentile relationship, 260, 261–64
Judaeans (term usage), xv
judgment. *See under* God (YHWH)
"justification by faith," 186–87, 196, 246
Justin Martyr, 158

Kant, Immanuel, 5
kingdom, messianic, 38–41, 43–45, 135

kingdom of God
God's homecoming and, 100
Jesus's vision and language of, 12, 30, 94, 170, 175, 221–22, 308n15
Judaean context for, 93–94, 104
vs. kingdom of heaven, 99–100
peaceable nature of, 167
third-century interpretations of, 180–81
kingdom of heaven, 4, 12, 30, 50, 56, 99–100
kings, as images of divinity, 51

Last Supper, 243, 244–45, 249, 250
Latimer, Hugh, 241
Law, 57–58, 59, 62, 166–67, 187, 262. *See also* sacrificial system, Levitical
Lewis, C. S., 13, 21–22, 188–89, 207
liturgy, 197, 257
Lord's Prayer, 222, 231–32
"Love Divine, All Loves Excelling" (Wesley), 126–27
Luke, Gospel of, 105–8
Luther, Martin, 187, 196

Marcionism, 159–60, 165, 171, 172
Mark, Gospel of, 95–98
Mary, 105
"The Mass," 241, 322n9
matter, 249, 250–51
Matthew, Gospel of, 98–105
Messiah, 88–89, 158, 168–70, 267–70, 300. *See also* coming king
Meyer, Ben F., 156
Michelangelo, 186, 197
Middle Platonism, 5
miracles, 94, 102, 104
Miracles (Lewis), 188
Mishnah, 181
Moltmann, Jürgen, 131
morality, 57–58, 59, 225–26
Moses, 34–35, 42, 57, 59–61
Mount Sinai, 57, 59
multiculturalism, 275. *See also under* church
mutual indwelling, 109–10, 120
mutual welcome, 270–72

Nadab, 59, 60
Nathan, 65
Neoplatonism, 5, 176, 185, 186
nephesh, 13, 14, 15, 308n19
new creation, 283, 298. *See also* creation, promised filling of; Zion, YHWH's return to
church as working model of, 146, 195, 252–53, 273
crucifixion and, 254
decline of biblical hope and, 272–73
gift of the spirit and, 140–42
God's homecoming and, 140–41
God's love and, 282, 294
as inheritance through salvation, 11
multiethnic nature of, 265, 268–69, 270, 282
OT–NT continuity regarding, 21, 103
Reformers' deemphasis of, 187–88
resurrection and, 46–47, 112, 118, 169
sacraments and, 236, 252–54
in third- to fifth-century theology, 182, 183, 184
Newman, John Henry, 197
New Testament
authority claims in, 212
Emmanuel promise in, 66
God's homecoming as central claim of, 22, 47–48, 128, 223–24
"heaven" and "soul" in, 11, 12–13, 15, 16

New Testament claim of OT promises
    fulfilled, 48, 162–63
  apparent exceptions, 114–28
    "at home with the Lord," 121–22
    "citizens of heaven," 123
    "depart and be with the Messiah,"
      122
    "eternal life," 124
    "in Abraham's bosom," 125–26
    OT–NT "shift" (*See* this-worldly to
      otherworldly "shift")
    "room in my father's house,"
      116–21
    "till we cast our crowns before thee,"
      126–28
    "today in paradise," 114–16
    "treasure in heaven," 124–25
Nicene-Constantinopolitan Creed, 174
Nietzsche, Friedrich, 189

Old Testament. *See also* Israel's scriptures
  de-emphasized in church teaching, 150
  going-to-heaven framing lacking in,
    19, 27, 34–35, 36, 46–48, 52, 150
  hermeneutic approaches to, 150, 152,
    160–62
Origen, 161, 181, 183, 319n14

parable of the rich man and Lazarus,
    125, 203
paradise *(refrigerium)*, 114–16, 182, 204
Passover, 57, 244–45, 250
Paul
  on baptism, 202–3, 206, 238, 239–40
  on being "at home with the Lord,"
    121–22, 192–93
  on bodily death, 196, 206
  on bodily resurrection, 157, 204
  on faith of Abraham, 54, 55
  on God's faithfulness to fulfill
    promises, 156–57, 165
  on God's homecoming in the spirit,
    131–37, 223
  on God's spirit and human spirit,
    286–88
  on intermediate state between death
    and resurrection, 121–22, 193,
    284, 286–92, 295–96, 299
  multi-ethnic vision for church, 258–77
  multiethnic vision for church (*See also*
    church: multiethnicity in)
  OT–NT continuity for, 156–57,
    159–61, 165–66, 167, 170–71
  personal vocation of, 301
  understanding of salvation, 11
  view of soul, 14, 15
Pausanias, 118–19
Pelagianism, 247
"penal substitution" doctrine, 311n23
Pentecost, 108, 109–10, 137–39, 238
Peter, 165–66
Pharisees, 102
Philo of Alexandria, 5–6, 158, 179
Pilate, 144
Plato, xiv, 5, 158, 308n18
Platonism
  authority of scripture and, 153
  church teaching shaped by
    beatific vision, 190, 191, 192
    death, 169, 283
    "eternal life," 124
    heaven and earth, 68, 150
    purgatory, 199, 200–201, 205, 207
    salvation, 150
    soul, 6, 13, 14, 15, 16, 150, 181,
      200–201, 308n18
  development of, 5–6
  foreign to Jesus and early Christians, 191
  going-to-heaven story rooted in, 6
  intermediate state between death and
    resurrection and, 283, 292
  OT–NT disconnection and, 149–50,
    153, 154

theology influenced by, xiv, 5–6
C. S. Lewis, 13, 188–89
fragmentation of gospels, 94
orthodox theologians, 200
Reformers, 186–87
theological education, 199
third- to fifth-century theologians, 177, 181, 185
Plotinus, 5, 185
Plutarch, 5, 6, 13
Polkinghorne, John, 291–92
prayer, 202, 203, 227, 231–33, 297, 302–4
priesthood, royal, 21, 52, 53, 194, 209
"principalities and powers," 168, 169, 276
prophets
highlighted by gospel writers, 95, 101, 103
on YHWH's return to Zion
linked to repair of all creation, 73–85
prophesied, 72–73
Protestantism. *See also* Reformers
anti-ritual/anti-tradition bias in, 58, 178, 238–39, 246
authority of scripture in, 211–12, 274
on intermediate state between death and resurrection, 198–99
Jewish "works-righteousness" rejected by, 188
view of eucharist in, 248–49
psychē, 13–14, 15–16, 19, 191, 308n19, 309n30
Psychopannychia (Calvin), 198
purgatory, doctrine of, 184, 205–6. *See also* paradise
biblical scholarship and, 199
dominance of, 196
driven by going-to-heaven story, 189, 195–96, 197–99, 205
homecoming and, 201, 209–10
lack of scriptural support for, 201–4
medieval development of, 196, 197, 198
need for punishment or purification in, 195–96, 205–8
persistence of, 207
platonic influence and, 199, 200, 205
reformers' opposition to, 196–98, 206
vs. sanctification, 206–7
purgatory, true, 209

Rahner, Karl, 197
Ransom of the Soul, The (Brown), 181–83
"rapture," 23. *See also* second coming
Ratzinger, Joseph (Pope Benedict), 203
Reformers
concept of sacrifice for, 248
doctrine of purgatory opposed by, 196–98, 206, 292
on Eucharist, 242, 251
going-to-heaven story shared by, 186–88, 198, 257, 292–93
refrigerium, 115, 182, 204, 296
Rehoboam, 70
resurrection
anticipated by filling of church with spirit, 17, 134–35
biblical meaning of, 27, 157, 169
first-century Judaean understanding of, 157, 169–70
"heaven," "soul" and, 7, 15, 16
of Jesus, 46–47, 112, 118, 157, 168–69
new creation and, 46–47, 112, 118, 169
purgatory and, 197–98, 199
as salvation, 204
in third- to fifth-century theology, 182, 184
Ridley, Nicholas, 241
ritual, 58, 246, 247

Romans, letter to, 11–12
Romans Road, 11
"room in my father's house," 116–21
royal priesthood, 21, 52, 53, 194, 209
ruach, 19, 139, 284–86

Sabbath, 104, 166, 253
sacrament, 234–35. *See also* baptism; Eucharist
sacrifice, 247–49
sacrificial system, Levitical, 62, 248–49
Sadducees, 313n9
salvation
  baptism and, 239
  as bodily resurrection, 204
  early church's understanding of, 4, 151–52
  vs. going-to-heaven story, 115, 204
  heaven and, 124, 125
  Law and, 57–58
  new creation as inheritance in, 11
  prayer of, 227
  this-worldly *vs.* otherworldly frames for, 4, 151–58
Samuel, 63, 105
sanctification, 206–7
Saul, 170
scapegoat, 248
Schmemann, Alexander, 234
Screwtape Letters, The (Lewis), 13, 22
scripture. *See also* Israel's scriptures; New Testament
  authority of, 152–53, 210–13
  distortion of
    in creeds, 185
    by going-to-heaven story, xi–xii, 22–23, 304
    by platonic framework of heaven and soul, 17–18
  ethnic separation and translations of, 257–58
  God's homecoming central to, 10, 20–21, 54
  heaven-and-earth metaphysic in, 8–9
  historicity of, 4
  OT–NT continuity, 21, 48, 89–91, 162, 163, 167
  OT–NT differences, 162–70, 177
second coming
  bodies transformed at, 23, 309n36
  early Christians' cautious approach to, 281
  God's homecoming and, 23, 131, 139, 223, 298
  misconceptions of, xi–xii, 22–23
  purpose of, 281
  in the spirit, 119–20, 282
second Exodus, 236, 237, 245
secularism, 188, 200
"seeing God," 191–93, 209–10
segregation, 264, 274
Sermon on the Mount, 99–100, 102, 104, 165
shamayim, 8, 28–29
Shammaite School, 181
Shekinah, 88, 322n15
Sheol, 15, 308n23
Signorelli, Luca, 319n19
sin
  finished by death, 206, 207–8, 295, 296
  forgiving and retaining, 112, 143–45
skēnē, 108
"sky," 8, 9–10, 29–30
Socrates, 5
Solomon, 35–36, 45, 47, 65, 66, 67–69
Song of the Three, 15
soul
  beatific vision and, 13–14, 191
  biblical meaning of, 12–16, 308n22
  human spirit and, 201
  in intermediate state between death and resurrection, 13, 15, 198, 283, 284, 287, 292

platonic misconception of, 6, 13, 14, 15, 16, 150, 181, 200–201, 308n18
purgatory and, 198, 200–201, 205, 207, 208
theological development and, 183, 186, 187
translation issues, 13–15, 308n22
space, 249–50, 251
spirit of God
baptism and, 137, 210, 237, 239
"breath," "wind" and, 285–86
creation and work of, 141–42, 143, 236
early Christians equipped by, 37, 110–11, 131, 139–40, 145
eschatological work of, 281–83
fulfillment of OT promises by, 45, 88, 131, 298
present fulfillment of cosmic promise by, 129–30, 141
in promised filling of all creation, 134, 282, 301–2
gift of
cleansing and atoning before, 142–43
as "down payment" on new creation, 223, 290, 295–96
filling of all creation anticipated by, 86, 129–31, 134–37, 146, 195, 252, 282, 298
filling of church (*See under* church)
glory-filled Tabernacle, Temple and, 108, 109–10, 112, 132–36, 138–39, 238
God's homecoming anticipated by, 130–31
in Jesus's breathing on disciples, 111–12, 140, 141–43
in NT (Acts, 137–39; Gospel of John, 139–46; Pauline epistles, 131–37)
at Pentecost, 137–39, 238
true self and, 295–96
God's homecoming in, 145–46, 282, 283, 298
declared in evangelism, 222–23
early Christians' understanding of, 4, 10, 16–17
with and within Jesus's followers, 91, 129, 134, 137–46
multi-ethnicity and, 260–61
vocation and, 213–15, 301–2
human spirit and, 286–88, 290
individual spiritual experience and, 132, 137–38, 139
present filling of heaven and earth by, 28, 31, 32, 86
shaped by own work, 291–92
sustaining between death and resurrection (*See* intermediate state)
term usage, xv
vocation and, 297
YHWH's return to Zion and, 79, 113, 301–2
Stephen, 284
"story," 4
"substance" *vs.* "accidents," 251

Tabernacle
cleansing of, 62
construction of, 58, 60, 61, 66
creation and, 20, 61, 108
divine promises and, 47
as heaven–earth intersection, 9, 37, 61–62
idolatry and, 60–61, 63
Jesus and, 91, 108, 109
YHWH's departure from, 60–61, 63–64
YHWH's presence in
as dwelling place of God, 20, 35, 36, 59, 60–61, 62
and gift of the spirit, 108, 109, 112, 132–36, 138–39, 238
and promised filling of creation, 43, 61, 62–63, 85–86, 134, 135

Temple
Ark of the Covenant and, 64, 66–67
building of, 65, 66–67
church as new Temple, 109–10, 136, 138–39
with worldwide scope, 138, 165–66, 264, 295
cleansing of, 143
creation and, 18–19, 20, 37, 45, 50–52
destruction and rebuilding of, 45, 69, 70–71, 88
as heaven–earth intersection, 9, 18–19, 35–37, 68, 70, 109, 117
human vocation and, 51–52
Jesus as replacement for, 64, 91, 108–9, 117
Jesus's confrontation with, 47, 97, 106, 165, 249, 250
purpose of, 47
Solomon's prayer of dedication, 35–36, 47, 67–69, 312n32
YHWH's departure from, 45, 71, 72
YHWH's presence in
and gift of the spirit, 108, 109–10, 112, 132–36, 138–39, 238
and promised filling of creation, 38, 45, 47, 86, 90, 108, 109, 135, 136
Temple as dwelling place for YHWH, 35–38, 51, 63–65, 66–67
YHWH's return to (*See* Zion, YHWH's return to)
temples, non-Israelite, 18, 50–51, 52
Tertullian
on "intermediate state," 16, 115, 204, 205, 296
Jesus as Messiah for, 158
new-creation focus of, 181–82, 183, 200
theology
educational challenges, 93, 175, 199
German liberal, 174
medieval, 184–85, 188, 190, 196–98, 200, 239
Reformation (*See* Reformers)
scripture *vs.* tradition in, 178, 192, 212
third- to fifth-century, 172–80, 181, 185, 213
theōsis, 296
this-worldly to otherworldly "shift"
vs. early church understanding, 158, 162, 164, 167–70
going-to-heaven story dependent on, 154
lack of historical support for, 155–56, 157–58
lack of scriptural support for, 150–53, 156–57, 162, 164–71, 175
as later church teaching, 23–24, 89–91, 149–50, 153–55, 158, 163–65
time, 249, 250, 251
"today in paradise," 114–16
Tower of Babel, 53–54
tradition, 178, 192, 212, 213
transcendence, 37, 68, 208
transubstantiation, 241–42
"treasure in heaven," 124–25
Trinity
as early Christian framework, 178
Harnack's demotion of, 174, 176
homecoming theme grounded by, 213, 304
in intermediate state between death and resurrection, 296–97
Tyndale, William, 187, 198

violence, 167, 168
vocation of church, 4, 194–95, 302, 303
vocation of humans

as agents of God's purposes for creation, 52–54, 144, 209
death and, 297
Eucharistic context for, 254
heaven-and-earth metaphysic and, 51–52, 97, 209
homecoming theme and, 19, 51, 53–54, 194, 213–15
humility of, 303
as image-bearers, 20–21, 47, 51–52, 144, 209
living in preparation for God's homecoming, 19, 53–54, 194
polarization of, 211
as royal priesthood, 21, 52, 53, 194, 209
shaped by spirit for, 297
worship and, 246–47
Voltaire, 204

Walls, Jerry, 208
Wesley, Charles, 126–27
"wind," 285–86
Wisdom of Solomon, 179
"works-righteousness," 188, 246
world. *See also* earth; heaven
as bipartite, 8, 320n28 (*See also* heaven-and-earth metaphysic)
creational monotheistic view of, 4, 46–47
as God's desired home, 12, 18, 20, 52
as sacramental, 234–35
World as Sacrament, The (Schmemann), 234
worship
as celebration of God's homecoming, 219–22
evangelism and, 222
Exodus, Exile and, 57, 58
human flourishing and, 221
human vocation and, 246–47
prayer as expression of, 233
sacraments and, 234
unity in, 272, 273–74

Zedekiah, 70
Zion, YHWH's return to, 299–300
coming king linked to, 40, 83–84, 88–89, 92, 95–97
God's homecoming and, 283
Jesus's embodiment of
completed at second coming, 131, 298
early Christians' understanding of, 88–89
as gospels' main theme, 92, 94–95, 224, 252
gospel writers' understanding of, 98, 105, 106, 108, 112, 130
and non-Judaean access, 263–65
in public career, 131, 223–24, 252
spirit's role in, 79, 113, 301–2
trinitarian context of, 300–302
judgment and, 40, 84–85, 86
regarded as unfulfilled in Israel's scriptures, 84, 86–88
as specific focus of cosmic promise, 40, 71, 73–85, 86, 88, 89, 90
David and Temple as context for, 64–71
Genesis to David as context for, 49–64
worldwide scope of, 76, 301
zōē aiōnios, 124

INDEX OF BIBLICAL PASSAGES

Note: Page references for notes, such as "166n22," point to the text page when the biblical citation appears in the endnote. This type of page reference points to the endnote when the note itself contains substantive discussion or related passages (i.e., "317n22").

Old Testament

GENESIS

1, 20, 47, 51, 52–53, 54, 66, 143, 282
1–2, 18–19
1–3, 51
1–11, 301
1:1, 35n18
1:2, 71, 79, 138, 236, 285
2, 52, 142, 143
2:1–3, 141
2:7, 141, 284, 285
2:10–14, 141–42
3, 53
3–11, 53, 58
4:17, 53
11, 301
11:1–9, 53
11:4, 53
11:5, 53
12, 166n22, 317n22
12–15, 54
12–22, 19–20
12:8, 55
15, 166n22, 317n22
15:6, 54
15:13–16, 57
15:17, 55
17:1, 55
18:1–22, 55
18:22, 55
28:12, 55
28:13–15, 56n8
28:16, 56n9

EXODUS

3:5, 57
3:7–10, 57
3:18, 57n11, 311n11

5:1, 57n11, 311n11
9:29, 28n3, 309n3
10:9, 57n11, 311n11
12:12, 57n11, 311n11
19, 52n3
19:4–6, 58–59n12
19:5, 28n3, 309n3
19:9, 67n32
20, 47, 58, 59
20:11, 35n18
20:24, 36n22
21–40, 58
23:20, 85
24, 59
24:9–11, 59n14, 191n3, 319n3
32, 70
32:8, 70n40
33:1–3, 60n19
33:12–16, 61n20
33:17–23, 191n3, 319n3
33:20, 59n16
33:23, 59n16
34, 136
34:6–7, 42n35, 310n35
40, 47, 58, 59, 66, 108, 138, 249
40:34–35, 43, 61n21

LEVITICUS

9:4, 42n33
9:23–24, 42n33
10:1–7, 60n18
16, 248n17
17:11, 62n24

NUMBERS

10:11, 41–42n31
13:23, 252n21
13:25–14:10, 42n32
14, 41–42, 44
14:10–12, 42n33
14:13–14, 42n34
14:17–18, 42n35, 310n35
14:20–23, 43n36
16:22, 284n9, 323n9
24:17, 180
27:16, 284n9, 323n9
33:4, 57n11, 311n11

DEUTERONOMY

4:39, 33n8
10:14–15, 33n16
12:11, 36n22
26:15, 33n14
27–29, 301

JOSHUA

2:11, 33n8
4:1–24, 56n10, 311n10

JUDGES

3:10, 296n25
6:34, 296n25

1 SAMUEL

2, 63
4:3, 63n25
4:6–9, 63n26
4:19–22, 64n27
4:21, 72
5, 64n28
6:13–7:1, 64

2 SAMUEL

7, 89
7:11b–16, 65n29
11, 66n30
14:7, 144n22, 316n22

1 KINGS

3:9, 144n22, 316n22
5–7, 66
8, 70, 138, 233, 264
8:6, 10–11, 66–67n31
8:10–11, 67n31
8:10–13, 27–30, 35–36n19
8:12–13, 67n32
8:13, 264n8
8:16, 36n22
8:20–21, 36n23, 67n33
8:27, 67n34, 80
8:27–30, 35–36n19
8:29, 36n22
8:29–30, 68n35
8:39, 264n8
8:43, 68–69n36, 264n8
8:48, 36n20, 69n37
8:49, 264n8
8:54–61, 36n21
8:59–60, 69n38
9:3, 36n22
9:6–9, 69n39
11:36, 36n22
14:21, 36n22
22, 300

2 KINGS

6:17, 9n8
12:28, 70n40
17:5–41, 70n41
18–19, 66, 70
19:15, 35n18
21:7, 36n22
22–23, 70
23:27, 36n22
25, 70

2 CHRONICLES

6:20, 36n22
7:16, 36n22
12:13, 36n22
33:7, 36n22

EZRA

9, 84
10, 84

NEHEMIAH

9:6, 35n18
9:19–20, 133n5
9:20, 112n35

JOB

34:14, 284n9, 323n9

PSALMS

2, 96, 158, 166n22, 167, 317n22
2:7–9, 55n6, 311n6
8, 209
11:4, 33n10
23:6, 219n2
24:1, 28
27:4, 37n24
31:5, 284
33:5, 28
33:13–15, 33n10
42, 50
42:5–6, 11, 14n22, 308n22
42:11, 14n22, 308n22
43, 50
43:3–4, 50
43:5, 14n22, 308n22
47, 166n22, 317n22

50:12, 28n3, 309n3
66:9, 292
72, 39, 43–44, 45, 47, 84, 113, 134
72:1, 43–44
72:3–4, 44n38
72:8–11, 44n39
72:12–14, 44n40
72:15–17, 44n39
72:18–19, 44n41
72:20, 43n37
74, 70
74:7, 36n22
89:11, 28n3, 309n3
96, 76, 134
96:10–13, 30–31n4
98, 76, 134
98:7–9, 30–31n4, 309n4
99:1, 33n9
102:25, 35n18
103:19, 33n10, 33n11
104, 30
104:21, 27–30, 46n43, 310n43
104:24, 286n13
104:24, 31, 28
104:29–30, 284n9, 286n14, 288, 323n9
104:31, 28
104:31–32, 46n43, 310n43
106, 229–30
110, 167
115:15, 33n13
119:64, 28
132:8, 51n2, 311n2
132:14, 51n2, 311n2
137, 70

ECCLESIASTES

3:21, 284n9, 323n9
5:2, 33n15
12:7, 284n9

ISAIAH

2, 40
2:2–4, 38–39n25, 269
2:4, 39
2:12, 281n3
5, 105n20
5:29, 269n13
6, 30, 138, 191n3, 234, 300
6:3, 28
7:14, 99
9, 39, 40
9:2–7, 268
9:6–7, 39–40n27
11, 38, 39, 40, 44, 46, 47, 80, 84, 97, 104, 113, 134, 135, 158, 237, 268, 269
11:1–10, 270
11:2, 79
11:4, 269
11:9, 8n7, 40n28, 135n11, 270
11:10, 268
19:1, 57n11, 311n11
22:5, 281n3
35, 103, 104, 105
35:1–6, 74n7
35:4, 86n28, 313n28
40, 75, 76–77, 237, 302
40–53, 224
40–55, 74, 75, 77, 88, 101, 104, 113, 229, 300, 301
40–66, 89, 250
40:1–2, 302
40:1–11, 299–303
40:3, 300, 302
40:3–5, 299n30
40:4–5, 10–11, 75n8
40:5, 86n29, 223
40:6, 300, 302
40:8, 77n10, 300, 303
40:9, 223, 321n5, 324n32

40:9–11, 302
40:10, 301, 302
40:10–11, 75n8, 223
40:11, 301, 302
40:27–29, 303n34
40:27–31, 304n35
40:30, 303
42, 96, 237
42:5, 284n9, 323n9
49, 166n22, 301, 317n22
49:6, 301
52:7, 223, 263, 321n5, 324n32
52:7–8, 101
52:7–10, 76n9
52:8, 86n30, 108, 223, 224, 263, 313n30
52:10, 101
52:13–53:12, 76, 101, 263
53, 168, 226, 245
53:1, 301
54, 76, 245
55, 223, 245
55:1–3, 250
55:1–9, 101
55:3, 89n39
55:6–7, 30, 76
55:8–11, 29
55:10–11, 10n9
55:10–13, 77n11
55:11, 303
56–66, 104
57:15, 34n17
57:16, 284n9, 323n9
59:15–16, 20, 77–78n12
59:20, 78n12
60:1–3, 19, 78n13
60:19, 78n13
61, 86
61:1–3, 78–79n14
63, 132
63:9, 79n15
63:11, 112n35
63:11–14, 133n2
64:1–2, 79n16
65:1–16, 80
65:17, 40
65:17–25, 80
66:1, 33n12
66:1–2, 80n17
66:15, 22, 80n18
66:22, 80n18

JEREMIAH

4:23, 71n42
23, 32
23:23–24, 31n5
31:44 LXX, 107n25, 314n25
43:13, 57n211, 311n11
46:10, 281n3
48:44 MT, 107n25, 314n25

EZEKIEL

4–8, 72
9, 72
10–11, 45n42
10:1–32, 72
11:22–25, 72
34:23–24, 88n38, 313n38
34:25–31, 73n6
36:35–36, 73n5
37, 186, 284
37:5, 284
37:9, 285n11
37:14, 285n12
43:1–2, 4–5, 72–73n1
43:4–5, 73n1
44:1–3, 73n2
47, 142

47:1–12, 73n3
48:35, 73n4

DANIEL

6:10, 36n20
7, 99, 152, 167, 269
9:20, 36n20
12:1–3, 27n2
12:2, 198n15

JOEL

1:15, 281n3

AMOS

5:18, 281n3

MICAH

4:1–3, 38–39
4:3, 39
4:4–5, 39n26

HABAKKUK

2, 44
2:9–11, 56n10, 311n10
2:12–14, 41n30

ZEPHANIAH

1:14, 281n3
3:14–17, 81n19

HAGGAI

2:4–5, 133n3
2:4–9, 82n20
2:5, 112n35
2:6–9, 133n4

ZECHARIAH

1:16, 82n21, 312n21
2:10–13 MT, 82–83n22
2:14–17 LXX, 82–83n22
8:2–3, 83n23
8:3, 312n21
9:9–10, 14, 83–84n24
9:14, 84n24
12:1, 284n9, 323n9

MALACHI

3, 237
3:1–3, 84–85n26
4:5–6, 85n27

New Testament

MATTHEW, 98–105

1:23, 99n10
3:3, 223n6, 321n6
3:11, 210n32
5:3–12, 100
5:8, 191
5:17, 104
5:20, 100
5:23, 87n34
5:28–41, 143n20
6:30, 124n16
8:4, 87n34
8:11, 166n22
10:28, 167n29, 317n29
11, 313n28
11:2–15, 105n20
11:4–6, 103n17
11:7–15, 105n21
11:12, 275n18
11:28–30, 105n22
12:31–32, 104n18
16, 144

16:26, 14n20
17:10–13, 105n21
18, 143
18:10, 191n3, 319n3
18:20, 243n15
19:21, 124
19:28, 130
23:18, 87n34
24:36, 281n4
25:14–30, 106
27:37, 114n3, 315n3
28:18, 99n11
28:20, 99

MARK, 95–98

1:3, 223n6, 321n6
1:7–8, 96n6
1:11, 96n7
1:14–15, 223n6, 321n6
1:15, 144n23
5:20, 105
7, 166
7:19, 166n25
9:2–13, 97n8, 313n8
9:11, 97n8, 313n8
10, 170
10:21, 124n16
10:35–45, 169n34, 194, 237n6
14:58, 109n29
15:26, 114n3, 315n3

LUKE, 105–6

1:32, 105
1:35, 105
1:68–79, 105
3:4–6, 223n6, 321n6
3:18, 223n6, 321n6
7:50, 152–153n4
8:23, 138n13, 316n13
8:39, 106n23
8:48, 152–153n4
9:51, 138n13, 316n13
12:4–5, 167n29, 317n29
12:13–21, 13
12:20, 13–14
12:33, 124n16
16, 125
16:16, 275n18, 323n18
16:19–31, 125n17, 203
18:23, 124n16
19, 116
19:11, 106
19:11–29, 106
19:41–44, 47n45, 224n7
19:42–44, 107n25, 314n25
19:44, 106–7
23, 167
23:34, 166n26
23:38, 114n3, 315n3
23:42, 114n2, 133n2
23:43, 114n3
23:46, 284n7
24:13–35, 158n10
24:21, 168
24:25, 107n26
24:25–26, 163n18
24:27, 163n19

JOHN, 108–12

1:1, 108, 141
1:3–5, 286n13, 324n13
1:14, 47n46, 108, 117, 140, 142n17, 143, 219, 294
1:18, 59n15, 294, 311n15
1:23, 223n6, 321n6
1:33, 109n32, 314n32
1:45, 143n21, 316n21
1:51, 109
2, 109
2:19, 109n29
2:21, 47n46, 109n30, 117, 142n17

3:5, 12n15, 308n15
3:5–8, 109n32, 314n32
3:34, 109n32, 314n32
4:23–24, 109n32, 314n32
5:28–29, 118
6:63, 109n32, 314n32
7, 142
7:37–38, 142n18, 316n18
7:37–39, 109n32, 142n16, 314n32
7:39, 142
11:35, 294
12, 109, 143
12:20–32, 143n19
12:30–33, 112
12:31, 167n29, 317n29
12:31–32, 226n12
13–17, 237
13:1, 230n17
13:2–20, 294
14, 91, 117, 140
14–16, 109n32, 314n32
14:1–3, 120
14:1–4, 116
14:6, 117
14:9, 108n28, 224, 293
14:12, 140
14:15, 324n31
14:15–20, 110
14:18–21, 23–26, 28, 119–20
14:23, 10n10, 117n7, 119, 237
14:23–24, 140n15
14:23–26, 120
14:28, 120
14:30, 167n29, 317n29
15, 210
15:26–27, 110–11n33
16:7–15, 111n33
16:8–11, 145n24
16:9, 145
16:10, 145
16:11, 144, 145, 167n29, 317n29
16:13, 177
16:33, 167n29, 317n29
17:4, 141
18, 145
18:36, 111, 125
18:40, 294
19, 145
19:11, 144, 211n33, 320n33
19:19, 114n3, 315n3
19:30, 141
20, 120, 140–41, 142, 143, 220, 323n5
20:1, 141
20:12, 109n31
20:15, 112n36
20:19, 141
20:19–23, 91n40, 109n32, 142n18, 314n32, 316n18
20:21, 238n7
20:21–23, 112n34, 139, 294n23
20:23, 143, 145
20:31, 143n21, 316n21
21:22–23, 120

ACTS

1, 107–8, 138
1:11, 131, 139
2, 137, 138, 139, 220, 282n5
2:1–4, 108n27
2:2, 138
2:42, 241n10
3:19–21, 130
3:20, 131
3:21, 139
4:8, 139n14, 316n14
4:31, 139n14, 316n14
6:3, 139n14, 316n14
6:5, 139n14, 316n14
7:55, 139n14, 316n14
7:59, 284n8
7:60, 166n26
8, 167
9:17, 139n14, 316n14

11:24, 139n14, 316n14
12, 224n8, 321n8
13:9, 139n14, 316n14
13:52, 139n14, 316n14
14, 224n8, 321n8
14:17, 10n9
17, 224n8, 321n8
17:24, 26–28, 258n2
17:26–28, 258n2
23:8–9, 15

ROMANS, 11–12

1–8, 266
1:1–5, 267
1:3–4, 135
1:18, 11n12, 308n12
3:21–8:39, 54
3:22, 271
3:23, 58
4:11–12, 16–17, 271n15
4:13, 55n5
4:16–17, 271n15
5:2, 11
5:17, 194n7, 282n6;323n6, 319n7
6, 238
6:1–11, 240
6:7, 206
8, 11, 23, 124, 134, 136, 186, 207, 231, 252, 269, 270, 282, 298
8:1, 206n24
8:8–11, 282n6, 288
8:9–11, 121, 135, 288n18, 295
8:12–30, 55n5
8:13, 291
8:15–17, 26–27, 287–288n17, 289
8:16, 14n21, 308n21
8:18–25, 131
8:18–28, 187
8:18–30, 11, 32, 134, 255n24
8:18–39, 209
8:21, 135n9
8:22, 134n7
8:23, 134n8, 135, 252n20, 322n20
8:26–27, 288n17
8:30, 252n22
9–11, 17n27, 266
10:2, 170n36
10:4, 159–60
10:6, 11n12, 308n12
10:12, 271
11:1, 277n19
12, 167
12–16, 266
12:2, 248
12:19–21, 166n26
13:1–7, 211n33
14, 135, 166, 166n24, 270, 271, 317n24
14:1, 270
15, 266–72, 274
15:5–6, 271
15:6, 136
15:7, 270–71, 272
15:7–9, 12–13, 267–68
15:7–13, 135, 166n27, 266–67
15:12–13, 268, 299n29
15:13, 46n44, 136, 270, 291

1 CORINTHIANS

1–2, 224n8, 321n8
1:23, 163n16
2:2, 243n14, 322n14
2:11–12, 287n15
2:11–16, 14n21, 308n21
3, 290
3:10–15, 203
3:12–15, 21n33, 309n33
3:15, 204
3:16, 136
5:5, 284n10
6:16–17, 19–20, 287n16

6:19, 136
6:19–20, 287n16
8:1–3, 10n11
10, 238
10:1–2, 236n5
10:17, 255n25
11:20, 241n10, 322n10
11:26, 243n13, 249n18
13:12, 192
15, 121
15:3, 91
15:3–4, 243n14, 322n14
15:11, 239n8
15:20–28, 17n26, 20, 131, 169n32
15:28, 8n7, 124n15, 136
15:29, 202n20
15:50–53, 23n36, 309n36
15:51, 198n15
16:22, 232n19

2 CORINTHIANS

1:22, 252n20
3–5, 245n16
3:6, 160n15
3:12–4:6, 136
3:18, 126n19, 127, 315n19
4, 207
4:6, 137n12
5:1–5, 295
5:1–10, 121
5:4, 23n36, 121, 309n36
5:4–5, 290n22
5:5, 252n20
5:6–8, 193, 289n21
5:7, 192
5:8, 115n4, 121, 315n4
6:16, 136
10:5, 177n5
11, 193
12:1–7, 193
12:4, 115n5

GALATIANS

1:1–5, 135n9, 316n9
2:11–21, 166n23, 317n23
2:15, 277n19
2:19–20, 206
2:19–21, 295
2:20, 230n16
3:1–4:7, 271n15, 323n15
4:1–11, 179n7
4:21–5:1, 165n20

EPHESIANS

1:10, 12n16, 215, 260, 262, 291, 308n16
1:14, 252n20
2, 261
2–3, 259–66, 268
2:1–10, 260, 261
2:8, 261
2:8–10, 226n13, 321n13
2:11, 261
2:11–22, 166n23, 249n19, 260, 261, 317n23, 322n19
2:12, 262
2:13–15a, 262
2:14, 263
2:15b–16, 263
2:17–18, 263
2:19–22, 264
2:21–22, 295n24
3:9–10, 265
3:10, 276
3:16–19, 265–66
3:19, 296n26
4:8, 263

4:10, 266n10
6, 244

PHILIPPIANS

1:3, 115n4, 315n4
1:23, 193
1:23–24, 289n20
3, 123
3:2–11, 157n7, 277n19, 317n7
3:20–21, 23, 123, 131

COLOSSIANS

1:5, 124n16, 315n16
1:15, 59n15, 293, 311n15
1:15–20, 286n13, 324n13
1:27, 249n19, 322n19
1:29, 239n8
2, 238
2:11–3:11, 240
2:15, 167n29, 317n29
3:3, 206, 295
3:3–4, 289n19
3:4, 298
3:11, 260n5

1 THESSALONIANS

1:9–10, 225n10
1:10, 131
4:14–18, 291
4:15, 198n15
4:17, 198n15

1 TIMOTHY

6:16, 200

2 TIMOTHY

4:8, 124n16, 315n16

HEBREWS

12:14, 191

JAMES

1:21, 308n19
5:20, 308n19

1 PETER

1:4, 124n16, 315n16
2, 52n3
2:9, 194n7, 319n7

2 PETER

3:10, 21n33, 309n33

1 JOHN

3:2, 192, 298

REVELATION

1, 52n3
1:6, 194n7, 319n7
2:7, 115n5
3:20, 23n37, 228–29, 228n14, 309n37
4, 126, 127
4:1–2, 9n8
4:10, 126n19, 315n19
5, 52n3, 126, 127
5:9–10, 11, 254n23
5:10, 21n32, 194, 194n7, 309n32
6:2, 167n29, 317n29
6:9, 13n19
6:9–11, 16
7, 273–74
7:9, 166n22, 317n22

7:9–10, 258n1, 322n1
19:1–8, 167n29, 317n29
19:11–21, 167n29, 317n29
20:4, 13n19, 16
20:6, 21n32, 194n7, 309n32, 319n7
21, 23, 127, 186
21:3, 10, 20
21:5, 20
22, 23, 128
22:4, 10, 191

Deuterocanonical Works

WISDOM

1:6–8, 31n7
1:7, 31n6, 309n6
3:1, 15
3:7–9, 15
12:1, 31n6

SIRACH

50, 87

PRAYER OF AZARIAH

64, 15n25

2 MACCABEES

2, 86
2:7–8, 86–87n32
7, 167
12:39–45, 201
12:43, 201
12:45, 201

Old Testament Pseudepigrapha

PSALMS OF SOLOMON

18, 170

Mishnah

ABOTH

3:2, 322n15